Studies in Multilevel Planning....III

Methodology and Database for Decentralised Planning

STUDIES IN MULTILEVEL PLANNING

General Editor : B. N. Yugandhar

Forthcoming Volumes
By Amitava Mukherjee

Techniques of Decentralised Planning
A Perspective Plan for Hill District
Manual of Decentralised Planning

Already Published

Researches in Decentralisation
Foundations of Decentralisation

STUDIES IN MULTILEVEL PLANNING : III

METHODOLOGY AND DATABASE FOR DECENTRALIZED PLANNING

PART - A

With Special Reference to District Planning in India

AMITAVA MUKHERJEE
Advisor
District Planning Unit
Lal Bahadur Shastri
National Academy of Administration
Government of India
Mussoorie

General Editor : B.N. Yugandhar

HERITAGE PUBLISHERS
New Delhi (INDIA) 1991

ISBN 81–7026–157–0 (Set)
81–7026–165–1

Published by B.R. Chawla, Heritage Publishers, 4C, Ansari Road, New Delhi - 110 002
Laser Typeset at Compofast, 7/33, Ansari Road, New Delhi - 110 002 and
Printed at Cambridge Printing Works, B-85, Naraina Phase II, New Delhi -110 028

TO

My Fiercest Critics

(With Gratitude)

Who Urged Me On To Work
Even Harder

CONTENTS

Gram : "ACADEMY"
Telex : 0585–243
Phone : 91-01362-2289 (O)
91-01362-2369 (R)

LAL BAHADUR SHASTRI
NATIONAL ACADEMY OF ADMINISTRATION
(GOVERNMENT OF INDIA)
MUSSOORIE-248179 (INDIA)

FOREWORD

When my colleagues and I, send out of the portals of this great Institution, with pride and fulfillment, the young officers of the Civil Service every year, to serve the half-clad, half-fed people, whom we so proudly own and constructively call " Indians", we struggle to provide the future of Indian bureaucracy with at least three things :–

One, a thorough indoctrination that they are creatures of the *Constitution of India, t*hat they owe allegiance to the Co*nstitution of India* only and that they are mandated to "defend preserve and protect the Constitution of India as established by law". First. Last. And Always. The true pride of a Civil Servant lies in so doing : in nothing else !

Two, we equip them with both "a penon and a sword" to battle it out in the dust and pelf, in the fields and the factories or wherever they may happen to be in the eventful and diverse careers ahead of them and

Three, an outlook fundamentally geared towards looking at what India would look like decades hence and strive towards making that vision of a grand India a reality.

This Volume (third in the series) is addressed towards equipping these Civil Servants with a "penon and a sword" in the realm of planning, whatever be its dimension and wherever they may be. The necessary condition for the successful execution of any task at hand is good planning, grounded firmly on a struggle to plan effectively at the micro level, shall have a spectrum of alternative scenarios to look into, examine and choose from. India's great diversity with regard to its cultural, social, economic, ethnic, religious, ideological, geographical and historical dimensions demands a diversity of approach each appropriate to different agglomerations and habitats, both in space and in time, for the incremental variations in their well-being. The labours of this Academy would be considered validated if we could drive home that the administrators of tomorrow have to understand and internalise the truths enjoined in the seven edicts repeated below:–

"Go to the People
Live with Them.
Serve Them.
Respect them.
Plan with Them.
Start with what they know.
And Build on what they have."

Yugandhar
(B.N. Yugandhar)
General Editor
&
Director

Lal Bahadur Shastri
National Academy of Administration,
(Government of India)
Mussoorie
23rd Sep., 1990

PREFACE

This is an exercise in assimilation.

We are at an exciting crossroad in our economic history. When the democratic fabric of the country is passing through its painful adolescence to maturity, its experimentation with developmental effort is increasingly moving towards lesser reliance on "macro-dynamic" and more on activisation of the "micro-dynamic". This "micro-dynamic" is nevertheless as varied, as multi-coloured and as multi-dimensional as our social structure itself. The activisation of this "micro-dynamic" through decentralisation, decentralised planning and decentralised administration has to take myriad paths depending upon what "micro-dynamic" is sought to be activated in what social order. There is scarcely any need to reinvent the "wheel": prescriptions have been worked out with care, precision, a lot of thought and laborious effort, and it is all there. Small wonder then, that in our context over twenty methodologies have been worked out for decentralised planning. While it has not been possible to include all the methodologies in these three parts (A, B and C) most of the major ones have been put together. It would be a rewarding experience to draw upon the richness of each of them according to the individual needs of the situation and planning. It is in that hope that these two parts are presented.

The issue of database would warrant a few brief comments. The database requirement of each methodology admittedly would be different and to some extent unique. The issues pertaining to database of each methodology have accordingly been dealt with in conjunction with the relative methodology and not separately. This would impart completeness to the methodologies and leave the continuity of the theme unimpaired.

In part A, Chapter I, we have reviewed quickly some of the important methodologies of decentralised planning which could not be included here but which nevertheless are seminal contributions.

In Chapter II, we have discussed the District Development Scheme of Visvesvaraya. It was first thought that the entire scheme could be placed in an appendix for its seminal ideas. Subsequently, it was felt that the methodology implicit in the scheme envisaged by the District Development scheme should be culled out and placed in a proper perspective, in keeping with the general tenor of the work.

The earliest attempt at district planning made by Gadgil is in Chapter III. His approach consists of four inter-linked aspects: (1) physiographic plan, (2) plan for the conservation of natural resources, (3) plan for productive activity, and (4) programme for the provision of adequate employment.

The methodology of Sulabh Brahme et al. is in Chapter IV. Brahme et al. emphasised scientific management of resources and provision of adequate employment to the mass of workers in the region and in the process increase internal potential rate of growth. They also emphasised retaining of growth impulses in the region through providing forward and backward linkages in the non-agricultural sector of the region.

The methodology suggested by K.N. Raj enjoins that the approach to district planning can be same as that of the national economy because the basic variables in terms of which the operation of an economy is usually subjected to judgement and to which planning targets and policies are generally related directly or indirectly (production, prices, income distribution, consumption levels, rate of saving and size and composition of capital stock) are the same whether one has in mind the economy of a district or of a nation. This is discussed in Chapter V.

In the preparation of plan for Rayalaseema region, Venugopal Reddy started with the most desirable growth rate of income and the corresponding investment requirement, and sector-wise allocation of investment was determined on the basis of the potentialities. For example, the primary and secondary activities in agriculture and allied activities were delineated on the basis of agro-climatic conditions. The development of secondary sector in selected centres was determined on the basis of the structure of the primary sector. The level of availability and the gaps in social services were obtained through growth centre approach. Chapter VI is a discussion on this Rayalaseema methodology.

Chapter VII has the A.V.A.R.D. methodology which underlines the preparation of the well known plans like the Mushari plan and the East Block plans. By and large the approach has been to cause growth through development of agriculture and agro-based industries, within an integrated area plan framework. Considerable emphasis on employment for the "Antyodaya" family and the non-working womenfolk in the rural sector imparts the plan the texture of "target group" approach.

We wish to guard ourselves against being misunderstood. The A.V.A.R.D. is not a methodology in the strict sense of the term: it is more in the nature of steps for drawing up a plan. Yet it has been included here for the "implicit methodology" that can be filtered out of it (as economists were busy filtering "growth models" out of Keynes' writing) and because of the impact it had on decentralised planning in this country.

In Chapter VIII is the summary of the methodology prescribed by the Report of the Working Group on Block-Level Planning. It clearly has emphasised the criticality of land development, organisation of the poor and the inventory of resources leading to a "status paper" acting as " instruments" of planned development.

Desai et al. chose employment generation as the basic instrument to tackle the problem of poverty even if there exists a trade off between employment and growth. This methodology was applied to the Dharampur experiment, and is discussed in Chapters IX and X.

In Part B, Chapters I, II and III are the methodologies followed in West Bengal, where the institutional arrangements for the articulation, formulation and administration of the plan at the district and sub-district levels have been fairly well stabilized. The methodologies focus on achieving development through raising the consciousness of the people, through eliminating the state of "assetlessness" of the rural poor and through socio-economic transformation of the social framework.

The NIRD apporach of Chapter IV belongs to the Growth Centre approach advocated by Lalit Sen and others for a very long time. It is the traditional approach of the Hyderabad-Mysore nexus.

The Working Group on District Planning argue that sub-regionalisation within the district is important to work out strategies for correcting intra-district imbalances in development. The report suggests three major objectives in preparing district plans; (1) Increasing productivity and growth in output; (2) Removal of poverty; (3) Removal of unemployment. This methodology has been detailed out in Chapter V.

A discussion on the methodologies of district or sub-district planning would be imcomplete without a discussion of methodologies adopted by Misra and Sundaram. Chapter VI is the action oriented approach to rural development of R.P. Misra and K.V. Sundaram. This approach is area planning approach by and large, with a hierarchy of targets.

Chapter VII and Chapter VIII deal with Inter-active Output Oriented Methodology and the Process Methodology of Local Level Planning advocated by Prantila and Bendavid-val respectively. Clearly enough, these methodologies provide a flavour of what planning at the district and sub-district level would look like, once urban economies expand in the district boundaries.

The Gujarat Model and the Karnataka Model are detailed in Chapters IX and X respectively. These are the two states where district planning has been successful, with the former model of older vintage. The single most important element of the Karnataka Model is its nearly unique system of monitoring plan implementation all along the line.

In part C, chapter I a review of the existing scenerio in various States in India with regard to District Planning is laid out. Based on these and the methodologies outlined earlier, our methodology is laid out in chapter II, which may be adopted by various States. We may add here, without fear of contradiction, that except for one or two notable exceptions, no State has adopted a well set methodology for District or Sub-District Planning.

It is hoped that these pages would provide a fairly rich cafeteria of methodologies for planning at the district and sub-district levels to choose from. It is believed, one may repeat even at the cost of suffering the structure of being repetitive, that the diversity of the needs of planning mirrored by the various parts of the country could be met by these "multi-coloured" and "multi-faceted" approaches and methodological instrumentalities. Some of the methodologies, it may be mentioned, are based on the "laboratory" of blocks and some have been generated within the confines of districts. Nevertheless the basic logic, tenets and analysis of the two "sets" are inter-changeable without materially impairing the super-structures and their applicability.

In the preparation of this work I have received the help, assistance and comments of large number of institutions and individuals. To each one of them I am beholden.

Particular mention must be made of the support received from Shri Arun Sinha, Joint Secretary to Government of India, Planning Commission, New Delhi and Professor Harvey Demaine, Associate Professor, The Human Settlements Division, Asian Institute of Technology, Bangkok. To them I am deeply thankful. Two most distinguished scholars of micro-level planning in India, Dr. K.V. Sundaram, Consultant and Project Co-Manager, Food and Agriculture Organization of the United Nations, at Nepal, and Dr. R.P. Misra, Professor of Geography, Delhi School of Economics, University of Delhi, have always been a source of inspiration.

Shri S.G. Kale, Secretary to Government, Planning Department, Government of Maharashtra and Dr. Dinesh Mehta, Director, School of Planning, Centre for Environmental Planning and Technology, Gujarat University, Ahmedabad, deserve my best thanks for all their assistance. Shri M.N. Roy and Shri Umesh Sarangi, District Magistrates of Midnapore and Nasik respectively have always responded to my requests with speed and "alarcity". They are thanked.

The American Planning Association, Chicago; Iowa State University, Cedar Rapids, Iowa, and the Asian Institute of Technology, Bangkok, have provided generous help. I am grateful to them.

Shri B.N. Yugandhar, Director, Lal Bahadur Shastri National Academy of Administration, Mussoorie and the General Editor of this series, has been a source of great support and his insistence to look ahead has provided strength to this venture. To him I am most grateful. Shri Lalit Mathur, Joint Director, Lal Bahadur Shastri National Academy of Administration, Mussoorie is thanked for all the courtesies shown. My staff at the District Planning Unit, have supported me very ably, and they deserve my thanks, particularly Shri Mahesh Kumar Tyagi for the excellent work done by him.

The errors both of commission and omission that remain are mine. And the opinins expressed in the volume are mine and do not is any way reflect either the view of the Government of India or of the L.B.S. National Academy of Administration, Mussoorie.

Amitava Mukherjee

Lal Bahadur Shastri
National Academy of Administration
(Government of India)
Charleville
Mussoorie
23rd January, 1991

CHAPTER I

METHODOLOGIES IN DECENTRALISED PLANNING : A SURVEY

I. INTRODUCTION

Decentralisation of planned efforts, in the Indian context has been in circulation for last several decades and had, to be most charitable, a mixed fortune though it quite never went out of focus altogether. With the change in the perception of the political executives (which is "inelastic" to political dispensation) that the people are no longer prepared to accept whatever is thrust upon them from above (the "supply-side" development programme)[1] and the rather belated acceptance of an early realisation, that the people must be consulted in any effort directed towards the upliftment of their lot, (even where the Leviathan lives and breathes) have brought about a resurgence of interest in decentralised planning.

A review of the fluctuating fortune of decentralised planning would reveal that till the publication of the *Report of the Working Group on District Planning*[2] there was considerable vacillations about the appropriate unit of planning (which has been summarised in Volume I in this series[3]). There were serious attempts made at developing various methodologies for planning at various area levels, below the State, more particularly at block levels. In subsequent years starting with the Report itself, methodologies for district planning were evolved and the models of a few states[4] where district planning had either a "longish tradition" or was implemented early, have emerged.

The celebrated facts that our country is very diverse and have political executives with different political hues, need no elaboration. Against this backdrop, in one sense or the other, all these efforts have been meaningful and some even seminal. While it has not been possible, immediately perhaps, to put into operation the various methodologies that evolved, they are nevertheless important contributions in the evolution of decentralised planning in this country. They are as relevant today as they were when they were thought out, and their applicability in some environment or the other, continues to be thoroughly valid and undiminished. It is, therefore, worthwhile having a look at each of them in detail.

II. CHOICE AND CAVEATS

The problem faced in working out the scheme of this book is the basic problem of economics, namely, that of choice relating to the problem of "surplus" : surplus in methodologies. A fleeting glimpse at some of the more important methodologies would be particularly rewarding before attempting at solving the "choice problem". In so doing certain caveats are in order here. *First*, we are looking at the "methodology" of decentralised planning and not, what I call, "engineering of plan formulation" which lie in the larger domain of the "Manual", which will be final volume of this series. We are not, therefore, additionally as well, concerned with the procedural details involved in framing a decentralised plan. It is essential to recognise that while procedural details may vary but the approach or methodology of planning may remain the same. *Second*, decentralised planning here connotes planning at the sub-state level. The methodologies discussed here accordingly relate to district planning, block-planning, village planning and area planning. Though district planning in this country, generally, is geared to the rural sector, conceptually it need not be so, which explains why we have examined at least one methodology which includes the urban sector as well. *Third*, those methodologies which may not have widespread applications in the Indian context but nevertheless provide useful insights in planning at lower levels have been reviewed here in this chapter with their outstanding characteristics, and those methodologies which have or are likely to have widespread bearing under Indian conditions have been dwelt upon in detail in chapter II and thereafter. *Fourth*, the term "methodology" in this volume has been used in a wider context and is deemed to partake "approaches with distinct theoretical underpinning" as well and therefore, the two terms are used inter-changeably.[5] *Finally*, all the methodologies have been deliberately discussed, irrespective of their vintage, in the volume in the "present tense" to emphasise the fact of their contemporary relevance in a country with "unity in diversity": the India of today that we have inherited from our ancestors.

III. THE REVIEW

(a) The Conventional Planning Methodology

In practice most local level development plans are formulated following the sequence of conventional planning, which certainly offers comfort to planners because of its comprehensiveness and its consistencies. The conventional methodology has the following steps:[6]

(i) Preliminary recognition and definition of problems of the planning area.

(ii) Decision to act and definition of the planning task.

(iii) Data collection, analysis and forecasting.

(iv) Determination of constraints and objectives.

(v) Formulation of operational criteria for design.

(vi) Plan design.

(vii) Testing of alternative plans.

(viii) Plan evaluation.

(ix) Decision-taking.

(x) Plan implementation.

(xi) Review of plan developments through time.

It may be useful to briefly elaborate each step here before proceeding further.

(i) *Analysis of existing conditions is the first step,* usually divided into three parts, namely; environmental analysis, resource analysis, and value analysis. The environmental analysis deals with the socio-economic and political changes, institutions, sectoral needs and technological developments; resource analysis is related to the managerial, economic, technical and financial capability of the area; and value analysis is concerned with the socio-cultural issues and aspirations of the local population, all of which are directed towards identifying the problems and opportunities faced by the area under planning, and the requisite projections of socio-economic variables are usually done to highlight the problem likely to be faced by society in the future.

(ii) *Objective and target setting* stage draws heavily from value analysis as seen from the background of the problems and opportunities faced by the planning area particularly as revealed by both the environmental and resource analysis. Target setting, is the quantification of what is to be achieved during the planning period, following the objectives, and is generally influenced by the estimated values of socio-economic variables in the planning area.

(iii) *Strategy and policy formulation* step utilises essentially the results of resource and environmental analysis. Though several strategies could be generated from the results of analysis done in the preceding two Steps, yet the matching of the competence of the people in the area with the opportunities available to them, given the objectives and targets of the Plan, is what is sought to be achieved while deciding upon strategy and policy to be pursued.

(iv) *Identification of programmes and projects* is considered important in order to achieve the objectives or targets of the plan, which is not difficult provided the objectives and targets are specific enough to pinpoint the class activity or activities essential to reach the target. At the local level, it is very important to specify the location of the project and size, that is, spatial planning is as critical as sectoral planning, where both the strategy and policy expounded in Step 3 could be used. If the policy is emphasising priority to depressed areas, and the strategy calls for massive infusion of services or commodity flow, then whereas the former could indicate the probable location, the latter would provide glimpses of the size of the project. Prioritization of programme and projects usually commences in Step 4.

(v) *Resource requirement evaluation* is the next step which essentially entails the estimation of the cost of the selected programmes and projects. Cost standards and the resource requirements when working with Step 5 hold the key to successful planning. Alternatively, it is satisfactory if the sources of fund proposed to be taken recourse to for implementing the projects be clearly spelt out in the plan.

(vi) *Phasing and implementation* step essentially outlines the scheduling of the project implementation and defines the administrative responsibilities in the implementation of projects, where an enumeration of the framework of coordination during the implementation phase is possible, which is done generally by specifying the linkages of the different Ministries, government departments or development agencies, involved in project implementation, because generally activities of government agencies could either be complementary or supplementary to the effective implementation of a development project.

There are several variations of the conventional approach to planning. Nevertheless, the logic employed is essentially the same, usually dividing economy into sectors and the plan is formulated along sectoral lines. The neat compartmentalization of the planning process is quite pronounced. Thus because the results of Step 1 is an input to Step 2 and so on, the solution of the identified problems seemingly has to wait until the planner have gone through the drill of all the steps and the plan printed.

In practice the process is flexible. Projects could be immediately identified during the Analysis of Existing Condition Step and submitted for funding. The modified form of the conventional approach is schematically presented in Figure 1.1.

The process of skipping some steps of the conventional planning approach via the initiation and implementation of impact projects, would make the framework more responsive to immediate local needs being planned for, which may provide an answer to the criticism that the conventional approach has not worked under field conditions. The most significant thing to note in the above modification, however, is the effort to make the process more active. For example, in a real life situation people may at times get puzzled as to why after the problem has been identified and the solution agreed upon, one has still to wait until after the document has been completed and distributed for the implementation of the project to start. It is apparent, however, that the modification essentially underlines the circular nature of planning and indeed the completion of other steps is not a condition precedent for commencing on a new one, and it is even possible to work on all the steps concurrently.

(b) The Problem-Oriented Methodology[7]

Suggested by Waterston as a possible remedy to the apparent inability of the Conventional Planning to produce results, the Problem Oriented Methodology is exactly the reverse of the conventional model, with the emphasis directed to the identification and implementation of projects that provide solutions to problem or are what have been called, impact projects. The steps of the Problem-Oriented Methodology are:

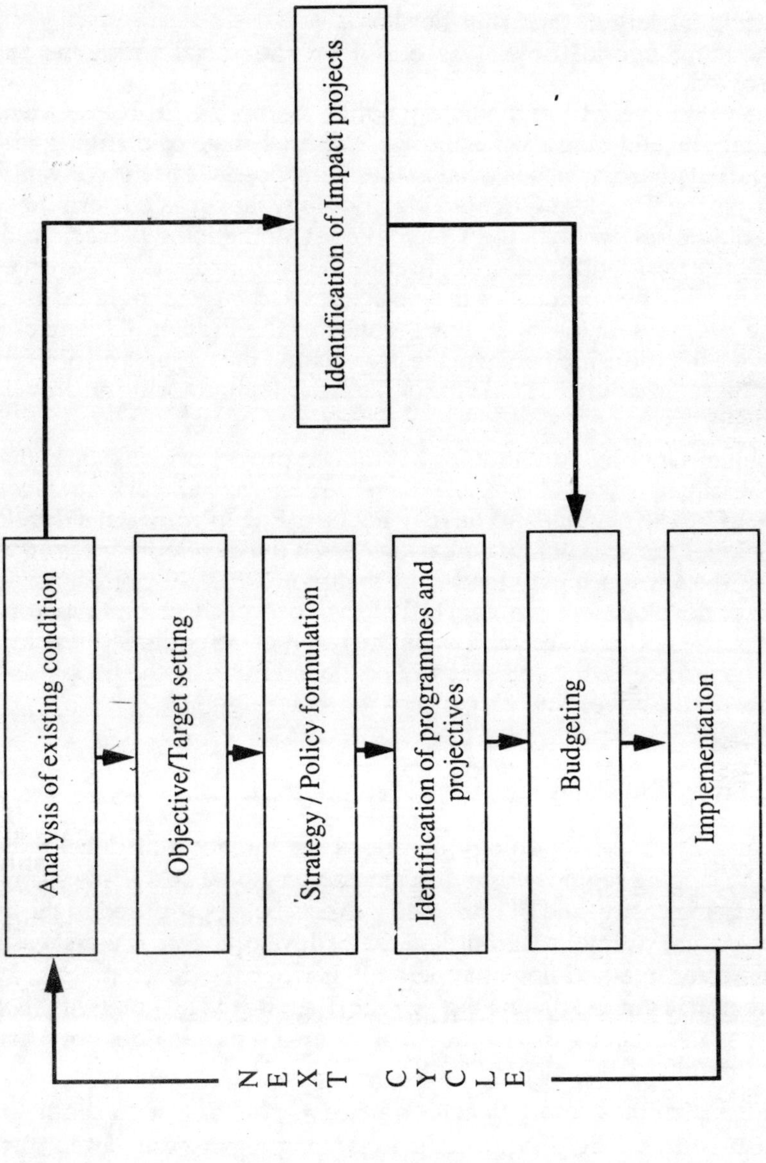

Figure 1.1 *The conventional Planning Approach Modified to Accommodate Impact Projects*

(i) Identifying the essential social problems to be resolved;
(ii) Reconciling these with available resources;
(iii) Selecting projects and policies to help solve the problems;
(iv) Devising a strategy for resolving the problems·
(v) Setting the targets (and time horizon);
(vi) Choosing overall objectives based on the social problems to be resolved.

The discerning eye will immediately notice that in the Problem-Oriented Approach, targets and objectives appear at the final stage of planning rather than at the initial phase, which is what makes it the opposite of the conventional approach. In the "Problem-Oriented Methodology the project determines the targets and objectives, while in the Conventional Methodology objectives and targets influence the identification of programmes and projects."[8] However, it is clear that in both the approaches the objectives and targets could be used to validate the progress of the plan, but because in the Problem-Oriented Approach the interrelationship between the projects and the targets and objectives is probably more pronounced, the role of the latter in monitoring and evaluation is probably greater.

The Problem-Oriented Methodology is indeed project-oriented, and therefore the general path of development which the area may embark upon could be lost sight of by the planner and he may not be trying to work out a development scenario for the area before embarking upon the development programmes. Thus, "the approach may tend to be symptomatic in its prescription for the solution of development problem rather than preventive or anticipatory".[9] Nevertheless, the approach certainly has the merit of being direct. In simple terms, it is the projects in the end that will be looked upon by the people as the manifestation of the government's concern for their plight.

(c) "Trial & Error" and Comprehensive Methodology

The "Trial and Error" Methodology describes the initiation of development projects in the lagging regions without systematic regional anslysis, which has the pitfall of being costly, and of unrelated projects being proposed in the area which do not usually remove the bottlenecks of development. A worst case of the "trial and error" methodology in operation is when the development of the backward region is pinned on one big project. Despite the fact that this shows government's interest in the development of the area, a project does not usually hold the key to the development of the region.

Countries sometimes resort to comprehensive planning with the help of foreign consultants, but because the data in lagging regions are not in plentiful, the planners will find out on completion of the plan that the situation in the country has already changed and the utility of the voluminous study may have been marginalised by then. An already difficult situation is made still worse by the fact that such a comprehensive plan is seldom updated, which makes it a costly but useless exercise with flux of time.

It is apparent that most developing countries usually need an approach that is free from the drawbacks in the "trial and error" and comprehensive planning methodologies, where the planning will be judged from the following criteria: (a) action orientation, (b) reduction in analytical work, (c) integration of programme elements, (d) flexibility of planning, and (e) participation of the population.

(d) Reduced Planning Methodologies

A methodology which would possibly satisfy the above criteria is the Reduced Planning Methodology, which is the result of various consulting activities in lagging regions by the German Development Institute, Berlin. Reproduced in Figure 1.2 are the planning phase and planning steps employed in this methodology.[10]

There are six phases in the methodology of which the initial four phases are as follows:

(a) Delineation of the region or area to be planned for. For countries like India where planning region and administrative region are co-terminus, there is little likelihood of there being any problem in going to the next step. If the area is yet to be delineated, then use of the national strategy for the development potentials of the area as the frame of reference for delineation would be satisfactory, which initiates the process into the next phase.

(b) Regional Analysis, as stated above, is the second phase, where basic information on population structure, economic base of the region, and socio-political structure is analysed, which is expected to provide an understanding of the factors of under-development of the region and some grounding for selecting key sectors of the regional economy.

(c) Goal Analysis Phase is the next phase, which is designed to focus on the major problem of the region as the base for working out a development strategy, which in turn, is the basis for prioritization of development goals, either within or outside the ambit of development strategy.

(d) Sector and Project Analysis, which distinguishes the Reduced Planning Methodology allows key sectors to be identified and used in the planning drill. The key sector identified, basically by looking at the development strategy chosen, leads to the identification of Key and Support Projects, which form the "project complex" for the planning area, whose schematic outline is shown in Figure 1.3.

These phases are essential, but not in the same sequence, and depending upon the planner's decision, any one can constitute the starting point. Once these first four phases are gone through, "project complexes" can be constructed in terms of spatial inter-connections, through the movement of food, migrations of people, etc. The fifth phase will be the construction of a qualitative goal-achievement matrix that facilitates ultimate choices and determine the develop-

Phases	Steps	"Entrances"
1. Delineation of the region	1.1. National strategy for regional development	Entrance I
	1.2. Development potential	
	1.3. Delineation	
2. Regional Analysis	2.1. Population	
	2.2. Economy	
	2.3. Socio-political structure	
	2.4. Factors of under-development	
3. Goal Analysis	3.1. Identification of goals	
	3.2. Development strategy	
4. Sector and Project Analysis	4.1. Selection of key sectors	Entrance II
	4.2. Identification of key projects	Entrance III
	4.3. Identification of support projects	
5. Elaboration of RDP	5.1. Construction of project complexes	
	5.2. Spacial development concept	
	5.3. Goal achivements of project complexes	
6. Implementation of RDP	6.1. Alternative implementation sequences	
	6.2. Organizations for implementation	
	6.3. Participation of population	

Source: *Peter P. Waller, "The Reduced Planning Approach for Regional Development Programs in Lagging Areas" in Avron Bendavid-Val and Peter P. Waller (eds.), Action-Oriented Approaches to Regional Development Planning, New York: Praeger Publishers, 1975, p.21*

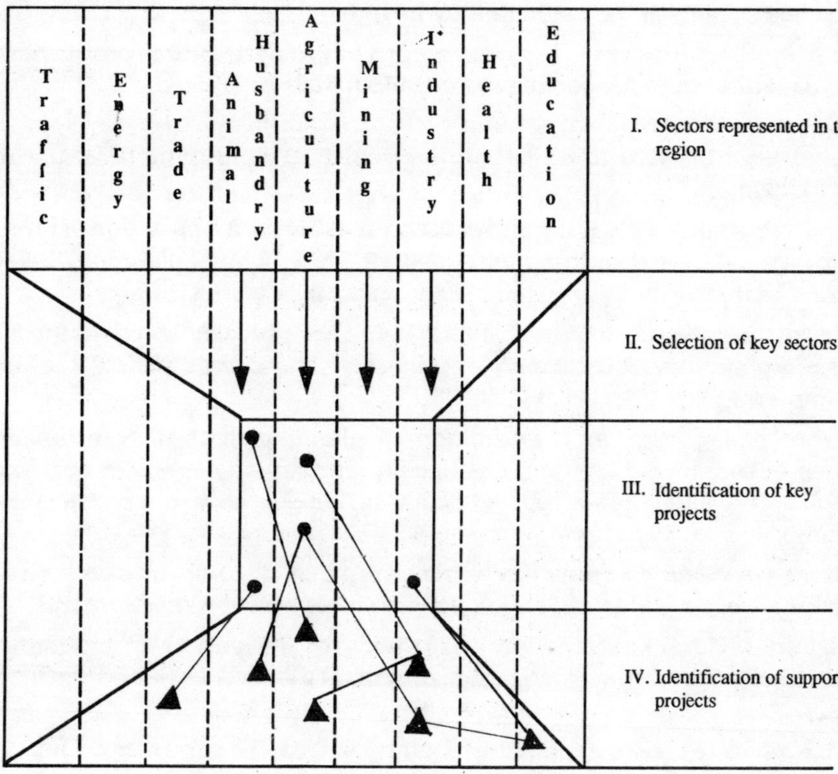

Figure 1.3 *Identification of Projects*

ment plan and finally comes the implementation of this development plan at which stage participation of the population is envisaged.

Not much literature is available about the performance of plans prepared through these methodological phases, though it has been applied in several countries. There are, however, three things about the methodology which need comment: *one,* the pragmatism it imparts to planning at lower levels; *two,* its emphasis on popular participation; and *three,* its flexibility.

(e) Rehovot Approach

The assumptions of the Rehovot Approach[12] are that:

(a) there "exists a common denominator to be derived from successful examples of rural development", and (b) "providing an economic livelihood on the basis of old and new possibilities" is the central aim of planning. Based on these assumptions, development is perceived as a gradual process, "a process of transformation, which occurs in definite sequences and is not erratic: from subsistence farming to diversified — and later to specialized — and automated farming".[13]

The basic tenets of the methodology include:

(i) A system of services, because no growth in agricultural production is achieved without the supporting system adequately organized.

(ii) A diversified regional economic resource base because for development to come about, there must be non-agricultural employment and rural industrialization.

(iii) Decentralized planning and decision-making for mobilization of human resources must have their loci at intermediate level regional planning, thereby implying that priority setting is not predominantly a vertical affair.[14]

The distinguishing features of the Rehovot-approach are described by phrases like 'simultaneous action', 'step-by-step', and 'cross function', the latter term implying:

(a) inter-planning tier coordination of planning, that is, co-ordination between village-level planning, area-level planning (analogous to our Block level planning) and supra-area level planning, (analogous to our districts level planning);

(b) inter-sectoral coordination of planning, that is, co-ordination between agricultural sector, industrial sector, service sector and other sectors; and

(c) intra-sectoral coordination of planning at the project or programme level,[15] like between minor irrigation project, HYV seed farm and fertilizers subsidy.

There are five phases in planning itself which may be summarised thus:

(a) Collection and collation of basic data; delineation of region and areas and diagnosis of the problems of the area under the instant planning exercise.

(b) A rough approximation of the region(s), and development of a "macro-plan" (within the contours of the general national plan) for the area under planning.

(c) Drawing up of micro-plans, planning from below, for the area under reference in the instant planning exercise.

(d) Transformation of socio-economic programmes into a spatial and physical plan for the region.

(e) And, finally preparation of concrete projects for implementation, directed towards solving the problems of the region under attack.

The Rehovot Approach has been successful in Israel, because the planning process at lower tier of planning in Israel always had a surfeit of human and financial resources which is normally not the case in the under-developed countries. Granted that resources are scarce in the underdeveloped countries, the methodology seems less appropriate, despite the assertion that the protagonists of the methodology firmly believed, it to be "an effective tool, if not the only one for solving the pressing problems of the rural areas... in all cases, where for any reason all the prerequisites of the development plan cannot be met, there exists no practical and operable alternative".[16] One merit of the approach, however, is its applicability being independent of any specific political system; it is dependent rather on the effectiveness of governmental organizations and institutional arrangements.

(f) P4- Micro-Regional Methodology

Van Raay elaborated his so-called P4-Approach for Regional Planning,[17] where planning for the local economy is perceived as a normative art, and stresses the importance of making a more efficient use of existing institutional arrangements, organizational arrangements and socio-cultural resources. He remains largely unpersuaded that the prescriptions (completely new creations) of the planning process will automatically be better than the malady sought to be cured, and is convinced that few 'desirable' changes are also 'feasible'; too many things within too short a time and with too little resources is impossible and chose, therefore, to advocate working within the given system, rather than trying to attempt at its thorough-going overhaul.

van-Raay thought that the planner should have both eyes open, ready to manipulate regional potentials to address changing needs, and be partners in a political process. The P4-Approach contains guidelines for coming to grips with complex planning environments for improving and increasing planner's capacity. In developing countries the planning approach should ensure:

- (a) that a long-term perspective for the plan to impart planning a sense of direction;
- (b) that the time frame is modest for the actual planning effort;
- (d) that active people's participation in the preparation and implementation of the plan is forthcoming;
- (e) that given the paucity of human and financial resources the problems which are ranked highest in the scheme of priorities be dealt with first;
- (f) that quick action be taken to set right the urgent problems as prioritized short-term action programmes, with due allowance for recurrent costs and maintenance requirements;
- (g) that limited use of sophisticated and quantitative measurements are made with emphasis on common sense, intuition, imagination, and popular participation; and
- (h) that continuous evaluation and adaptation, are fully recognised.

The P-4 Approach enjoins a rolling planning process, commencing with the identification of an initial focus of attention, based on a quick assessment of immediate problems, possibilities and long-term needs, followed by a deeper examination and intervention with added emphasis on, and attention to, the long-term perspective. The P-4 approach favours substitution of comprehensive development plans by short-term action programmes, spanning over one to three year periods in the early phases of the planning.

The ultimate aim of sub-national planning is rational and imaginative temporal and spatial allocation of scarce resources to achieve progressively expanding objectives of economic growth, social justice, environmental quality and spatial organization. Therefore, the obvious methodological choice for engaging in decentralised sub-national planning, is "ongoing interactive process of comprehensive analytical orientation and selective action," which is structured around four main entry points namely:

(p1) policy environment;

(p2) problems and potentialities;

(p3) priority clusters; and

(p4) project complexes

which constitute building stones of the plan, since basic understanding, recommendations, "action-evaluation and future perspectives are as synchronic and eqaully important elements of a flexible process of learning, intervention and adaptation."[18]

The P4 Approach first demands a comprehensive analysis of the pertinent policy areas and strategic choices (p1, Policy Environment), and then explore the possibility of structuring the regional and rural issues and problems in a five to five matrix, (p2, Problems and Potentials), focussing on:

(a) the density, age, sex composition, activity structure, and growth of population;

(b) macro-organizational arrangements, like relative position of socio-political power of various groups and power status structure of society per se;

(c) the socio-cultural environment, including the social and psycho-cultural attributes of a population; prevailing production systems and technological means, customs, usage and practices; and

(d) the natural and physical environment.

In the p4-Approach, priority setting p3, (Priority Clusters) starts with a recommended fact finding survey, and a quick selection of feasible priority-areas for sub-national rural planning is envisaged and a method for so doing is provided for. Control, manpower burden, recurrent commitment, spatial demand, time lag and coherence are the criteria laid down for selection of feasible priority areas.

Similarly in p4, (Project Complexes) projects that are thought of as being most critical to the attainment of stated objectives of planning, are listed and subsequently clustered by time-frame, space and need.

The p4-Approach has a clear distinct identity vis-a-vis the so-called 'pure-action oriented' or reduced planning approaches. The regular examination of both the original reference points and initiated actions, against the backdrop of the overall context, enjoined in the p4-Approach helps to ensure that the principle of only temporary subordination of certain priority areas vis-a-vis others remains valid.[19]

Finally it is also distinct in its micro-regional perspective because the methodology accepts that these functional micro-regions are the basic building blocks of the larger socio-spatial system, and constitute the intermediate level at which sub-national development programmes can be meaningfully applied. The greater the land-use specialization, the higher the need for support functions requiring allocations of substantive acreage for their efficient operation like transporation, service centres, irrigation, reservoirs and soil erosion control. Conversely, land-use diversification may go on till a point is reached where volume of production is adversely affected by a generalists' approach undermining the planning process, putting into jeopardy potential growth and the provision of basic needs. The two opposing but complementary forces of spatial structuring dealt with in the analysis amongst themselves co-determine the distinct identity of sub-national development planning and catered for intervention.

In planning terms, a dual perspective, viz., that of community and micro-region is considered necessary. Self-reliance, resource-orientation, and self-control have been made imperative elements for community behaviour for its very survival, but the methodology believes that the conditions of the poor cannot be segregated from the changing values and norms of society at large. The community and its associated territory cannot be conceived of as the exclusive sphere of life in a modernizing society, which explains largely, why an integrated micro-approach to development should encompass concurrently several communities and be concerned with inter-relationships and complementarities in an area that is progressively organized as a functional unit, or "minimal basic building block", which has been called the micro-region, to be treated for the purposes of planning as an integrated whole.

The need for governmental and non-governmental checks and balances at the micro-regional level is very important, with downward accountability of officials as one of its features. Self-reliance and self-control should be sobered by such a mix of checks and balances.

A population base of 25,000 to 50,000, preferably 50,000, should ideally be the size of a micro-region, under this methodology, because the sets of services and provisions that are critical for developing its self-reliance and ensuring viability hovers around 5,000 to 10,000 families. It is apparent that minimal improvements at the grassroots level will be essential if a rural base is to emerge that is responsive and sensitive to, and is capable of, modernization. Development should be planned in terms of the micro-region as a whole, so that several centres and their hinterlands are dealt with simultaneously, and arbitrary project planning is avoided.[20]

(g) Selective Spatial Closure

The Selective Spatial Closure (SSC) methodology conceives local and regional development at sub-national level to be processes which can be promoted by the devolution of power to local and regional 'communities', to enable them to plan the development of their own resources vis-a-vis their own needs, and to offset exogenous relationships having a negative impact on them, an argument that is grounded on an evaluation of regional policies in both developing and developed countries.[21] The world-wide trend (when the methodology was developing) towards centralization has exacerbated the economic, social, cultural and political backwash effects on specific regional communities. Hark these words:

> "... spatial disparities in material living levels in most marked and mixed economies have not decreased, or if they decreased at one level (e.g. 'the intra-regional or urban level'); and second, 'the subjective perception of conditions of living by concrete regional communities seems to show growing discontent on the part of sub-national groups (including local and regional ones) about the increasing impact upon them of exogenous economic and social determinants... and their ability to resist them and to shape their own destiny within large and still expanding economic and political systems".[22]

This methodology is based on neo-populist notions of development and like the neo-populists, there is a great deal of concern for the ill-effects of centralization and large-scale organization.[23]

Stohr restates and refines the Selective Spatial Closure as predominantly "endogenous regional development" in peripheral areas, because it is thought that traditional sub-national policies have not succeeded, and they have not succeeded because of the numerous changes in external conditions for sub-national development, like the fall in the rate of aggregate economic growth, fall in the availability of public funds, adoption of new technology for decentralized patterns, and the increasing pressure for people's participation in the process of plan formulation and plan implementation.

The Selective Spatial Closure, however, has the following advantages:

(a) the development of less developed areas; promotion of territorial identity;

(b) favouring of development that is not primarily based on spatial extension or spill-over effects;

(c) self-reliance and reduced dependence on sizeable public financial inputs;

(d) energy and resource savings; the broad mobilization and mutual interaction of regional resources, rather than their selective 'combing out' for large-scale economic circuits;

(e) differentiation and diversification according to economic and non-economic factors and criteria such as "regional cultural characteristics, regional identity, regional participatory structures, environmental conditions", and so on, rather than the indiscriminate application of "standardized models", like the "the urbanization/industrialization model";

(f) progressive increase of endogenous regional problem-solving capabilites, replacing "the focus away from external assistance and externally-defined goals";

(g) promotion of small-scale social, economic, political, and ecological circuits;

(h) progressive flexibility of regional social systems, particularly in terms of their adaptive and innovative capacity;

(i) enhanced role for lower (local and regional) "decision making levels in the development process and increased popular participation."[24]

"Selective self-reliance and endogenous regional development", are thought of as being synonymous with Selective Spatial Closure Methodology, which requires that local economy has the "the internal ability and external possibility of territorial communities to mobilize fully their internal resources and endogenous development potential in economic, socio-cultural, environmental and political terms".[25]

The following preconditions and constraints (which are summarised in Stohr's own words) are essential for the success of the methodology:

a. political preconditions and constraints:

- a decentralized power structure and provision of broad access to scarce resources;
- neutralization and control of external mediating functions;
- establishment of a continuing territorial adjustment and learning mechanism;
- external aid only for limited periods and for providing self-reliant structures;
- willingness on the part of central government to at least tolerate—if not promote—self-reliant local/regional development.

b. Socio-cultural preconditions and constraints:

- promotion of a broad autochthonous intellectual elite and their integration into the regional society;
- territorial socio-cultural identity on the basis of historical ties or, alternatively, on the basis of sharing a common future goal;
- endogenous learning capacity as a precondition for free and symmetric information flows without unilateral dependence.

c. Economic preconditions and constraints:

- sufficient endogenous resources (particularly natural ones) and internal markets;
- diversified and decentralized economic structure;
- high degree of internal economic interaction within regions;
- communal instruments facilitating innovations and reinvestment of surplus value in region itself.

d. Finally, ecological constraints and preconditions are listed, such as self-regulating mechanism and restriction of "territorial expansionist tendencies".[26]

The preconditions are the real weaknesses of the this methodology because these foregoing preconditions are the common range of objectives which a sub-national development plan attempts to achieve in a developing country. Instead of indicating how the objectives of a development plan could be reached, the objectives are presented as preconditions, and if the preconditions were satisfied, all development planning exercises would be dysfunctional. The feasibility of the desirable preconditions is left unassessed, and the empirical foundation of the approach is clearly weak.

(h) The Agropolitan District Methodology

Friedman and Douglass were the first to suggest the Agropolitan District Methodology,[27] which is a strategy of accelerated rural development, revolving around "the formation of small politically empowered urban-agrarian-districts, which should solve the impending crisis of development and the designing of development processes, which respond to local needs",[28] which emanates from the conviction that rural development can be achieved by "empowering regions with the means of controlling institutional arrangements and ownership patterns internally and bargaining externally for allocation of national resources on a par with metropolitan and other regions".[29]

Originally the Agropolitan District Methodology envisaged the creation of a network of local government units within a country, the agropolitan districts, which would entail:

(a) a devolution of power and change in cente-local taxation arrangements to provide each unit sufficient autonomy and economic resources to plan and develop its own self;

(b) land reforms and return of wealth to the members of each agropolitan district; and

(c) the commitment of central government to support financially, materially, and technically, the locally initiated developments, and commitment of the central government to undertake projects of national significance and for ensuring inter-regional equity in the allocation of development funds. The contours of Agropolitan Districts were drawn up as being rural areas having an effective population density of at least 200 per km, in which a town of between 10,000 to 25,000 people would normally be located and the district area would lie within the area circumscribed by a commuting radius of between 5 and 10 km, (or approximately one hour's travel time by bicycle), yielding an overall size of population ranging between 50,000 to 150,000, a majority of whom would initially be farmers.[30]

In geographical terms the Agropolitan District would approximate the Community Development Block in India, but what distinguishes the Agropolitan District is the emphasis on effective political power and self-government, implying avoidance of an identification with field administration units.[31] Friedman and Douglass conceived the developmental efforts of Agropolitan Districts as involving social facilities, infrastructure, agricultural improvements and light labour-intensive industry. Indeed the distinct identify of the Agropolitan Development strategy emanates from presence of industries within the districts and the devolution of political decision-making to local level.

From a strategy originally designed in the context of economies with levels of urbanization below 20 per cent, rural population density patterns exceeding two hundred people per square kilometre, a settlement pattern of clustered villages and towns, and conditions of extreme poverty[32] for accelerated rural development, the Agropolitan District Approach became 'a basic-needs strategy of territorial development', having relevance for both Asia and parts of Africa, which highlight the shift in thinking from "functional" planning to "territorial" planning for lower tiers in a multi-level planning system. Agropolitan Districts are still defined as units of local government within which development programmes will be formulated and implemented, but stress now is on the boundary of districts being co-terminus with a local community or interest, or in Friedman and Weaver's terminology a "primordial unit of territorial integration".

Three basic conditions are said to be essential for successful agropolitan development: selective territorial closure, the community ownership of productive wealth, and the equalization of access to the bases for the accumulation of social power.[33] Selective territorial closure, should be applied at the relevant territorial level, be it the district, or the region or the nation, for preventing the out-migration of resouces, which is essential to ensure that the benefits of local development accrue to the local masses. And the last two conditions must be satisfied for ensuring that the whole local community benefits from development efforts, otherwise "even the initial effort is not likely to be made, and the productive potential of the community will be realized only in part".[34]

Production within the Agropolitan Districts, should be directed towards meeting basic needs, and follow the principles of self-reliant development, to create a diversified local economy, and for meeting local needs as far as possible from local production. Development should be a self-financed phenomenon to the extent possible and developmental efforts should attempt at mobilization of local natural resources, within the boundary conditions set by the need for conservation of ecosystems, with heavy reliance on local knowledge. 'Social learning' is to be promoted to enhance the capacity of the local masses to solve their own problems and to pass on the message that unless the development forces are based fundamentally within the economy, development can never be pervasive and long lasting.

It becomes clear that in the Agropolitan District Development Approach no mathematical models and techniques are sought to be used, as heavy reliance is placed on transactive planning, and policies and actions are formulated and implemented through interpersonal dialogue, where a whole lot of mutual learning ensues.

The need for projects of national significance, and small-scale projects which are basic-needs oriented, within the Agropolitan Districts is very great. This approach also envisages national investments in industries which can complement the development programmes formulated and implemented within the Agropolitan Districts. Thus Friedman and Weaver argue that alongside concurrently with the cellular economy of the districts, an urban-based corporate economy would exist, whose industries would not compete with the agropolitan industries, but develop "backward and forward linkages with the thousands of small industries in agropolitan localities".[35]

The Agropolitan District Development Methodology is seemingly "a policy of planned industrial dualism" with small-scale technologically appropriate labour intensive agropolitan industries operating side by side with technologically advanced, capital-intensive large-scale industries. The large-scale industries, can achieve agglomeration economies and were thought of as being best located in close proximity to each other, forming industrial complexes or *growth poles*, while the agropolitan industries need to be protected from the onslaught of the larger, technologically advanced industries. Therefore, growth poles formed by the large scale industries should form regional enclave economies at major ports or in other suitable locations and need not be spatially integrated with agropolitan development.[36]

The co-existence of the parallel economy and an Agropolitan District Development Strategy, however, raises additional theoretical questions which have not been satisfactorily considered by the agropolitan development strategists. It is unclear as to how basic and intermediate industries, as well as projects of national significance will be financed and operated, when the clear emphasis is on avoiding increasing dependence on the outside world. This problem is not intractable, but the formulation of Agropolitan District Development strategy is weakest at precisely the point where neo-populist development theory requires the most careful argument.[37]

IV. ANALYSIS OF THE LOCAL LEVEL PLANNING METHODOLOGY

It is difficult to decide either way about the relative efficacy of the planning methodology discussed in the preceding sections. The only effective way to determine the efficacy of a planning methodology would be to compare the outputs of these methodologies and their relative implementability. Nevertheless, a few observations which may be of use in deciding upon the most desirable properties of the reviewed planning methodologies would be in order here.

First, a planning process is relatively neutral with regard to the substantive contents of the plan, that is, the methodology. It tells planners the approach to adopt and phases to follow but no criteria are laid down for the quality of outputs from each of these phases and approaches.

Second, because planning methodology generally influences the logic or presentation and formulation of a plan using a particular planning methodology may differ significantly in focus relative to another plan using a different methodology. Thus, a plan formulated by using the Reduced Planning Methodology will be different from one using the Comprehensive Methodology.

Third, the data requirements of each planning methodology generally differ but by and large, the consensus is that the comprehensive planning or the conventional methodology, requires a larger amount of data input than that of the Reduced Planning Methodology or the Problem-Oriented Methodology. However, some plans using the Conventional Approach usually employ additional data as a cosmetic in the plan document, that is, the information that the data produce has no bearing on the substantial issues that need to be addressed to in the planning process. Thus, the data analyzed and presented may have no connection with the formulation of strategies or identification of programmes and projects.

Finally, the logical sequence which the various planning methodologies suggest does not exclude simultaneous or overlapping operations among the phases. "The linearity of the approach is by no means inflexible. Interactive operations to segment of step or to a particular step may even produce a better plan".[38]

V. REVIEW OF REGIONAL METHODOLOGIES

There has been numerous studies in this country on the regional dimensions of the Indian economy at the district and sub-district levels. It would be impossible to review all of them in this Chapter (because that is beyond the scope of the both) nevertheless a few are reviewed here for providing a fleeting glimpse of the diversity of the studies and/or the variety of the methodologies adopted.

(a) *Study of Sunam and Samana Blocks* in the districts of Sangrur and Patiala in Punjab undertaken by the Punjab Agricultural University, Ludhiana, is one such study, which is in the nature of a diagnostic study without plan for action. The agronomical and hydrological aspects of the study and the emphasis mainly on working out a viable infrastructure framework for agricultural progress is quite important. The various constraints operating at the micro level core examined and through such analysis it indicates the variables affecting development at the grass-root level. A locational hierarchical system of service and growth centres in the area has been worked out to provide the organizational framework for agricultural development, based on certain simple methodologies evolved by the Pilot Project studies on growth centres to which we shall turn later. Employment aspects and social factors in development were however not considered in the project.

(b) The research, planning and action project in *Naurar Wastershed in Bhikiasen Block of Almora District* (U.P.) undertaken by the G.P. Pant University of Agriculture and Technology is another important study in the nature of some research studies undertaken by an inter-disciplinary group, without attempting a detailed plan. This is on problem-identifying and problem-solving research and action, and contains studies of fragmentation and dispersal of holdings, employment structure and migration of rural labour, consumption, investment and financial structure, alternate resource use plans for representative farm situations and representative sub-watersheds, and study of credit requirements under different levels of technology and so on. The framework of analysis and the various techniques employed for analysis, such as the use of aggregative linear programming models and partial budgeting techniques for formulating alternative resource use plans at farm and sub-area levels are important aspects of this study. "The alternate cropping patterns suggested for different sizes of farm holdings and the economics of farm management worked out for each case illustrate the in-depth investigations required in each particular locality to promote sound agricultural planning".[39]

(c) *"Operation Bharani"* by the University of Mysore is worth looking at. This is an on-going rural development project undertaken by the University of Mysore as a research-cum-action programme in Hunsur Taluk, Mysore District, to accelerate rural development in these areas, by adopting different kinds of strategies like multipronged attack, synchronized action, popular participation, catalytic intervention, growth centres strategy, strengthening the weak etc. A survey to identify the basic minimum needs of the villages forms part of the survey.

(d) Two other *District Studies of Jhabua* (M.P.) *and Dharmapuri* (Tamil Nadu) which are in the nature of techno-economic surveys with indicative plans worked out in a 10 year frame, by the Institute of Public Opinion is also worth mentioning. The study takes into account the resource configuration, and the socio-economic condition of the people also, but, the discussion soon reverts to traditional economic analysis (and the people recede into the background) but attempting to estimate Gross Domestic Product of the District and the emphasising maximum production irrespective of the contribution of other factors involved. The planning strategy and programme formulation are directed at:

(i) encouraging flow of entrepreneurial and specialized skills;

(ii) inducing flow of capital; and

(iii) development of infrastructure. Planning for social changes, although recognised in principle, is not consciously reflected in the plan.

The Jhabua study caused a special survey about the nature of indebtedness of the tribal population, and envisaging doubling of district income, based on development of irrigation facilities and increasing agricultural production including a large scale programme of livestock, poultry, and pasture development. Estimates of the total number of employment opportunities to be created as a result of these plan proposals have been indicated.

The Dharmapuri entitled as "Employment-oriented survey", is essentially based on secondary sources of information, with thrust of development of dry land farming and rapid development of medium and large scale industries. A study of employment trends have been provided and sectoral targets of employment have been worked out for the 10 year perspective. An employment gap has been worked out as mainfested in terms of full-time unemployment, under-employment and seasonal unemployment and low productivity employment in the unorganized self-employed or household sectors, without explicitly indicating the methodologies of employment estimation.

(e) Several *Block-level Studies* numbering twenty, were prepared by the *Pilot Project on Growth Centres* during the Fourth Five Year Plan covering all types of area conditions. Such as green revolution areas, backward areas, tribal areas, hilly areas, trade-commerce-oriented areas and so on, were chosen for conducting pilot studies in growth centres, for working out the optimal scheme of hierarchy of growth centres for the most economical and efficient provision of goods and services and to specify the functional gaps in the physical and institutional infrastructures of these centres and related settlements.

The methodology adopted is as follows: Detailed surveys were conducted of all the settlements in the block, including the survey of households, market centres, small-scale and cottage industries, educational institutions, health centres and sub-centres, transport and communication linkages and the shopkeepers. Based on settlement systems analysis for measuring the centrality and identifying the hierarchy of places using computer and simpler techniques, a General Settlement Plan (GSP) was formulated, as the first step in the planning procedure, to show the various levels of hierarchy of settlements with their service areas, service-area population, weighted average distance to the settlements they would serve and the maximum distance to them from any settlement falling within their service areas. The GSP indicated the gaps in the provision of institutional facilities which should be filled up and the communication links which should be established to enable the selected centres to function effectively.

The GSP was followed by a General Transport Plan (GTP) seeking to:

(i) improve the accessibility of the growth centres to their service areas;

(ii) connect the lower order centres with the next higher order centres in the settlement hierarchies; and

(iii) relate them, where necessary, for the development of the area with external connections outside the block.

The sectoral plans for the sectors of agriculture, industry, health and education were then worked out, with thrust on the identification of programmes (based on the availability of resources) to be located in the growth centres. Finally, to reconcile the possible differences between sectoral plans, the general settlement plan and the general transport plan, an integrated area plan was worked out.

The Growth Centre Plan of the 20 selected blocks is confined to recommendations for selective investment at the chosen places in order to fill the gaps and make up the deficiencies in the physical and institutional infrastructures in rural areas, which makes its partial scope and the sectoral plans are confined only to those sectoral activities which have a locational implication without giving details of the total programme. The Growth Centre Plan does not specifically deal with the employment aspects of the area programme, and tells us nothing about the mechanics of distributing the benefits of the economic and social facilities among the weaker sections of the population.

(f) In 1972, Government of India initiated *Pilot Intensive Rural Employment Projects (PIREP)*,[40] in 15 blocks in selected districts in different States, which partook the nature of action-cum-study projects for providing lessons to formulate future policies in the field of rural employment. The projects were of three years duration from 1972-73 to 1974-75. The evaluation reports of these pilot projects are available. For the purpose of this review, three project reports were considered. (i) Nayagram Block, Midnapur District (West Bengal), (ii) Trithala Block, Palghat District in Kerala, and (iii) Alirajpur Tribal Development Block, Jhabua District (Madhya Pradesh).

The methodology adopted for the areas has been simple. An area profile including various aspects such as rainfall, climate, population, working force, agriculture, irrigation, livestock, agricultural wages, industry, roads, markets, warehousing, co-operation, literacy and education, medical and health facilities has been given. Since the purpose of the project was to provide employment in a phased manner to people in the age group 15 to 59, willing to work and not requiring skills of a high order, a household survey was conducted in the selected blocks to ascertain the number of such persons in the area. The guidelines for such surveys were provided by the Government of India. In the second step, a three year programme of providing jobs in schemes leading to the creation of productive assets was drawn up, where the labour and material components in such schemes were to be in a prescribed ratio of 70:30 similar to what has been prescribed for the present Jawahar Rojgar Yojana, with the labour component now raised to 50 per cent. The mix of activities in the various projects undertaken by and large, consisted of irrigation works, road programmes, afforestation programmes, social conservation works, pasture development and the like. The schemes were prepared by the technical departments of the government, without the choice of works being based on any scientific cost benefit analysis, but on a subjective judgement by the concerned technical departments. The major elements in this action-oriented programme were: conducting an unemployment survey, preparing an employment budget, registering workers, formulating work projects and implementing these projects.

The evaluation of PIREP projects have shown:

(i) that the formulation and selection of work projects were not done on the basis of an area plan;

(ii) that the project has not succeeded in creating a resource base for generation of self-sustained employment, as it was not based on a long-term development programme;

(iii) that the institutional and organizational arrangements to put through the programme hindered the implementation of this project;

(iv) that the mix of projects selected and implemented were not necessarily the optimum;

(v) that in some cases the much required other complementary investments by different departments were not forthcoming; and

(vi) that an employment programme for the rural areas has to be part of a larger and comprehensive exercise in area development planning.

(g) *Project Reports prepared for the Comprehensive Area Development Programme (CADP) of West Bengal,*[41] particularly for Deganga (District 24-Parganas North) and Tamluk-I (District Midnapur) are of interest to us. Under this programme, in the *first phase*, the development plan is drawn up on a macro basis taking the area as a whole, and in the *second phase*, the macro plan is fitted with plan and programmes based on minute details of both physical and socio-economic conditions of the smallest planning unit namely the village, with more direct and more extensive involvement of local people confined to second phase.

The method of preparing the plan during the first phase consisted of constituting different Working Groups, whose work was co-ordinated by a Steering Committee, both of which consisted of a number of technical experts of the district, with the basic information required for the plan being furnished by the relevant Working Groups and some information (particularly the felt needs of the people) being also collected from the local people through discussions held at the village level.

The development plan drawn on the macro basis provides broad by the amount and type of credit, power and other inputs necessary for realization of the production and employment potential for the area. Starting with resource inventory, the irrigation potential of the area is explored in detail. The plan recommends the most suitable overall cropping pattern for the area keeping in view the production maximization target, irrigation arrangements, credit-marketing system, storage and agro-service facilities, aggregate input requirements, peasants' training arrangements, subsidiary occupations like dairy, poultry, fishery, types of rural industries that may be started and so on. The overall capital and recurring costs of the project and economic viability of different kinds of production activities in the area have all been worked out in the plan and proposals for growth centres and service centres have been included.

Employment aspects have been duly considered in the project report, and the total labour requirements in the area for agricultural development according to the lines envisaged in the plan has been worked out, both month-wise and crop-wise in detail. Thus, the employment opportunities likely to be created by the proposed agricultural and industrial schemes has been worked out. The fixed capital and the working capital requirements for the various programmes have been worked out and the sources of funding have been indicated.

(h) *Spatial Approach for District Planning A Case Study of Karnal District* by Sharma is a peculiar study.[42] The main objective of the study, which is essentially micro-regional in nature, is to analyse the process of a region's growth as a functional unit at the lowest level of organization of the economic activity spatially, taking the settlement hierarchy and space relations as constituting an expression of a region's physiographic structure, resource base (physical and human) and the state of development. The study is essentially as a prelude to an understanding of the complex relationships among different regional elements, requiring intensive field work preferably by sample surveys using specially prepared questionnaires.

In spatial planning from grass roots-level there is a need for vertical and horizontal integration and co-ordination of development activities. For instance the spatial framework of the development plan at the Block level should be viewed as a part of the similar effect for the larger areas unit like the District of which the Block is a complementary unit. The 'synoptic' or bird's eye viewpoint conveyed in the principles of regional planning finds its relevance in such studies. The study hoped that the techniques of analysis and findings of the study would serve to assess the approach to micro-level planning in the context of the integrated rural development strategy.

The unit area for the study of settlements, population and their attributes was the village. The data on land use and cropping pattern was on the tehsil basis. Since the objective of the study was to examine the hierarchic pattern of settlements, if any, it was considered essential to restrict the study to villages of more than 2000 population and all the urban centres. Empirical studies revealed that most of the services and facilities begin to occur beyond the population size of 2000. The findings of the study that a population of 3000 is the basic minimum level at which central function get located in settlements which justify its location was taken such a selective approach.

The study is based primarily on secondary data though field tours were undertaken. In the course of field tours, discussion with a number of people, connected directly or indirectly with the problems of space relations were held. The data were made available through different organizations of which the important ones are: the Directorate of Economics and Statistics; Directorate of Census Operations, Haryana; Directorate of Industries and Agricultural Marketing Board.

Christaller's Central Place Model and Losch's Model of Economic Landscape provided the necessary theoretical and conceptual framework for planned development examined in the study. There have been departures from the original and classical versions of these models. These theories are criticized for their limited applicability but according to the study they provide a frame for regional analysis. Central Place theory has three main elements; namely urban centres; their hexagonal market area; and transport networks. By substituting settlements for urban centres, zones of influence for hexagonal market areas, and movement patterns for transport networks, the study found that the theory can be made applicable to non-urban hierarchy also. Empirical studies on settlement functions both in the developed and developing regions revealed the existence of different tiers of settlement functions and distinct spatial and hierarchic patterns of consumer travel behaviour. The study urges that instead "over critical judgement on the geographical regularities, the number of central places and the size and shape of the trade and service areas, the behavioural assumptions of the theory should be accepted and the theory should be treated as normative for working out a locational model of central places". The present study of Karnal District is an attempt in examining the pattern hierarchy taking note of certain regularities in the distribution of settlements, relative uniformity of the agricultural landscape and the emergence of market towns and urban-industrial centres along the major routes converging on Delhi.

(i) *Strategy for Integrated Area Development Case Study of North Kanara District (Karnataka)*[43] by Bhat is a well known work by a well known of micro-planning expert. Bhat holds that Development Block, the District and sub-regions within States comprising groups of District/Development Blocks provide a basis for planning close to ground reality integrating and co-ordinating the plans, at these area levels, and only against this background that the merits of decentralised planning using sub-regions within States can be appreciated.

The study attempts to illustrate that all planning is for planning of land use and settlements in terms of an approach to integrated area planning. The physical resources, the human settlements and their attributes in the area need systematic analysis in terms of their spatial distribution pattern of association potentials. The concept of a resource inventory needs elaboration in a spatial context unlike a huge data inventory that is now being built up at different area levels and departments thanks to the access to computer facilities.

Social facilities and amenities and economic activities need to be analyzed as an exercise in locational analysis, where the application of Central Places and Growth Centres, have been dominant, but these have been 'foot loose' because the resources and their levels of utilization influencing the pattern of emergence of nodes or central places have hardly been considered in a spatial context.

Emphasis on environment, programmes to alleviate poverty, IRDP (Integrated Rural Development Programme) intended to create durable assets and several ad hoc plan programmes (e.g. SFDA, Small Farmer Development Agency) need to be built in our studies in Integrated Area Planning or else they may degenerate to the situation where they can neither be treated as micro-regional studies nor as exercises oriented to planning.

The concept of Integrated Area Development in the study lays stress on spatial integration of development activities, which has been lacking (according to Bhat) in the procedure adopted in the planning process at all the levels of the political-administrative framework, namely the national, state and District levels. The approach to spatial integration itself has often been spelt out and practised differently by specialists from different social sciences and by the planners and by the administrators. The approach to spatial integration, the study emphasizes should be attempted at different scale of the geographical surface ranging from the micro (comparable to the size of a District and below) to macro (group of states or parts thereof) levels with appropriate levels of aggregation or dis-aggregation of activities according to their relative importance. At the micro level the geographic space provides a spatial framework which is realistic, where all the human settlements can be plotted on a map and their spatial patterns of distribution, linkages, social services and facilities and economic activities and their inter relationship can be studied as a part of the evolution of the region as a functional-economic entity. Similarly, the resource base—particularly of agriculture, forestry, minerals, water and power can be evaluated in terms of their area coverage in the geographical surface. In fact, the strategy for integrated area development implies integration of human settlements, population and its attributes included with the resource base; and the necessary conditions are provided by the spatial framework mentioned above.

It is against this background of the conceptual framework that the present study is an attempt to highlight the spatial aspects of the strategy for integrated Area Development of a district in Karnataka.

A good deal of confusion also exists in the planning literature in India regarding micro-level planning, Area Development, Integrated Rural Development and so on. The present study in its spatial view regards the twin facets of rural and urban aspects of development as inter-related. Viewed from this consideration the urban centres and a large number of rural settlements are to be treated as "nodes" which are necessary for integrated development of the areas at the level of Development Block (village clusters) and the District, Village being the lowest or local unit of planning.

(j) *Planning Unit Areas for Integrated Rural Development Studies in Integrated Rural Development*[44] by M. Vivekananda Rao attempt to understand the prevailing distribution pattern of amenities and services and the contact pattern of villages on other places for marketing and employment with a view of judge the minimal planning unit without resorting to a large scale expansion of the present basic amenities and services, keeping in view the norms for providing them. Further, in view of the non-feasibility of providing other rural amenities and services to the 'minimal units' at the present level of development, an attempt is made to identify an area for providing some of these at a reasonable distance from the 'minimal units'.

The present study attempts to identify primary planning units at grass-root level for Integrated Rural Development by taking into account the present level of development of amenities and services and the existing contacts for marketing and employment. The starting point for the analysis is the village. The study traces the linkages in terms of dependency of sample villages of the district has been studied by Dr. V.M. Rao, based on data from District Census Hand Book, 1971, and therefore, it can be seen as an extension of that study which takes into account the dependency of sample villages on other places. In this study the terms functions, amenities and services are used interchangeably, and "threshold population" and "hinterland population" are used in the analysis to identify hierarchy of functions. The hinterland population for various functions is estimated under certain assumptions as the study is based on a randomly selected sample and the data pertain to the nearest place of availability of various functions is studied through skewness of distance distribution (the distance from sample village to the place where the function is located). In the study the location aspect of functions is considered and not the spatial preference of the villages, but, the spatial preference are reflected in marketing and employment contacts. The study has, additionally taken into account only the availability of functions but not their qualitative aspects.

The results of the study are given in four sections with the first section dealing with amenities and services, the second section dealing with marketing, the third section dealing with employment and the fourth strategy.

(k) *Integrated Rural Area Development Planning A Case Study of Backward Area*[45] by Singh is also of interest to us. The concept of 'integrated rural areas development' has now been unanimously accepted by our planners, economists, geographers and sociologists as the most effective tool for a comprehensive development programme covering all aspects of economy and all sections of society. The present study entitled, 'Integrated Rural Area Development and Planning of Ghasipur Tehsil' is the outcome of detailed and intensive study and attempts at providing a comprehensive framework for a coordinated and balanced development of the entire region based on its resource potentials and man-power, to provide a better standard of living and employment to the people of the region through the optimum utilization of land and irrigation potential, proper arrangements for agricultural credit, livestock improvement, marketing facilities, provision of better health and education and development of transport system. In order to achieve these goals, the quantitative as well as qualitative approach has been adopted to evaluate the development potential of the study region and strategy of 'growth centre' used as development policy instrument.

The present study, except its theoretical part, is primarily based on the field observation, official records, available literature, personal knowledge and analysis of data and various other information. Apart from using data from secondary sources questionnaires were used for collecting some primary statistics.

(I) The study by Amitabh Kundu and Moonis Raza[46] for rural electrification programme for two districts of Madhya Pradesh, namely Bastar and Chandrapur, is a class by itself.

In Bastar and Chandrapur districts where the total number of inhabited villages is around 3,000 each, a study of all the villages from the angle of assessing their potential for electrification is difficult. The rural electrification schemes according to the stipulated norms by REC are generally prepared for a block or a cluster of villages falling in one or more blocks. This study, simply provided a broad planning frame to estimate how many electrification schemes can come up in these districts by a target year under the given constraints of finance and electric power.

The projections for the study is made in several stages. The future number of connections and connected load under different users' categories have been obtained through regression analysis, based on several alternative linear formulations as indicated below:

(i) Data on connected load over different years have been used to project the electricity requirement by the target year under various load categories using time as the basic explanatory variables.

(ii) Econometric models using a number of socio-economic variables have been used for explaining the inter-block and inter-village variations in the connected load and number of connections for the most recent year for the study, namely 1976-77, which has then been used for projection purposes.

Thus we see that the regression models based on cross-sectional data have been constructed at two levels: first, the model has been prepared on the basis of the block level data; and second, the village level data for the 50 villages have been used to estimate regression equations separately for the two district, where as some of the variables used in the first model had to be dropped because of the non-availability of data. The secondary data relating to cultivated area, net area sown, number of water points, etc., have been collected through primary surveys in case of each of the selected villages to build up this predictive model.

(iii) A time-series profile of trend of the number of connections and connected load has been obtained for electrified villages for five years, which has been used for making projection of load and connections for an average village in each block. This average figure times the number of villages to be electrified gives the relevant number of connection or connected load for each block.

(iv) For assessing the potential of industries based on agricultural produce, first the production of the relevant crops has been estimated for 1983. After deducting the projected demand for final consumption the amount available for intermediate use has been worked out which will determine the upper limit of the capacity for the agro-based industries assuming no export (from the district) of raw material. Similarly, surplus (for intermediate use) for forest-based and other industries has been estimated. These projections ultimately help in estimating the total power requirements for industrial sector in the districts. As the distribution of future industrial units within the districts are important in the formulation of rural electrification schemes, the important places and their hierarchy have been found out using simple statistical methods of aggregation.

(v) Input coefficients of power for various industrial units have been used to estimate the requirement for electricity based on the number of units of different industries, i.e., commodity groups.

The alternative projections for electricity consumption, connection, etc. for various usages based on different methods enabled us to examine the validity of the results and discuss the relevance of alternative assumptions. In case of significant difference between the different projections, further analysis has been carried out to identify the reason for such anomalies, and an attempt has been made to get more realistic set of projections.

These projections have then been cross-checked in terms of the availability of crucial resources which define the upper limit to capacity. For instance, there is a limit to the ground water potential in different parts of the district, and a realistic projection for the area under different crops and productivity of land has to be set within the constraint of ground water potential. While projecting the projection of different agricultural crops essential for the agro-industries it is necessary to ensure that the area under different crops and the per hectare yield etc., are not taken to be higher than the upper limit imposed by the soil and climatic conditions, which would in turn provide a cross-check on the number of industrial units and their production capacity.

Another important consideration in making these projections was the future strategy of development pursued by the Government. The provision of subsidy for promoting agriculture and industries in a district by the State Government has a vital role to play in this regard. The Rural Electrification schemes can succeed only when such measures are taken in a well-coordinated fashion.

(m) *Service Centres in Rural India Policy, Theory and Practice*[47] by Wanmali is one of the major works in this regard. This study is placed within the growing field of interest in government policy and its impact on the distribution of rural services in the Third World. There are several themes running through the study. Some of these are (i) models and theories of service provision, (ii) state policy in service provision, (iii) role of government and private sector's ion service provision, (iv) impact of rural development programmes of the government on the regional economy, (v) role of spatial planning in rural India particularly at the district, and sub-district levels, and (vi) impact of resource base on the pattern of service provision.

The study is based on the field survey undertaken in 1978-79 in Milryalguda taluka of Nalgonda district of Andhra Pradesh. A similar survey which was conducted in this area about ten years ago provides the bench mark against which the the findings of the present study are examined. The study area is a part of command area of Nagarjunasagar Hydro-Electric Project on the River Krishna. A part of the study area cannot be irrigated and, therefore, is dry. The analysis of the impact of policies of government and private sectors, in the area of service provision, on the dry and the irrigated tracts of the Taluka can be of some interest. In addition to being of practical value to the Development of the Government of Andhra Pradesh, the exercise has a much wider relevance. Further, it facilitates a more rigorous examination of the theoretical models of regional development than any so far attempted in the Indian context

The dissertation concentrates upon a critique of the urban and industries based models of spatial development in India, a critique of the modified growth pole hypothesis of Misra, Sundaram and Rao. The work comprises, inter alia, of description of the study area and the analysis of its regional economy (irrigation, cropping pattern, change in population, and in population size, distribution), the analysis of service provision in the study area (locations of rural and retail service, use of these services, service centres, structure of service centres, service areas, service population sex distribution of service provision), the analysis of the spatial impact of service provision (per square mile incidence of rural and retail services, sectoral and spatial view of this process), and a spatial model for rural development which is based on the rural-urban view rather than the current urban-rural view. What makes the discussion interesting is that it studies the change in the same region, in the same villages, and in the regional economy, after a gap of almost ten years.

The foregoing review is by no means exhaustive; it is at best illustrative. There have been several other very major contributions like the Chitradurga study[48] of Misra and the Raichur Plan[49] by Lalit Sen et. al. which portray major methodologies in district planning, but they could not be discussed here. The EMPOV model of the UNCRD, Nagoya Japan by Ranjit Dhar et. al.[50] and the Western Ghat Project[51] also have distinct though specialised methodologies of their own. By and large we have been guided in our choice by the turn considerations of their replicability and the wider canvas of aplication. Twenty one methodologies have been discussed in this study in all.

Notes and References

1. Mukherjee, Neela and Mukherjee, Amitava: *Supply Side Analysis of Poverty Alleviation Programme* (Mussoorie: Lal Bahadur Shastri National Academy of Administration) 1990, manuscript).

2. Government of India: *Report of the Working Group on District Planning* (New Delhi: Planning Commission) Vols. I & II, 1984.

3. Mukherjee, Amitava: *Researches in Decentralisation* (New Delhi: Heritage Publishers) 1990.

4. Gujarat, Karnataka and West Bengal are examples in point. These "methodologies" have been discussed in this volume. G. Thimmaiah is of the opinion that the issue of methodology has crystallised in Karnataka and Gujarat only, which view is not shared by us. See G. Thimmaiah: "India", in Maetz, M. and Quieti, M.G.: *Training for Decentralised Planning Lessons from Experience* (Rome: Food & Agriculture Organization) 1987.

5. Misra, R.P. and Sundaram, K.V.: *Multi-Level Planning for Integrated Rural Development in India* (New Delhi: Heritage Publishers) 1980, have defined "methodology" along these lines, which we have followed here.

6. Lichfield, N.; Kettle, P. and Whitebread, M.: *Evolution in the Planning Process* (Oxford: Pergamon Process) 1975, p. 19-21.

7. Misra, R.P. (ed.): *Local Level Planning & Development* (New Delhi: Sterling Publishers) 1983, p. 80.

8. *Ibid.*

9. Misra R.P. (ed): *Local Level Planning and Development* (New Delhi: Sterling Publishers) 1983, p. 81.

10. Basic source: Waller, Peter P.: "The Reduced Planning Approach for Regional Development Programmes in Lagging Areas" in Bendavid-Val, Avrom and Waller, Peter P. (eds.): *Action Oriented Approaches to Regional Development Planning* (New York: Praeger Publishers) 1975.

11. See Misra, R.P.: *loc. cit*, p. 84.

12. Weitz, R.: *Integrated Rural Development: The Rehovot Approach* (Rehovot, Israel: Settlement Study Centre) 1979.

13. Institute of Social Studies Advisory Service: *Theory and Practice of Regional Rural Development and Planning* (The Hague : Institute for Social Studies)1986, P. 148-149.

14. *Idem.*

15. *Idem.*

16. Weitz, R.: *op. cit.*

17. Raay, H.G.T. van: *Regional Planning for Integrated Rural Development* (The Hague : Institute of Social Studies Advisory Service) 1981.

18. Institute of Social Studies Advisory Service: *op. cit.*, p. 154.

19. *Ibid.*, p.156.

20. Raay, H.G.T. van: *Integrated Development of Kedah Region, Malaysia* (The Hague: Institue of Social Studies Advisory Service Mission Report) 1984.

21. Institute of Social Studies Advisory Service: *op. cit.*, p. 158.

22. Stohr, W.B. and Todtling, F.: "Spatial Equity: Some Anti-Theses to Current Regional Development Doctrine", in Folmer, H. and Oosterhaven, J. (eds.): *Spatial Inequalities and Regional Development* (Leyden: Nijhoff) 1978.

23. Gore, C.: *Regions in Question, Space, Development Theory and Regional Policy* (London: Methuen) 1984.

24. Institute of Social Studies Advisory Service: *op. cit.*, p. 160.

25. Stohr, W.B.: "Selective Self-Reliance and Endogenous Regional Development Pre-condition and Constraints", (Wien : Wirtschfts Universitat) Discussion Paper No. 19, 1984.

26. *Ibid.*

27. Friedman, J. and Douglass, M.: "The Agropolitan District Approach", in Lo, F.C. and Salih, K. (eds.): *Growth Pole Strategy and Regional Development Policy: Asian Experience and Alternative Approaches* (Oxford: Pergamon Press) 1978.

28. Douglass, M.: "Territorial Dissolution and Alternative Regional Development for the Central Plains of Thailand", in Stohr, W.B. and Taylor, D.R.F. (eds.): *Development from Above or Below: The Dialectics of Regional Planning in Developing Countries* (Chichester: John Wiley) 1981.

29. *Ibid.*

30. Friedman, J. and Douglass, M.: *loc. cit.* 1978

31. Friedman, J.: "The Active Community; Toward a Political Territorial Framework for Rural Development in Asia", in *Economic Development and Cultural Change*, Vol. 29, 1981.

32. Friedman, J. and Douglass, M.: *loc. cit.* 1978.

33. *Ibid.*, p. 195.

34. *Idem.*

35. Friedman, J. and Weaver, C.: *Territory and Function: The Evolution of Regional Planning* (London: Edward Arnold) 1979, pp. 204-205.

36. Friedman, J. and Douglass, M.: *loc. cit.* 1978 p. 183.

37. Gore, C.: *Regions in Question, Space, Development Theory and Regional Policy* (London: Methuen) 1984.

38. Prantila, B.: "Review of Local Level Planning Process", in Misra, R.P. (ed.): *loc. cit.*, p. 93.

39. Misra, R.P. and Sundaram, K.V.: *Multi-Level Planning for Integrated Rural Development in India* (New Delhi: Heritage Publishers) 1990, pp. 120-127. This is basic source for the recital of this section and of the four sections to follow.

40. *Idem.*

41. *Ibid.*

42. Sharma, A.N.: *Spatial Approach for District Planning* (New Delhi: Concept Publishing Co.), 1980.

43. Bhat, L.S.: *Strategy for Integrated Area Development*, Case Study of North Kanara District (New Delhi: Concept Publishing Company) 1987.

44. Rao, Vivekananda M.: *Planning Unit Areas for Integrated Rural Development* (New Delhi : Ashis Publishing House) 1980.

45. Singh, B.N.: *Integrated Rural Area Development and Planning,* A Case Study of Backward Areas, (New Delhi: Anupama Publications) 1988.
46. Kundu, Amitabh and Raza, Moonis: *Indian Economy, the Regional Dimension,* Centre for the Study of Regional Development, (New Delhi: Jawaharlal Nehru University), 1982.
47. Wanmali, Sudhir:*Service Centre in Rural India,* Policy Theory and Practice, (Delhi: B.R. Publishing Corporation)1983.
48. Misra, R.P.: "District Plan for Chitradurga", being Part II, of Misra, R.P. (ed.): *District Planning A Handbook* (New Delhi: Concept Publishing Company) 1990.
49. A part of Raichur Plan is at Annexure-XI of Chapter XV.
50. Dhar, Ranjit and Rao, M. Rammohan: *The Empov Model* A Supply Side Model for Rapid Employment Promotion and Removal of Poverty in Developing Countries, with an Experiment in Bangalore District (Nagoya, Japan: United Nations Centre for Regional Development) April 1983.
51. Government of Kerala: *Report of the Task Force-I, Appointed by the Steering Committee on Western Ghats Development Programme* (Trivandrum: Government of Kerala) 1989.

CHAPTER II

DISTRICT DEVELOPMENT SCHEME

(VISVESVARAYA METHODOLOGY)[1]

I. INTRODUCTION

In an undeveloped country, like India, there is need for improvement and development in many directions: improvement under communication, housing, water supply, sanitation and other social wants. All these needs however, should be subservient to economic advancement, because, if production from agriculture and industries is increased, there will be allround rise in income which will enable the people to raise their standards of living. "Animalities are fundamental". As a first step, therefore, the masses have to be provided with opportunities of earning a reasonable income to provide themselves with the physical wants.

The immediate object of the proposals outlined here is to urge that "at least one district in every Indian Province be taken up for intensive development by planning", which will not put any appreciable strain on the resources of a local Government. The district chosen may need financial support for the first four or five years or so for development planning, after which the experiment ought to be self-sustaining.

II. MAIN LINES OF DEVELOPMENT

"The basic wants of a family may be taken as six in number — Food, Clothing, Housing, Education, Recreation and Amusement, and Work". As vast masses of the rural population lead a hand-to-mouth existence any scheme for ameliorating their condition should aim at making provision for the necessities of life. If the standard of living of the poorer classes who constitute more than 75 per cent of the population is raised, the standard of living of the middle and upper classes will rise automatically.

III. DATA

The information is to be collected in statistical tables for each residential area or region by means of surveys which will reveal approximately, the productive capacity and income of the area, and show whether the income earned is sufficient or not to provide the people with the minimum wants of a healthy and decent existence.

The tables and information gathered will reveal: the total population of the district, its average annual income; the proportion of income that is distributed between the various occupations and the proportion of people employed in various occupations. Changes and adjustments from time to time for the maintenance of a proper balance of the composition of occupations amongst those who are employed and secure a progressive rise in the standard of living.

The survey and statistical statements collected will reveal how the average individual income in a village, town or city stands as compared with that needed for normal subsistence. Evidence suggests that at the present the income of an average family is in the neighbourhood of about 62 per cent of what they need and for three-fourths of the rural population, the average does not seem to exceed even 30 per cent of what they need. The first endeavour should, therefore, be to provide gainful occupations and services to people so that they can secure the minimum income for every family in the district, necessary to have the bare necessities of life, by even Indian standards.

The statistical statements resulting from the surveys will indicate to trained minds, the specialists and the experts, the directions in which industries and employment should be increased or multiplied in order to raise the income.

The district economic council and the development office superintendent and their expert staff will be assisted considerably by the statistics so collated in advising the local village councils about the directions in which their productive activities should be extended and strengthened for increasing income substantially.

IV. AIM OF DISTRICT DEVELOPMENT PLANNING

The appalling amount of unemployment and particularly under-employment allround is due to a wrong conception of life, that work is an unpleasant necessity (rather than one of the six wants of a healthy family life), the ignorance of the population, lack of guidance by public leaders of Government and the utter absence of economic planning and organization.

"The aim of the district development scheme is to lead the people to work under discipline, to take up the most profitable occupations within their reach, to double their average income and mitigate their existing poverty and distress. In their very attempt to double their present average income, the people of a district will acquire the initiative, vigour and co-operative effort necessary to provide themselves with their further wants".

Steps should be taken to provide temporary relief to the poorest classes by organizing for their benefit new units of work and new employment opportunities as an emergency measure.

The main lines of development to be pursued in District Development Planning will include the following policies and measures:

(a) The people should be induced and trained to develop an attitude for harder work, more methodical way of working and in closer co-operation with their neighbours to increase production.

(b) A survey of economic conditions should be carried out to find out the present shortcomings which afflict the people; the directions in which reforms should be affected and remedies which are necessary and to create and select occupations for them.

(c) Occupations which generate the highest remuneration or profit should be chosen.

(d) The district should be equipped with appropriate institutions, directing staff and policies to promote development.

(e) Elementary education should be spread rapidly, particularly among the adult population, because without education and an informed public, it would not be possible to attempt at building up efficiency or prosperity.

V. DISTRICT ORGANIZATION

The population of an average district in British India is about one million souls. The total yearly income of such a district, may be taken to be about Rs. five crores. The aim of District Development Planning is to double this income within a period of seven to ten years, which is proposed to be done on the footing of a carefully thought out plan and programme and with the aid of an agency specially chosen for the purpose.

The superintendence and control of District Development Planning and its implementation will be invested in a development officer and his staff working in close association with a district economic council, made up of seven to twelve members, nearly half of whom will be elected by the people of the district. The executive work of the district economic council will be attended to by the district development officer, who will have two deputies and a staff of some twelve assistants, who will be expected while working in close cooperation with the council, to execute orders handed down by the State or provincial government concerned.

VI. PLAN TYPOLOGY

The economic council will take into account the material and human resources, available in the district while preparing the plans and schedules of work to be executed in each official year. The council will also prepare a Five-Year Plan embodying forecasts of developments in various aspects of the district's economic life for the ensuing five years, including the year for which a working plan and budget are prepared.

The three essential parts of a district development scheme are: a plan, schedule of works and a budget, all of which will be constantly undergoing revision and development at the hands of the economic council and the district development staff. The plan, the schedule of works and the budget will be prepared in accordance with the provisions of the scheme and the instructions of the controlling authority in the provincial or State government concerned.

The services of qualified public-spirited citizens who volunteer for this scheme may be utilized in a capacity to be decided by the district development officer either as individual officials or in committees constituted for local objects (under the scheme) and will be subordinate to the development officer and will be subject to all the rules and discipline expected of them.

VII. VILLAGE AND TOWN ORGANIZATIONS

To encourage self-government among the rural masses it will be convenient if a group of villages, perhaps 10 or 12 in number, are treated as a village union or unit and operated together, the combined population of which may vary between 5,000 and 10,000 with the office of the village council established in a centrally situated village within the group, and of seven to twelve members, elected for a one year term at a time from amongst the most competent residents in the area, by an electoral college of headmen of families residing in it.

The elected Chairman of the Council will be responsible to the District Collector and to the district development officer for the performance of all the duties assigned to the village council under the scheme.

The village office will keep record of statistics of production and income of the population of the constituent villages and prepare a report embodying the necessary statistical tables at the end of each year, which will indicate the income in each village and the average income per family and per head of population in the whole cluster of villages.

Under the advice and instructions of the district development department, the village council will draw up a list of raw materials and other resources available for generating employment to local labour; of industries and trades which require encouragement in the coming year; indicate the amount of capital and material needed and ways and means to obtain them. The estimates and plans when prepared will be submitted to the district development officer for approval and after obtaining of necessary sanction the proposals will be implemented.

The villagers will be encouraged to concentrate attention on gainful occupations, and new activities in the village will include extension of irrigation, use of fertilizers, establishment of new industries, expansion of old industries and promotion of trade to increase income and revenue of the village population.

Concurrently, under the advice and direction of the development department, a forecast of production and income for the ensuing period of five years may be prepared and in some villages attempts will be made to achieve 50 per cent increase in income by the end of the fifth year of the programme.

Such increase may not be possible in every village, but in some villages, by rapid nurturing of new industries the income could be increased by more than 100 per cent.

In the case of the agricultural population, income is certain to fall in some years on account of bad rainfall or in a lesser degree by excessive rain or heavy floods or inundations. It is, therefore, advisable to increase employment in industries and other occupations. The results of each year will be maintained in suitable statistical tables, registers and reports, copies of which will be kept in the village council office, and also in the district office of the development department.

In every district in each such town and city, an urban development council should be established to encourage the growth of industries, trade and other occupations and to collect and record statistics of production, service and income. Detailed methods of development can be worked out for each city and town, having regard to the nature of its occupations, commercial activities and aptitudes.

VIII. OCCUPATIONAL AND PRODUCTION SURVEY

Almost the first work of the development department should be to investigate: how the people of the district are employed, how many of them are in agriculture, how many of them are in industries, trade, transport and other services and what is their aggregate income in each of these classes of occupations. For a true picture of the resources and earning capacity of the people, the distribution of the total population and income distribution in the respective occupations is essential.

A survey of industries should have a high priority, because they typify occupations which have been neglected in the recent past which is why they are likely to generate handsome returns in the future, if undertaken at once and pursued along correct lines.

The first labours of the survey would, therefore, be to collect data for industries in each cluster of village and in each urban unit in the district area under the following heads:

(i) Number of establishments or separate units of work;
(ii) Capital invested;
(iii) Labour employed;
(iv) Products and their value; and
(v) Per capita value of industrial output in each unit area.

An assessment of existing industries in the district should be made and a list should be prepared of other new industries that can be profitably established, which will be among the earliest results of the development programme.The next most important work would be a comprehensive survey of occupations in the district, under four classes as under:

(i) Industries and crafts;
(ii) Agriculture and allied occupations;
(iii) Trade and transport; and
(iv) Services, professional, public, domestic, etc.

This survey should generate information under each of these groups of occupations regarding products (if any) and their values, total population including dependents maintained and the amount of income in each group. Thus the income, or the approximate income, of the entire population of a cluster of village, town or city can be worked out and statistical tables of total income, per capita income and other data for the entire district can be prepared. Simultaneously, a register should be prepared of able-bodied persons who are unemployed, and of approximate number of people who suffer from under-employment or seasonal unemployment, which are necessary to provide a complete idea of the economic situation in the district.

A glance at such data will show how heavily agriculture is overweighted and how great is the necessity to afford relief to the soil by transferring the surplus population now dependent on agriculture to industries and other gainful occupations. An occupational survey of the kind suggested above is likely to reveal the following more obvious defects in the economy of the State

(i) that the people are insufficiently employed and, although prepared to work, their opportunities of obtaining suitable employment and earning a decent living are limited;
(ii) that the income of the people in most districts, save in irrigated tracts or industrial neighbourhoods, is below what is necessary for a normal healthy existence;
(iii) that for want of mass education and training the people do not have courage to start new enterprises and skill to secure new sources of income; and
(iv) that for lack of proper business environment, credit and co-operation are at a discount and new business undertakings are of necessity slow to take root.

IX. AIDS TO DEVELOPMENT

Sound policies, institutions, equipment and administrative practices can all help in the production of commodities and services, which may be considered under two heads, namely:

(i) Principal Aids, and
(ii) Subsidiary Aids.

The principal aids to development are aids which are practically indispensable for the purpose of district development and partake the nature of banking facilities, statistics, tariff protection, mass education and travel conveniences. The subsidiary aids are commercial museums, exhibitions and fairs, research, marketing and transport facilities, workshops and training institutions, and commercial and trade schools.

(i) Principal Aids

Government should use its good offices to make available capital in the district for purposes of production by raising the capital required wholly or partly in the district itself, to reduce the exorbitant rates of interest on loans prevailing in the rural tracts, ensuring at the same time that the security of the loans advanced is not jeopardized.

One of the greatest needs, if not the greatest, for the encouragement of industries, is protection against undesirable imports and dumping by foreign countries. For tariff protection to local producers and manufacturers, the Government departments concerned should keep examining the issues pertaining to protection and make representations as required, from time to time, both to Provincial and Federal Governments and Legislatures.

Mass education should be vigorously pushed forward along with development activities. "Real economic progress cannot be secured, and, when secured, will not long survive unless backed by a well-informed enlightened public opinion". Here, there will be obstacles because the richer land-owning classes are opposed to their tenants receiving education through fear that they might get out of control. Local travel agencies managed on business lines, if brought into existence, will materially assist further inter-communication and commercial intercourse, and help to promote unity between all parts of India.

A large number of well-managed hotels should be established in towns and cities and lodging houses should be established in centrally situated villages subsidized by village councils. With model hotels established in cities and towns and model lodging and boarding houses established in villages, the pace of business life of a district will be appreciably quickened.

(ii) Subsidiary Aids

There should be a commercial museum with adequate staff—one at least at the headquarter station in each district both to exhibit sample products, chiefly to serve as patterns for local manufacture and to serve as an agency from which should emanate all proposals for holding periodical exhibitions and fairs in the principal towns and business places in the district.

In agriculture, a wide range of experiments in scientific methods of production, fertilizers, eradication of pests, marketing problems, crop insurance, utilization of farm wastes, irrigation and the like, should be provided for and a laboratory should be established in many a modern industry for regulating manufacturing processes, because raw materials are required to be tested and finished products made to conform to standard specifications.

Some organization is needed to provide the illiterate cultivator with adequate marketing facilities because currently due to the ignorance of the cultivator, the middle man takes advantage of his helpless position and buys the produce of his labour at a low price and sells it at rates advantageous to himself in the nearest town or city.

Both for products of new industries and for transport of raw or semi-raw materials intended for manufacture, railways should be induced to charge low freight rates, and wherever rates are disadvantageous to industry they should be brought to the notice of the Central Government for redressal.

An experimental and demonstration station may be usefully established at the headquarter town of the district to impart instruction, say, in some half a dozen industries which are likely to prove profitable to the people of the district, and concurrently a central workshop should be maintained to give practical training in manufacture. Either classes should be attached to existing schools or separate trade schools should be maintained to give instructions in various occupations, such as weaving, tailoring, smithing, carpentry, and so on, and an elementary knowledge of economics should be imparted along with such training.

Seventy five per cent of the juvenile population passing through the educational institutions in the districts should have practical training of some sort, so that in their subsequent life span, every single individual among them may be either a producer or a worker, adding to the wealth of the district.

X. POLICIES AND IMPLICATIONS

From the foregoing, the following practical measures suggest themselves:

(a) Radical changes will be necessary in the economic structure and policies in the districts, if the present per capita income is to be substantially raised.

(b) Certain new policies and practices are recommended in the district development scheme directed at changing the economic structure in a district involving public control of the economic structure. Under the proposed scheme, this control is vested in the district development department and the district economic council working jointly. The ultimate control of the local government over all district development works will, however, remain unaffected.

(c) Selected men, whether officials or non-officials, should be trained and employed on the scheme, and only enthusiastic officials and popular leaders who can render disinterested public service should be chosen for the work.

(d) Among the officials and volunteers employed in the district under the development department, a reasonable proportion of the employees should, if possible, be persons who have been educated or have widely travelled abroad.

(e) New occupations should be started and old ones expanded as may be necessary, particularly those which would give an abundant supply of the basic wants of the population—in food, clothing and shelter.

(f) Units of production and business undertakings should be multiplied by bringing capital, labour, organization and managerial ability together, wherever there may be scope for income and profit generation.

(g) Because this scheme is confined to a district, minor industries should be brought into its fold.

(h) Lists or tables, should be prepared, showing how much grain, cloth, housing materials, educational and other facilities are available and how much more are needed by making estimates.

(i) Statistics of production particularly under agriculture and industries should be collected first and maintained in every village union, in town unit areas as well as in the district as a whole. Preparation of occupational statistics should follow.

(j) Statistics of changes in the occupational structure as far as can be ascertained should be published along with annual reports.

(k) Tariffs should be watched and adjusted from time to time.

(l) Rural indebtedness and exorbitant rates of interest charged by the money lender are evils which should be attacked and remedied at the very outset, wherever possible.

(m) Reform and re-awakening in universities is essential to train young men and women in the science of better living, so that a good proportion of them, after they pass through the university portals, may be able to enter farms, factories or shops and carry on business with success after a brief apprenticeship, if necessary.

(n) To make the people industry-minded and to create an atmosphere of progress, information campaign should be resorted to by writing and distributing leaflets, of public lectures, and other means of communication. The information to be disseminated ought to have bearing on:

  (i) past experience and present state of industries in India;

(ii) recent experience in the same field in progressive countries;

(iii) a knowledge of up-to-date machinery in common use; and

(iv) modern processes of production and the latest industrial and commercial practices.

(o) The public should be kept informed up-to-date, by widely circulating information, from time to time, about the true state of affairs in respect of the following:

(i) specific facilities and concessions given by Government to encourage industries;

(ii) the nature of and conditions under which expert advice provided by Government can be procured;

(iii) the distribution of population and income by occupations; and

(iv) maintenance of accurate current records and statistics.

(p) No efforts should be spared to start new units of work for the benefit of the large numbers of people who suffer from unemployment and under-employment.

(q) In both rural and urban unit areas, much of the success of the proposed scheme will depend upon the growth of the working capacity of individual families and citizens, which should be stimulated by well devised information campaign, by devising a system of incentive and disincentives and by other methods of encouragement, with the aid of public-spirited leaders and local committees.

(r) The co-operative spirit among the people should be particularly stimulated, opportunities being provided for them to work together in unison in production and profit-making occupations.

(s) And finally the district development department, with the aid of the economic council, should be able to check malpractices in business concerns by exercising a kind of paternal control and by bringing to bear on them the moral influence of the community.

XI. A CONCRETE PROGRAMME

There is at present neither any plan, nor any national policies, for solving new economic problems that emerge at various points in time, and planning on a national scale will require the active co-operation of the people and the support of the Government. Till such time when a national plan does not come into existence, individual districts whose administration is to some extent within the hands of the people themselves, may attempt planned development.

The district development scheme herein proposed gives the outlines of a desirable plan, aimed at making an intensive effort to increase production by persuading the people to work harder, and under discipline, to work more intelligently and effectively.

Size and Resources of a District

For purposes of illustration, the following hypothetical data may be assumed for a district in which the same may be brought into operation:

Area of District	5,000 sq. miles
Population	1,000,000
Annual Revenue to be made available for expansion of industries and for improving agriculture and developing occupations generally	Rs. 80 lakhs
Yearly Grant for maintaining the district development scheme	Rs. 5 lakhs

The cost of maintaining the development department may be taken at Rs. 5 lakhs for the first three years, of which Rs. 3 lakhs for a central workshop and other training institutions, all of which sum should, in the first instance, be met out of a provincial grant. If the plan succeeds, the income of the people will increase and so will the Government revenue, with it, from new industries and new avenue employment for the people. From the third year onwards, this grant may be reduced and eventually withdrawn.

Main Lines of Development

The five principal objectives of planning, in the present case, are—

(i) to ascertain the demand and supply of goods to the people;

(ii) to preach the gospel of hard-work and the value of co-operative effort;

(iii) to create new sources of production;

(iv) to bring work within the reach of every able-bodied citizen; and

(v) through these measures to double the income and standard of living of the people in seven to ten years time.

It is proposed that, to begin with, the scheme be limited to the reconditioning of one district at a time in each Province or State in the manner stated above.

District Organisation

This will consist of:

1. An Economic Council;
2. A District Development Department, and Budget; and
3. A Five-Year Plan.

The economic council may consist of seven to twelve members. District economic conferences will be held at regular intervals in the year where officials, experts, leading businessmen and active citizens from all parts of the district will be invited to participate. The district should be properly equipped with offices,institutions, policies, staff, and experts who would be able to guide the people in starting and in operating new units of work, in company formation and co-operative business practices and continue to do so till occupations are more correctly re-distributed. Certain Indian communities are particularly well versed in such activities, whose special knowledge, skill and practices in this respect might be advantageously put into a modern form and widely disseminated.

Village and Town Organization

The village councils and their headmen will administer a group of villages (with a population varying from 5,000 to 10,000) who will be allowed to tax themselves for the purpose. Panchayats, wherever they exist, may help them with funds to make a beginning. In the first three to five years, Government may subsidize the village councils but thereafter the councils should be made self-supporting.

The urban units will be provided with funds for their work by the municipalities or other local self-government bodies concerned, and as in the case of the village councils, they will be also aided by subsidies from the Government during the first five years. "Eventually when the village units are found working satisfactorily most of the functions of the district administration in the area may be safely transferred to village councils"

Survey and Statistics: A survey will be carried out of production, income, number of workers employed, and so on, in industries, agriculture and other occupations in each unit area and the district as a whole. Statistical tables will be compiled showing the distribution of population and income by occupations, to serve as a guide in planning for the future.

Aids to Development: Simultaneously certain facilities are needed to create an industrial and developmental atmosphere, such as banking facilities, statistics, tariff protection, mass education and travel conveniences.

Capital is required for new industries and for expansion and improvement of agriculture and subsidiary rural occupations. In the initial stages, the amount required may be taken at about the same figure as the total yearly revenues of the district. This sum may in most cases be raised, with the aid of a Government guarantee of interest for a term of years, from well-to-do classes of the population in the district itself. A beginning may be made by raising a loan equivalent to about 25 per cent of the revenues of the district for utilization as capital on minor and cottage industries, which may be gradually increased as demand rises for financing new ventures. The loan should be advanced, as far as possible, not by a Government department but by independent financial organizations, such as local trusts, branch banks or co-operative societies.

Citizenship Training: For training the people for industries and business life, a central workshop, an experimental and demonstration station, a museum, trade schools, commercial classes, farms, and the like, will be brought into existence as required. The cost of these, unless the Government itself comes forward to provide them, should be met by appeal to local industrialists and merchants, leaders and philanthropists backed by handsome subsidies and subventions by Government.

Development Schedules and Budget: Estimates of work to be done and their cost will be collected in the form of schedules for each unit area. Schedules of development for the initial year and approximate schedules for five years will be prepared for each village and each urban development unit first, and from these for the whole district. All works and improvements to be carried out in the year in the village unit area and in the urban unit area including training for industries should be brought on a schedule in this way and the budget for their execution based thereon, which should be duly approved by the district economic council and the development department before the commencement of the new financial year, and the requisite funds in each union should be raised by a local tax or supplied by a local Panchayat, if there be one.

Annual Reports: An annual report embodying the results of the surveys and other progressive measures undertaken in the district during the year should be prepared and copies kept on record in the offices of the local councils and in the district development office at District Headquarters. Copies may also be furnished to other offices as required.

Code of Rules: A code of rules for administering the district development scheme should be prepared and maintained, somewhat imperfect initially but as work progresses, it is bound to gradually improve with the experience gained in advancing the scheme.

XII. SUMMARY

Work is essential for the production of consumers' goods and services requiredto meet the various wants of a human family. Where more work is put into gainful occupations, more income will be generated, and the greater the income the higher would be the standard of living. Longer hours of labour, teamwork, discipline and skill put into labour, and better organization and planning would lead to increased production of goods and services. "To show the way to these various expedients is the object of the district development scheme here described".

The proposed district development scheme, is expected to provide an effective starting point for the economic reconstruction of the countryside, and the specific aim of the plan, to begin with, will be to stimulate the productive capacity of the district and double its income in seven to ten years time. Because of men, money and directing ability to implement district development scheme outlined here, on any large scale, may not be immediately available the scheme may be confined initially to one or two district(s) only in each Province and State.

Developments in such spheres like political, social or cultural areas, should be attempted by creating other independent agencies and not through the district development scheme. Such beneficial measures should be worked together and in close harmony but the immediate aim of the scheme under consideration is limited to economic betterment. Material wants should rank first and as they are fundamental to the very existence of the people, they should be treated as a class by themselves.

Erroneous traditions have to be radically changed and numerous modern practices and policies must be assiduously cultivated to make the people trust each other and co-operate more freely for attaining national aims and ends. And therefore, a district development department associated with a district economic council is proposed to correct defects in the economic life of the people and stimulate progress.

The scheme aims at securing bare subsistence wants mainly for the rural population and is intended for the rehabilitation of a district only.

There are too many people employed in some occupations and too few in others, and production is impeded, which explains why a balanced re-distribution of occupations is strongly urged.

To make up speedily for the past neglect to industry, special measures are contemplated to expand them and increase the proportion of the working population on them to three or four times its present strength.

Paucity of resources, in rural areas either for investment or for use as working capital for the volume of business essential to ensure comfortable working conditions for the people is quite marked. Steps should be taken to ensure the availability circulation of capital, even if it necessitates Government sharing unfavourable risks.

The average citizen should be educated and encouraged to work for the propose plan and induced by lure of income and profit to raise his economic status.

Notes

1. Basic Source: Visvesvaraya, M.: *District Development Scheme : Economic Progress by Forced Marches*, (Bangalore: Bangalore Press)1942.

CHAPTER III

INTEGRATED AREA-UNIT BASED DISTRICT DEVELOPMENT PLANNING

(GADGIL METHODOLOGY)

I. CONCEPTS AND CONSTRAINTS

The two primary requirements of district planning, according to Prof. D. R.Gadgil,[1] are: *one,* the knowledge of local conditions, and *second* the association of local people with the formulation and implementation of the plan. Both these aspects are implied in any development planning, but whereas in India the need of obtaining technical and economic knowledge, data and consultation with people before formulating planning at the national level is well recognised, there is virtually a complete absence of these elements, at the local level.[2] The gap in knowledge and information, is the most glaring at the district level, though some administrative statistics are available, depending on the system of land tenure and the method of maintenance of village records; some data are available regarding the distribution of holdings and cropping patterns, and some technical information may be available in places where the relevant surveys such as those relating to minerals) have been conducted, but for the rest, either technical information is inadequate or is irrelevant. For example, Agricultural Research Centres are few in a State and many districts have no such centres at all with the result that special problems of agricultural production technique cannot be dealt with, except on the basis of information relating to some distant area which may or may not be relevant, locally.

Without a minimum base of such knowledge and information, a plan of development for an area like the district cannot be built up, and while the minimal base will suffice only during the preliminary stages of planning, as planning takes root and it extends in coverage and intensity, the quantum and quality of information and data will have to be progressively increased. An appreciation, of the great importance for local planning, of agencies investigating into local conditions and collecting information on all aspects of socio-economic life and technical production and other activity of the district or the local area, is urgently required for making a proper beginning with district development planning; and provision for continuing extension of investigational and research activity in all the fields at the local level is a necessary concomitant to the continuance and growth of district development planning effort. Until detailed local knowledge is available to test and question the applicability of standard schemes and to provide the base on which to build alternative proposals, the chance of replacing the present approach to planning seems remote.

The second aspect, that of people's participation, in formulation and implementation of plans is equally important, because agencies which are employed for the conduct of research and investigation of the local situation will have to work in close unison with different strata in the local population, without which the success of investigational research effort, so dependent upon an understanding by the relevant element in the local population, will be jeopardized, and because the pattern and the priorities will have to be determined in relation to local needs, choices and opinions. It is true that in several of areas the scope of such choice would be limited, given that the decisions appertaining to the objectives to be pursued, the allocation of funds, the choice of agencies, and such other related matters, are made at higher territorial or planning levels which impose certain constraints on district planning, but it is as much true that within the narrow margin left, the choice should be made locally after a full understanding of the whys and wherefores of the foregoing constraints and their relevance to local choice by the people concerned.

Additionally, only through people's participation that motivation for appropriate formulation and early implementation of plan is created. Whereas the formulation of a plan may be related to technical knowledge and broader objectives, its implementation on the ground (once formulated) would be possible only with full local understanding and cooperation, which necessary condition further reinforces the need for local participation at the formulation stage. Greater wisdom and cooperation at the implementation stage would be forthcoming, if at the stage of plan formulation itself the local elements are fully associated in the process of plan formulation so that there could be widespread appreciation of what is being planned and what the exercise of planning is expected to achieve.

Ordinarily a district is unlikely to be economically homogeneous and district development planning must face problems of planning for a mixed or heterogeneous area, and therefore, it automatically follows that the basic preliminary work of at least some aspects of the district plan must be carried out in terms of smaller, homogeneous area units. While this unit should be small and compact, it should also be large enough to serve as a unit of integrated planning, which is why it must embrace within it a wide variety of economic activity typical of the particular rural economy and it must be capable of being treated as an integrated economic unit for the purposes of planning.[3] The most common factor of integration at this level of rural economy would be sale and supply activity, and where there is some commercialization of agriculture, such a unit may be identified as the primary market area, knowing that there are many obvious difficulties of definition and demarcation involved in the concept as a practical operative planning device and not as a theoretical utopia.

Whereas in terms of the existing situation the area unit may be identified as the market area, in terms of development planning it may be deemed as the lowest area-unit for the integrated provision of socio-economic overheads and services. Clearly enough, this approach to the definition of the lowest area-unit does not lead to an immediate ready, cut and dried identification of a planning area. In conceptual terms the market area has a centre or nucleus and by reason of specially convenient means of communication or otherwise, it serves a fairly well-defined surrounding area as the primary marketing, sale and supply centre. In planning for the future it would be convenient to start with such existing centres and provide, for the surrounding areas, the overheads which must precede development as radiating from the centres. One of the most difficult problems in planning (at the district and sub-district level) for widespread development is that of providing minimum socio-economic overheads everywhere, whose efficient and economic planning is an important task in the initial stages, which is why, it becomes necessary to identify convenient integrated area-units.[4]

Because planning is looked upon as involving coordination, formulation and execution of a number of socio-economic measures and activities for unfolding a given pattern of development, village as an unit of planning is ruled out. This concept of planning assumes at each level and in each sector, a strategy and a programme of economic activity in the state and public sector combined with a regime of fiscal, monetary, physical, and other measures of encouragement and inducement, of regulation and prohibition. The plan is integrated in the sense that the effect of the implementation of the plan is expected, to lead to the initiation and cumulation of different type of public and private economic activities to bring forth development along the warranted path. The national plan is supposed to integrate fully the plans of all tiers and authorities in all sectors. At each lower level, the State and the District, the plan is formulated within the total frame, with given objectives and external data or constraints, derived from the higher level plans. The district is considered here as the lowest area-unit of governmental planning, but because it is ordinarily too large and heterogeneous it would be difficult to formulate an integrated plan directly for the entire area of the district, which is why, while some elements of activity and some integrating factors would operate only at the district level, for the bulwark of primary production, dispersed industrial activity, rural trading and transport or urban activity oriented towards serving the rural economy, etc., the district has to be divided into convenient areas for formulation of an integrated plan for the lowest level area-unit, and the concept of the 'mandi' area is considered as the most appropriate for this purpose.

II. FORMULATION

Given the assumption that the district plan is not a summation of lists of departmental schemes,[5] that there is a minimal base of information and data regarding local conditions, an analysis of the main features of an integrated district plan and the procedures or stages by which it could be put together could be a convenient starting point. Subsequently, with administration organized in terms of activities of certain departments, any scheme or plan will have to be translated into departmental schemes for implementation, but to prepare an integrated plan is one thing in the first instance; its transformation into a series of properly coordinated departmental schemes is another, and the preparation of schemes for individual activity, and sub-activity of each department and then to put them together as a plan, is yet another set of things in the formulation of an integrated plan of a district. The stages or aspects of a district development plan that appear appropriate on the basis of some experience are as follows in the succeeding paragraphs.

Stage-I: The first stage appears to be that of the preparation of the physico-geographic plan of socio-economic overheads, particularly so at the district level, and granted that the main business of a district plan being to influence and direct the activities of thousands of small producers, action in this regard has two aspects: *One,* with regard to the provision of those basic services and amenities without which growth and diversification of economic activity will not come about, and *two,* the provision of those incentives and disincentives which lead to development of economic activity along the warranted path. The first requires, largely, public action in relation to planned provision of utilities and social services, which in our context has to be planned in terms of a physico-geographic frame, and includes the provision of communications which dominates economic activities in the initial stages of planning. Lack of means of communication is the bulwark of backward regions. The establishment of a system of communication integrating the area with all other areas and all locations is, therefore, the *first requirement* for a plan of development. Water, power, the development of economic organizations such as those of marketing and credit, storage and processing, which forms the basis of economic activity are other related essential pre-requisites for development, and social services, like education and health, form vital parts of the provision of socio-economic overheads.

The need to economize and obtain the best results from a given investment, forces on us the necessity of planning carefully, the provision of all these socio-economic overheads. Three requirements of this provision are obvious: *one,* that the spread must be such as to benefit all areas within the district; *two,* that the provision of the costlier utilities and services must be arranged from a hierarchy of convenient centres, and *three,* that in the determination of these centres and the areas served by them, to a large extent, existing patterns of marketing and other economic areas are followed. A physico-geographic plan is thus a plan:

(i) of communications and

(ii) of the development of a series of centres at and from which certain services and amenities are provided, ideas closely connected with the concept of the 'mandi' area unit discussed earlier.

The possibility of looking at location of these centres of services and utilities from two different points of view should be clearly noted. In the *first place,* the centre would essentially be the main centre of marketing and exchange in terms of a small or large area: exchange activities and the provision of the services which have to be most widespread would be the normal function of such centres. In terms of planning development, addition of furnishing technical assistance or the more modern institutionalized economic services such as of credit, storage and processing and of social services such as those relating to education and health to these functions are necessary, but from the point of view of a development plan, especially in relation to the growth of non-farm activity, a centre may be thought of as a centre of growth of industrial or other activity which helps to transform the economy of the surrounding region. Clearly enough, the concept and the location of a centre of this type would be different from that of the traditional centre. A district plan must provide for the development of well distributed centres of the traditional type for the entire district. The industrial development plan of the district may select some of these centres for intensive development of some types of non-farm activity, or find it necessary, for whatever reason, to develop other centres for particular purposes, but as the two types of centres will have different functions, the utilities and services located in them and the demarcation of their areas will follow different principles, in so far as the former will adopt a generalized common approach, the latter will be related to certain specific aims.

Stage-II: The second stage of an integrated district plan relates to the conservation and development of natural resources. A country dominated by rural economy, and where agriculture employs such a large proportion of the working force, that a development plan at the district level has to deal with the conservation, exploitation and development of natural resources and be built upon natural resources. The conservation and broadening of the natural resources base is an essential preliminary step in development planning, specially because large parts of these resources have been greatly neglected in recent decades. Conservation and development of resources, of soil, water and vegetation are extremely important for our agricultural inter-area economy. Problems relating to conservation of natural resources arise all over the country as a general phenomenon, but it is at once highly local, in the sense that there is a great variation in the characteristics of resources and the problems of conservation and development presented by them, and in the sense that full conservation and development of all resources necessarily entails detailed local action. A hypothetical division of the district into homogeneous economic areas will have to be made for this plan of conservation and development of natural resources and the 'mandi' area unit may be found convenient.

Stage-III: Against the backdrop of the physico-geographic frame of the distribution and placement of socio-economic overheads and services and of the plan for the conservation and development of natural resources, that the plan of development of production, agricultural and non-agricultural, is to be prepared as the heart of the planning process, can hardly be overemphasized.

Unlike action in relation to the provision of socio-economic overheads and conservation and development of natural resources, which area is largely influenced by governmental action or by cooperating groups of persons (baring a few exceptions) in the production plan, the operations appertaining to development of production are essentially those of individual agriculturists, artisans, etc. where planning action is, to a large extent, a matter of providing assistance and incentives to individual producers, which is what makes it important to think out carefully, what may be called the *objectives* and *strategies* of development.

Defining objectives is to spell out the particular immediate goals in each field both vis-a-vis the previous development and the future requirements of the district, which is best illustrated by the fact that at a given level of progress of cooperative activity it may be more important to look to the functioning of the cooperatives in relation to particular categories, such as tenants or artisans, than to seek universal membership. The concept of strategy is also illustrated by reference to rural industrialization, as for example, one may decide to focus initially on the development of processing in the cooperative sector and on the rehabilitation of traditional artisan industry, because, these may be of immediate importance and at once because they provide foundations for future progress. In another context, perhaps a programme of providing improved public conveniences in schools may be adopted for long term improvement of rural health habits.

Such problems of analysis and estimation will be encountered in each programme in this field. The agricultural production programmes today, give very uneven results, because no analysis takes place and because of utter disregard for local conditions. A three-fold classification of agricultural improvement programme is basic: *one,* deemed improvements which are locally accepted but not yet widespread, *two,* improvements proved to be useful locally but not yet accepted, and *three,* improvements which have to be tried out and established in the local environment. With regard to only the first one is a programme of propaganda and appropriate incentives indicated; in relation to second which is a large class, because of the limited extent of local adaptation effort so far, a systematic work in local adaptation and adjustment must have the highest priority. Programmes for the development of agricultural and non-agricultural productive activity have to be formulated to suit local circumstances and conditions and at once to suit the requirements of the different classes of producers. The widespread complaint that the benefits of agricultural programmes accrue to the more substantial cultivators, emanates from lack of differentiation in this regard. Existing programmes have to be specially adapted to, or special programmes framed for, the small-land holders and part-time farmers if the planning effort is to touch the lives of the teeming millions.[6]

Without distracting from the importance of agricultural production, it has to be mentioned that the activization of the rural economy demands a greater expansion of the subsidiary primary production and of industrial activity.

Intensification of agricultural production activity will generate employment and so on, for only the middle and large cultivators, who constitute less than half of the rural families. Therefore, for the small, effectively part time cultivators, the landless labourers, rural artisans and others, supplementary and new activities must be discovered, innovated or invented, a part of which would arise from planned programmes of the provision of socio-economic overheads and of the conservation and development of natural resources, but that would not be enough, and therefore, a greater part of such activities must be found in expansion of the field of non-agricultural primary production, like, animal husbandry, fishery, etc. Though the importance of this has been recently recognized yet no appropriate development has been planned, and the technical view, in this regard as in several others, dominates the field without reference to the needs of the economic situation, without much awareness that the situation demands the development, for example, of dairy and poultry activities in units and at levels which will be within the competence of at least the average small farmer, if not the landless labourer; and, if necessary, the individual small units must be supported by the requisite net-work of services and supplies. Finally, the rural economy will begin to move only if industrialization of the countryside is no longer regarded as only supplementary or incidental to other activities, but as the main result aimed at by the programme of industrial development.

Stage-IV: This naturally leads to a consideration of the immediate problems of non-producers. The provision of socio-economic overheads, the conservation and development of natural resources and steps to improve and encourage productive activity, all benefit those who have a minimum viable base of productive resources, but those who have no or little command over resources or no productive resources at all, cannot benefit directly from any of these programmes of development planning; and because there is little hope that the majority of this class of people having access, in the foreseeable future, to productive resources through such measures, say, as redistribution of land, *the programme* required for them is essentially that of provision of adequate employment. At the sametime, the position that the programme of providing employment for non-producers cannot be an additional rural works programme of the Planning Commission is not seemingly logical because the contents of a rural works programme cannot be different in character and the content from the programmes for providing socio-economic overheads or of conservation and development of resources or the maintenance of these or of existing works. Clearly enough a rural works programme which is conceived of as additive, will not be properly integrated with planned programme and will, to that extent, be wasteful of resources.

Stage-V: Dovetailing is a key element in this plan. The need to provide for adequate local employment through different channels of development programming thus imposes additional requirements on the process of plan formulation, in two directions: *firstly*, in relation to their spatial and *secondaly*, with regard to temporal distribution. The entire programme of additional economic activity directly undertaken by the government and the public sector, together with any expected increase in employment offered by the private sector, must generate total employment required. The size and the degree of labour intensity of planned public activity must be related to this objective and because the aggregative employment has to be properly distributed spatially and temporally, over the district, planned activity must be initially close in relation to specific local requirements. And then the generation of additional employment has to be looked upon not as appertaining to a particular year, but as continuing long-term requirement, and therefore, the employment requirement should not only affect the size and shape of the annual plan but also deeply influence the perspective plan, and indeed the perspective and strategy of all planning. The employment aspect of planning thus colours and orients the whole process, and has an integrating effect, because it gives direction, and magnitude, to a large number of planning decisions.

Stage-V: Prioritisation obviously is the next thing to look into because the requirement of dovetailing of the plans, also generates the problem of priorities. Broadly, priorities have to be determined by reference to scales of valuation and by accepted ideas appertaining to the route which planned development is likely to take. Conservation might be objectively given high priority, because conservation of resources is a condition precedent to development. Where simultaneous development of all areas is sought, a communication and services programme must be given high priority, and the problem becomes more complicated in connection with what are called "social welfare activities". A minimum provision of educational and health service for each citizen is an input required for a minimum performance by labour units, which implies that a considerable amount of educational and health expenditure would be treated as investment expenditure and not welfare expenditure. Obviously a great deal depends on subjective valuations and judgement, but a limit has to be placed on independent judgement in each local area in such matters, and an accepted framework of overall national objectives and a certain broad valuation, must inform all district plans.

The second important integrating factor, and at once the constraint, is the amount of financial resources available for the district plan, that limits the extent of effort that can be put forward within a period, and which makes planning meaningful because it provides the frame within which (given local, natural and human resources and the local interpretation of national objectives) the optimum effort can be made for the best utilization of the available financial resources. The strategy of the plan as a whole, or for the public sector, and prioritisation of schemes or programmes and allocations, are made fully with reference to this constraint. Without financial constraints the district development planning will be a mere compilation of a charter of demand, embodying desired schemes and projects which are not necessarily interconnected and in which no indication of logical relation or chronological order need be given. "With the constraint imposed by the overall financial limit, the interpretation of a district plan means essentially the spelling out of the logical relations between various sectoral and departmental plans and the chronological order in which within all of them together particular schemes will be initiated and completed."[7]

Stage-VI: A number of calculations of availabilities and balances of resources will have to be made. A programme of road construction of a given length and given size would require certain equipment and trained personnel; the programme for high yielding variety seed have to be based on a given complement of farms and farmers; for education and health programmes, buildings, equipment, teachers and nurses have to be made available in a given measure for any level of desired performance. Similarly the total building and construction programmes in all sectors in the district taken together would be subject to the overall limitation of availability of building materials, like the total output of bricks or the possible allotment of cement. Generally the entire plan, and in particular, the socio-economic overheads and the conservation plans, require labour as an essential input on a large scale, which makes it possible that the availability of labour would place a limitation on the size of these plans that could be accomplished within the given time frame. These calculations in physical terms serve two purposes: one, they indicate limits to possible performance and two, they give a clear view of the present challenge ahead of us, so that through, chiefly, a better organization the limits could be stretched.

The additional input in district planning that could be most readily made available in early stages of planned development is better organization, and in fact for success of new programmes of development, attention must be paid to problems of setting up and operating appropriate organizations. Two types of organizations, viz., the Panchayati Raj Institutions and the Co-operatives, in this regard would be particularly utilized but this is a general approach and it still leaves unsolved several problems. For example, if experience is any guide mere provision of a works programme does not, without a special organizational effort, benefit the target groups. The organization indicated for this purpose usually partakes the nature of Labour Contract Co-operative Society whose organizational pattern and functioning in a variety of contexts have not been experimentally determined. The situation regarding the major problem of the organization of small holders for agricultural production, for which cooperative farming appears to be the logical solution, is no different.[8]

Other organizational problems that arise in local planning, emanates from some aspects of land reforms, and sometimes, because of a mixture of public and private interest, such as, that of the management of a public utility like a tank which benefits only a limited number of people within the community and so on. There are some areas where new experimental effort requires mainly organizational improvisation, particularly so, with problems relating to the weaker sections of society or with problems of conservation or development of non-arable land where a number of departments such as forest, revenue and animal husbandry may be interested and where without arousing local interest and popular participation, no effective programme could be carried out successfully. The problems of organization loom excessively large where a departure from the traditional pattern is warranted or where the disadvantaged are sought to be benefited. "It is thus clear that in the formulation of plans and more particularly in the plan of implementation, attention has to be paid to indicating carefully the organizations entrusted with operation and coordination and, in many fields also to designing and experimenting with new types of organizations for the purpose."[9]

Stage-VII: The two aspects of the integration of plans that need to be specially stressed are coordination and synchronization. Any given objective like that of increasing agricultural production would clearly be linked with a large number of schemes and projects and activities of different departments: it would be interlinked, for example, with the conservation of land, development of water resources, construction of connecting communications, availability of power, supply of credit, institutionalization of marketing, guaranteeing of prices, setting up of co-operative processing units, supply of improved or High Yielding Variety seeds, supply of fertilizers, supply of pesticides, introduction of improved practices and implements, the provision of technical assistance and advice, extension services and research farms. This illustrative (not exhaustive by any standard) list brings forth the meaning of logical inter-relationship within the activities of different departments and agencies which are intended, either in part or in whole, to subserve one common objective. Given the plan size and the objectives, the extent and nature of each activity and its chronological order have to be determined in advance, closely relating it to all the other activities which it supports or by which it is supported. Without taking this dimension of mutual inter-relationship into account in the plan formulation there would obviously be disproportionately high expenditure of energy and financial resources in several directions, which would be wasted without the necessary support. Integration in the context of district plan means paying close attention to all these aspects of inter-relationships and emphasizing the need to maintain a proper degree of proportionality. In the absence of coordination and synchronization, implementation cannot be effective. The complementarity of different programmes and activities cannot bear fruit unless the activities provided for are appropriate and in proportion and unless also in each context, they are in fact undertaken and completed at the appropriate times. Synchronization of implementation of various aspects of programmes is critically important with regard to such objectives as annual agricultural production plans.

It is obvious that such a plan is not merely standard departmental schemes put together; it is much more, and hence if adjustments are required to be made in such a plan, much greater thought and labour need to go into it, than would be required in relation to a collection of departmental schemes which can be put together, cut down or joined together.

III. TASKS FOR EACH LEVEL

The preparation of a district development plan has to be undertaken chiefly at two levels, the district and the 'mandi' area level. While the overall frame, the strategies and the comprehensive works and schemes have to be planned at the district level, the details of the plans for conservation, production, etc. have to be worked for the 'mandi' area. Financial allocations, both spatially and sectorally have to be finalized, and distribution of schemes and programmes against the background of the employment criterion has also to be carried out, at the district level. Organizational problems will perhaps be uniform throughout the district, except in some areas like forest, wastelands or animal husbandry where there may persist local peculiarities. Integration, coordination and synchronization of plan activities will have to be undertaken appropriately at district and 'mandi' levels through the overall integrative effort will be in relation to the district plan.

The tasks at all levels are two-fold: *one*, that of marshalling all available information, qualitative and quantitative, and judging of requirements, feasibilities, logical priorities and chronological orders from a technical perspective and, subsequently, given the final judgement regarding programmes and priorities, the work of formulation of an integrated plan given all the limitation and constraints; *two*, that of taking account of differing levels of local competence, local knowledge, local attitudes, local preference and possible local reactions and responses. While the former will by and large be the responsibility of official or administrative agencies, and official and non-official experts, the latter can be achieved only by association of local leadership with the total enterprise: indeed the speed and the efficiency with which administrators and experts execute the first, will itself be greatly affected by the extent of interest they arouse in the local population in relation to it and the cooperation and assistance that they enlist from the local people.

Local participation in plan formulation and implementation can be harnessed essentially by entrusting a good deal of district development planning to local authority, like the Zilla Parishad in Maharashtra and Karnataka and in many other States. It may be noted that while the work of the administrator and the expert can cover the entire area of planning with near uniform efficiency, the interest and commitment of local leaders[10] and population may differ widely from area to area which obviously is a function of the education of local leadership and of its consciousness of the real meaning of national socio-economic objectives. From the perspective of possible variations in coverage and depth of local interests, it is essential to recognize that given national objectives and the total scope of the national plan of development, all aspects of it would necessarily be reflected in district planning, even though the local leadership may not be equally interested in all of them, for only then the general compulsions of the national frame would be useful in relation to continuance of minimum effort in those directions which fail to evoke full local interest. In the ultimate analysis, it is necessary to ensure that national objectives are, in fact fully accepted by local leadership everywhere, for no real social transformation is possible through development without full understanding and cooperation from local leadership and people in this regard. "Therefore, while in the initial stages, the national frame may serve a useful purpose, the full and meaningful pursuit of national objectives requires an educational effort in relation to local leadership which must be considered as extremely important and essential. In part, therefore, the process of district development planning must be understood as that of communicating, to local leadership and population, aspiration and ideologies with which the national plan is informed. On the other hand, the realism and the effectiveness of the national plan depend essentially on an understanding at the national level of the possibilities and difficulties of local planning."[11]

IV. SOME NEW ORIENTATION

At first inspection it may appear that the approach requires resources beyond what would be available and is too detailed for operationalisation, but a close scrutiny will reveal that this is not a fact. If experience is any guide effective rural work is impossible without coming to the brasstacks, and the agricultural production programme envisaged in this methodology is, basically the same as what is attempted in agricultural extension in any country. And then the personnel required for the field work detailed in this methodology are for the most part already positioned in the field in most districts in India.

There are chiefly two directions in which new inputs will be required: the first input is local survey and research in all fields, which is a completely neglected area, and a part of which can be filled by drawing on the resources of existing academic and training institutions in the district.[12] There are three phases to this work, namely:

(i) collecting systematic information in relation to each field and identifying problems;

(ii) conducting research locally, chiefly in relation to proving, adapting and adjusting standard prescription and solutions in relation to local conditions;

(iii) training local personnel engaged in plan formulation and implementation in specialized aspects of the work in each field. It is true that the existing academic and training institutions are not equipped for the task at hand, but no intractable difficulty should arise in making good this deficiency. For example, the staff of the department of economics or commerce in a local college could easily be trained to undertake the preliminary survey and then the subsequent continuous economic surveys, and to impart instruction to district staff in appropriate planning techniques. However, not only could local institutions play this important role in planning but they could also have their own efficiency and competence should greatly increase by this interface. A minimum programme of new institutions is unavoidable, as for instance each district must have one agricultural research-cum-demonstration centre but such action is an inevitable concomitant of development itself. As local planning becomes more detailed and more effective, support of systematic collection of more data and support of greater in-depth research in all fields will be inevitable. And with the progress of development planning, the resources and competence of local academic and training institutions must also further increase.

The second important input required is that of entirely new attitude and new method towards district planning, in atleast in two directions. The adoption of the problem-solving attitude towards all aspects of development planning by the partners in the process; and willingness to trust the judgement and competence of (and delegate authority to) personnel on the lower level have to be developed quickly. The new methods are those required particularly by the adoption of the problem-solving approach. Even if a beginning is made, with a standard departmental scheme as a convenient starting point, this approach requires scrutiny of every detail vis-a-vis local resource and local circumstances. Defining objectives, translating objectives into programmes of work and putting programmes in the form of a set of schemes, all require new methods of detailed work even where one starts working upon an old base. The putting together of plans, particularly what has been termed above as coordination and synchronization, will necessitate both evolution of new methods and a thorough analysis of the plan for implementation.

Effective district development planning will thus call for a better utilization of old resources, for a reorientation of the existing set-up and, above all for new attitudes and a readiness both to trust the people more at lower levels nearer to the ground conditions and to delve deeper into the problems at hand.

V. SOME COMMENTS

The reading of the methodology evolved by Prof. Gadgil in this short paper reveals the working of an outstanding thinker. Some of the thoughts expressed nearly a quarter of a centuary ago, are strikingly fresh even today and deserve to be read widely and seriously.

The methodology consists of four inter-connected dimensions:

(a) physico-geographic plan;

(b) plan for conservation of natural resources;

(c) plan for productive activity; and

(d) the plan for providing adequate employment opportunities.

First the need for data is clearly seen and the import of knowledge and information as distinguished from data is seen in no uncertain terms. Unlike many, he saw the need for an exhaustive data base but was pragmatic to urge that a beginning can be made with a minimum data and information base, and as the process of planning at the district level gets entrenched, the content and quality of data will progressively get improved. And in this the critical importance of investigational and research activity in all fields at the local level as a necessary concomitant to the continuance and growth of district development planning effort is very neatly put forth.[13]

The methodology, by implication, contributed to the debate on whether the district is the appropriate unit of planning, and at once by suggesting that "Mandi area" as the lowest area of planning, it synthesized the two opposing portent forces in an unique combination. The methodology for delineating the "mandi" or the "market area" suggested, conforms to the basic tenets of regionalisation[14] and was conceived of as a centre or nucleus, and because of specially convenient means of communication or otherwise, it should serve a fairly well-defined surrounding area as the primary marketing, sale and supply centre. And by conceptualizing planning as co-ordination, formulation and execution of a number of socio-economic measures and activities, for unfolding a given pattern of development, village as an unit of planning was rejected. The methodology, therefore, combines in one a system and a sub-system within the system for planning at the district and at the sub-district level. V.K.R.V. Rao's seminal observation in a different context that planning should be an attempt to "formulate a minimal unit for integrated development without an uneconomic expansion of the existing spatial structure of basic amenities and services",[15] seems to have been presaged years ahead of time.

The theoretical underpinning of the methodology seems to be in the realm of growth centres and diffusion. There has been severe criticism of these theoretical underpinning, in different context, but they seem to dominate a good part of micro-level planning theory even today. There are several approaches discussed in this book which still adhere to this theoretical framework including the N.I.R.D. approach, and no strong alternative theory has as yet been propounded to substitute the Growth Centre model. The "Growth Foci" formulation[16] is some break from the past but not quite and the "integrate growth foci" concept[17] is still extremely tentative. Thus the instant methodology attempted at internalizing a sound theoretical base on which to establish the district planning structure.

The methodology talks about local participation in the formulation and implementation of the plans, as was perhaps the case in every methodology of the time, but the finesse of the conception here was the subtle distinction between local participation, local interest and local commitment. While local people's participation can be ensured, their interest and commitment to plan formulation and plan implementation is another matter: the former relates to the "engineering of local level participation", the latter is in the domain of essence of participation. As it has been found in four gram panchayats of a State known for establishing institutional arrangement at the grassroots level, that though every class is represented in the Gram Panchayats, only the representatives of the relatively affluent class speak; the others are patient listeners. That is, local level participation has been arranged for, their interest in and commitment to the task at hand is ambivalent.[18] In an age where there is a deafening chorus about local level participation, taking cognizance of these niceties is likely to carry us much further.

The methodology seems most modern in its approach to environment in terms of conservation of natural resources. It speaks about conservation and development of natural resources: conservation comes first and development next; it does not speak about use or exploitation of natural resources only. The methodology admits of a great variation in the characteristics of resources, and the problems of conservation and development presented by them calls for local action. Not many planning methodologies have paid so much of attention to conservation of nature, and had such concern been pervasive in all our thinking since, the depredation of common property resources and forests on such a wide-spread scale, both before and after the "Green Revolution", for agricultural growth could perhaps have been prevented.[19]

The internal fabric of the mechanics was clearly seen. The timely advice that district planning was not a mere assimilation of schemes and that a schema of graded priorities must be spelt out, applies for the most part, in an overwhelmingly large number of district planning exercise currently being undertaken in the whole country. It seems the methodology was evolved is some modern day district planning cell in one of the several States, still struggling to find its moorings in this area.

Where the methodology failed to give us deeper insights lies in the realm of resource mobilization, resource devolution and resource allocation. Questions relating to powers to tax and borrow at the district level; the criteria for devolution of funds from the district to the areal unit of planning chosen; and the yardsticks that may be applied in allocation of these resources, did not receive a favourable treatment from the distinguished thinker. And what should be the institutional arrangements for ensuring people's interest and commitment to local level planning are areas that have been left grey. The methodology speaks about co-operativisation, but only of the farmers, leaving away the issues pertaining to organization of the poor landless or assetless agricultural labourers, whose need for an organization borders around, what for want of a better word we say, "ruthlessly urgent".

It would have been good to hear on these issue from a person who guided India's Planning efforts for many years. It looks like a paradox that a person who had such clear visions, in his subsequent writings virtually abondoned the course of district planning.[20] Curiously enough the exponent of this methodology despite his deep interest and thorough understanding of the interaction between agrarian structure and poverty, chose not to address himself to the questions appertaining to the inter-relationships between land reforms and district planning except in passing, in this methodology.

Nevertheless, it was indeed a pioneering work.

Notes and References

1. Basic Source: Gadgil, D.R.: *District Development Planning* (Poona : Gokhale Institute of Economics & Politics) 1966.
2. The terms "local level" and have been used inter-changeably, though in the literature on the issue "local level" is deemed to be a tier below the district level. See Nanjundappa, D.M.: *Area Planning and Rural Development* (Delhi: Associated Publishers) 1981.
3. The debate about the appropriate unit of planning still continues. See Mukherjee, Amitava: *Researches in Decentralisation* (New Delhi: Heritage) 1990, p. 12, for a very brief summary of the debate on what should be the appropriate unit of planning.
4. In an actual exercise conducted in the Wardha District it was found that such an area-unit, called in this case for convenience the 'mandi-area unit' usually covered a population of 15 to 20 thousand. The population and area coverage will differ from region to region depending upon the intensity of primary production, and the density of population. And then, as was the experience in Wardha, while in some cases the centres and the area served by them are fairly easily and clearly identifiable, in other cases, a selection among centres may have to be made and careful demarcation of areas undertaken. This has then to be done on the basis not only of the existing situation but also of projected future development. This is akin to growth centre approach or the growth foci approach of R.P. Mishra et. al. See Mishra, R.P., Sundaram, K.V., and Prakasa Rao, V.L.S.: *Regional Development Planning in India* (Delhi: Vikas Publishing House) 1974, and criticisms of the Concept in Wanmali, Sudhir: *Service Centres in Rural India* (New Delhi: B.R. Publishing Corporation) 1983, pp. 23-29.
5. Despite decades of struggle, most district plans, unfortunately enough, even today are an "agglomeration" of departmental schemes. See Government of India: *Report of the Working Group on District Planning* (New Delhi: Planning Commission) 1984.
6. Minhas has also recently re-emphasized the issue of a system of incentive and disincentive. See Yugandhar, B.N. and Mukherjee, Amitava: *Readings in Decentralized Planning* Vol. II, (New Delhi: Concept Publishing Co.) 1991 (forthcoming).
7. Gadgil, D.R. : *Loc. cit.*
8. Organising the poor continues to be a major concern even today. For instance.Kannan, K.P.: *Rural Proletarian Struggles: Mobilisation and Organisation of Rural Workers* (Oxford: Oxford University Press) 1988.
9. Gadgil, D.R.: *Loc. cit.*
10. Local level participation has not still been enlisted, because of the attitude of "we" and "they"; "I and them". See L.C. Jain's remarks at the *Workshop on Training for Decentralised Planning and Area Planning*, on 19th May 1990, at New Delhi organised by Association of State Training Institute, HCM Rajasthan State Institute of Public Administration, Jaipur.
11. Gadgil, D.R.: *op. cit.*
12. An idea operationalised in the preparation of "Agro-Climatic Plans" during the VII Five Year Plan. See Basu, D.N.: "Agro-Climatic Regional Planning Project: A Short

Background and Current Status", in Yugandhar, B. N. and Mukherjee, Amitava: *Readings in Decentralized Planning*, Vol. I (New Delhi: Concept Publishing Company) 1990.

13. Even till date we have not got rid ourselves of this problem, despite our total agreement with such provision. See Jahagirdar, D.V.: "District Planning: Some Difficulties", in *Papers Presented at the Seminar held on District Planning in Maharashtra : A Review* (Aurangabad: Department of Economics, Marathwada University) November 1988, pp. 137 to 145. See Government of India: *Report of the Committee of the Study Group on Information Gap* (New Delhi: Planning Commission) July 1989.
14. The latest attempt at delineation is the Agro-climatic Zoning. See Alagh, Y.K.: "Guidelines for Planning at the Agro-Climatic Regional Level", in Government of Gujarat: *Gujarat Eight Five Year Plan* (Gandhinagar: General Administration Department, Sachivalaya) September 1988.
15. Rao, V.K.R.V.: *Foreword* to Vivekananda, M.: *Planning Unit Areas for Integrated Rural Development* (New Delhi: Ashis Publishing House) 1980, p. VIII.
16. Misra, R.P.: "Growth Poles and Growth Centres in the Context of India's Urban and Regional Development" in Kuklinski, A. (ed.): *Problems in Growth Poles and Growth Centres in Regional Planning* (Geneva: U.N. Regional Institute for Social Development) 1972. For a scathing criticism of this see Wanmali, Sudhir: *Service Centre in Rural India* (New Delhi: B.R. Publishing Corporation) 1983, particularly chapter IV & V.
17. See Mukherjee, Amitava: 'Growth Centres: Need for Change in Approach", *Economic Times*, 13th January 1990.
18. See Westgard, Kristen: *People's Participation, Local Government & Rural Development* (Copenhagen: Centre for Development Research) 1986, and its review in the *Economic & Political Weekly*, 26th March, 1988 in the Section of Review of Agriculture.
19. See Hanumantha Rao, C.H.: "Agricultural Development and Ecological Degradation", *Economic & Political Weekly*, December 24-31, 1988, pp. A-142 to A-146 for an analytical framework of this disaster.
20. Kamath, A. R.: *Selected Writings and Speaches of Professor D.R. Gadgil on Planning and Development (1967-1971)* (Poona: Gokhale Institute of Politics & Economics & Orient Longmans Ltd., New Delhi) 1973. The book has a select bibliography of his writings, which does not indicate any substantial interest having been retained in the subject.

CHAPTER IV

APPROACH TO DISTRICT PLANNING[1]

(SULABH BRAHME APPROACH)

I. INTRODUCTION: WHERE WE WENT WRONG

The First Five Year Plan was remotely based on the Harrod-Domar model of economic growth. The Second Plan onwards we have adopted sophisticated techniques of planning in the form of multi-sectoral growth models, in the formulation, of the development plans. A four sector (or some say two sector) model developed by Prof. Mahalanobis was used in the formulation of the Second Plan, and similar models have been adopted in the later Plans, where the sophistication of the models have increased with each successive Five Year Plans.[2]

All growth models start on the premise that the growth process is already under-way and that the model can be used for making a plan for growth in the aggregate levels of production, consumption, investment and so on, but in the developing economies, the growth processes are not under-way and the task is to initiate the process of development itself, and therefore, the growth models lose much of their relevance. Secondly, the growth models suffer from over-aggregation in the context of an underdeveloped economy. Aggregation blindfolds planning to the sharp cleavage that exists between the 'modern' and the 'traditional' sectors in the underdeveloped countries, within almost every field of activity, a problem which the application of the growth models to the modern sectors alone, treating the vast traditional sectors as residual, cannot solve. And the assumption that most of the variables responsible for growth, or non-growth, can be quantified and fitted into an organized pattern of relationships, is unrealistic, because the basic problem in under-developed countries, is the gap in knowledge essential for quantification of these variables. Therefore, with all their statistical refinements the neat models of growth have failed to give additional insight into the problem of initiating and sustaining growth in our developing economy.

Thus while the econometrics of growth looks neat on paper, the unmeasurable socio-economic and political inter-relationship as expressed in the institutional set-up and the pattern of asset ownership in the society, cannot be taken account of in growth models. The institutional and organizational aspects of the structural changes envisaged in the transformation of the particular backward economy of ours remain uncared for. References to economic policies, like Prof. Mahalanobis's urge for an early decision on fixation of land ceilings and on redistribution of surplus land, have been made outside his two or four sector growth models that comprised the foundation of our Second Five Year Plan.

The planning effort in India is largely operated on the quantitative parameters and is confined largely to the modern sector while the non-monetized sector of the economy (the bulwark of the Indian economy) and the institutional frame in which the economy operates, have remained beyond the purview of the plan for development, which outlook is reflected in the prime goal of national planning defined as increase in the rate of growth of the Gross National Product (GNP). The pursuit of this objective has directed the planning effort to create conditions for expansion of private economic activity through public outlays. A growth-oriented approach together with the strategy of initiating economic expansion through development of basic industries, heavy industries and agro-industrial infrastructure in a mixed economy has led to a heavy dependency on foreign aids and loans, and adoption of a policy with regard to foreign private investment and subsidies to export industries, which leaves much to be desired. As regards industrial activity, the growth-oriented strategy combined with the reliance on private initiative for development led to adoption of capital intensive technology favouring the developed regions as locations for industries, and the economically strong groups as promoters of new economic, particularly so new industrial, activity.

II. NEED FOR REGIONAL PLANNING

The need for regional planning for backward regions is then often emphasized on the basis of extra-economic appeal for equity and justice, but it is necessary to realize that the reduction in regional disparities and acceleration of the rate of growth are not mutually exclusive, and are complementary to each other. The economic advantages of decentralized development and the economic costs of concentrated development both occur as accumulated effects over time, and, therefore, only a consideration of an adequately long period can the two be put in proper perspective.

The concentrated development approach emphasizes continuously rising investment in the development regions, but the external diseconomies of agglomeration will depress the overall efficiency of capital and increase the factor cost for the society thereby widening the gap between private productivity estimates and the realized productivity for the society as a whole. On the contrary, investment directed to increase the absorption capacity of the lagging region will draw within the process of production the yet unexploited productive resources and under-exploited productive resources of the region, and in the long run the social cost of sustaining a given rate of growth will be higher, the more concentrated the development is conceived to be.

The annual output of a given investment in the lagging region may not be as high as in the developed region implying a high capital/output ratio. A high capital/output ratio and therefore, a lower rate of growth may not however, necessarily imply that the total worth of the investment in opening up areas in the developing region, or in permanent improvements on land will prove to be far more productive in the long run than equivalent investment in improving the facilities in the overgrown regions only marginally. Therefore, considering an adequately long period, the economic cost and the social costs of economic development and the national space, as a whole, bears a direct relationship with the regional disparities in development.

Planned effort for the development of various regions is all the more necessary because of the vastness of the country, the diversity of resources and the glaring inter-regional disparities in the prevailing levels of development. Regional planning can be used for a more direct regulation of the development of different regions through providing appropriate guidelines and principles for regulation of the amount, composition and phasing of investments, and with the flux of time as the canvas of regional planning becomes smaller, a regional plan can encompass more specific suggestions about the locational pattern and, in view of the structural peculiarities of the region, indicate appropriate methods for organizing productive activity for sustained economic development of the region.

III. DELINEATION OF A REGION

For purposes of economic planning, a region may be delineated with reference to a number of relevant considerations: geo-physical homogeneity, or a common socio-economic history for example.[3] From the point of view of implementation of the plan policies, the planning unit may be so delineated as to be co-terminus with an administrative unit. Consistent with the need for homogeneity with regard to potential advantage of planned development, the region should be broad-based and endowed with the element of diversity, such that it will enable the integrated development of the region deriving its major strength from local resources and local market.

IV. OBJECTIVES OF PLANNING

It is necessary to recast the objective and orientation of economic planning, nationally and shifting the focus from the acceleration of the rate of growth in aggregate income to 'lifting the levels of living of the people'.[4] The planning at the national level must take the population of the nation as the basic parameter for formulating the plan, and the minimum contemplated level of consumption, at the level considered adequate when made available to the entire population, will generate the consumption vector depicting the quantities of different goods required to be made available for consumption. Planning then should work back from this vector, the pattern of production and of international trade, harnessing in the process, the resources of the country optimally for meeting the basic consumption needs of the entire community and to ensure a sustained improvement of the standards of living of the people. The level of adequacy for consumption would be defined in the relation to the level of development of the economy as a whole, and thus the level of adequacy for consumption will be revised upwards periodically and allowed to encompass new and better products, to the extent that they can be made available within the reach of the common mass.[5] The objective of planning, therefore, has to be expressed in terms of "the most appropriate utilization of the available productive resources to ensure a universally shared improvement in the levels of living based on meaningful participation of the people in the process of development".[6]

V. STRATEGY OF DEVELOPMENT

Economic development of a community, in the last analysis, may have to be traced to a sustained increase in the production of desirable output and increase in the productivity of the physical resources as a whole and that of the average worker. In a market economy, each and every output combination is a function of the structure of demand which depends on the income distribution, which in turn depends upon the ownership pattern of productive assets. The scope for increasing agricultural production as well as industrial production would, therefore, be a function of the level of domestic mass consumption, and the levels of incomes of the masses have to increase so as to absorb the increased outputs.

In India the growth of production is stagnating because the levels of income for mass of workers are not increasing due to lack of adequate expansion of productive employment in both agricultural and the non-agricultural sectors. Under the circumstances it has, at times, been advocated that income levels of the masses could be improved through direct transfer of income without disturbing the pattern of ownership of productive assets. However, such a strategy would create imbalances between supply and demand in the short run, causing a rise in prices and reducing the saving potential of the economy in the long run, thus cutting at the root of economic growth. A rise in the incomes of the mass consumers, will yield positive marginal productivity for labour and offset the adverse saving effect which would be less than what should be in the case of direct income transfer, provided such rise in income is based on higher demand for labour and higher employment. In the strategy of development, therefore, in the agricultural sector and in the industrial sector a combination of increasing employment and increase in the productivity of labour is of crucial importance.

In agricultural sector the developmental strategy adopted in India has laid stress on introduction of irrigation-fertilizer-tractor technology with a view to increasing agricultural production, but this new technology, which is capital intensive, is accessible only to a small section of the cultivators, whereby leading to increased inequality in rural incomes and deterioration in the conditions of the rural poor.[7] Thus the present strategy of agricultural development through its consequent impact on the income distribution in rural areas, destroys the economic basis for continued agricultural development, and at the same time, lack of expansion of non-agricultural activity does not leave many options open for the non-viable cultivators. A related malady in the agrarian situation is that the skewed distribution of the basic agricultural assets permits under-utilization or misutilization of land on the part of the big farmer, and at once the small farmer is compelled to indiscriminately use the land and other resources without due consideration to the long term ill-effects of such exploitation, whereby the natural resources of the community get malutilized, resulting in a social loss.

The crucial element in the agricultural strategy is to improve the income levels of the mass of agricultural workers by making adequate work available to them and through increasing their productivity, for which each agricultural worker must operate with adequate complementary factors in the form of land and related inputs. For the full benefit of improved productivity to accrue to the worker, it is imperative that the worker gets responsibility of managing productive resources. It is also imperative to strengthen the resource base in order to provide adequate work for a large number of agricultural workers which, brings forth the need for conservation, augmentation and enrichment of the natural resources and their scientific management. The alternative agricultural strategy suggested here is aimed at enlargement of the resources of the region in two directions: *one*, it will lead to physical augmentation of the resource through land reclamation, erosion control, water conservation etc., and *two*, it will result in conversion of a non-resource into a resource through activizing the hitherto dormant opportunities of production. For example, scientific management of land will enable the community to bring under cultivation land presently left as permanent fallows, or appropriate organizations will make feasible the productive use of livestock products like cow dung, bones etc., that are currently wasted, and at once, better utilization of the natural resources of the region and active participation of the agricultural workers in the scientific husbanding of these resources will be made a reality. The egalitarian income distributional consequences and the superior overall productivity effects of this strategy cannot be over-emphasized.

Agricultural activity with traditional methods of cultivation partakes the nature of an extractive industry depending more on the natural agro-climatic endowments, particularly rainfall, than on productive industry converting inputs into outputs in the true sense of the term through controlling the conditions of such conversion. Transformation of 'agricultural activity' into 'agricultural industry' as envisaged above is expected to yield overall increase in productivities through control of conditions of production, but, in activities where the basic productive factor, that is, land can be altered to only a limited extent, the scope for increasing productivity is also limited. In theoretical terms diminishing marginal productivity sets in much earlier in agricultural industry than in the manufacturing. The greater scope for increasing productivity in the manufacturing sector, makes transfer of labour from primary production to manufacturing activity an essential element in the development process.

VI. INDUSTRIAL STRATEGY

It may be underscored here that agricultural activity produces goods that are essential as basic necessities, which explains why increase in incomes may not get fully reflected in the increase in demand for agricultural commodities, but would lead to greater demand for new goods, mainly manufactured articles. If regional development is confined to agricultural development and if rising demand for manufactured goods is to be met by imports, income terms of trade to the region will deteriorate, which is why diversification and development of industries become important, even for the agriculturally prosperous areas.[8]

The advent of industry contributes to the evolution of social structure and way of life, and creates, and continually reinforces the dynamic resilience of the socio-cultural fabric of the country essential for material and social progress. The forces of change will remain weak, and if any betterment of human and material agents of development takes place, it will be lost to the regional community through their emigration to other regions that are industrialized, in the absence of industrialization of that region. Thus along with the agricultural development, the industrialization of the region has to be initiated and promoted in a planned manner.

It is crucial that the plan for industrialization is not reduced to a mere set of discrete proposals for manufacturing a number of industrial products, but that the whole scheme of industrialization is organically linked with the regional economy, be it the district, supra-district or sub-district economy, under reference. The economic impact of a proposed industry can be on the employment effect in the area, on income generated, on induced investment and several such areas. The dynamics of regional multipliers becomes more complex because of open channels of inter-regional trade. It would be necessary to assess the 'activity-interaction potential' of each of the industrial unit proposed, in the form of its 'backward' and 'forward' linkages, and to the extent that these linkages lie outside the region, the impact of the multiplier within the region would be weakened. The activity-interaction potential of a given increase in manufacturing activity, therefore, would be maximized where such leakages are minimized, if the chain is extended as much as possible within the region itself.

Planned development of resource-based industries appears to be the most appropriate instrument of initiating a process of sustained industrial development in a backward region, where such industries, when organized so as to be widely dispersed within the region, will help extension of manufacturing activity to rural centres, which will cause the interface of larger areas with the new processes and create a climate for innovation in the production activity in the rural areas. Resource based industries also have a strong bearing on the agricultural activity, because a valuable feed-back effect is provided by enhancing the efficiency of farm business through providing manufactured inputs and assured market for the agricultural produce. The increase in agricultural incomes that would ensue, will strengthen the local demand for a variety of manufactured goods, whereby making a further diversification of industrial activity possible in the region, which in its turn will cause the urban market for agricultural and horticultural products to be strengthened, providing increased access to diversification and commercialization of agriculture. It is also necessary to introduce specific modern manufacturing activity in the region after taking account of all backward and forward linkages to help modernization of the primary activity and the artisan craft in the region. It goes without saying that "a symbiotic relationship" could thus be developed between agriculture and industry and both the sectors can grow as mutually supporting sectors.

The distribution of non-agricultural activity over space is of crucial importance and must be worked out on the basis of the localization of agricultural activity and the distribution of population. Development of urban centres for performing the essential economic technology, for routing and storage of agricultural produce, for storage of agricultural input requirements, for being centres of manufacturing activity and administration, will have to be designed, so that these facilities come within the reach of the masses, because for the development of a well distributed expansion of economic activity in the region, a well designed urban network is an essential pre-requisite.

The urban pyramid for the region can be visualized to consist of major urban centres of regional importance at the apex, minor urban centres at the intermediate level, and rural-urban centres providing agricultural and related services to the rural population at the base. The major urban centres are the leading centres connecting the regional economy with the rest of the world; the minor urban centres at the intermediate level is the organic link between the urban and the rural areas of the region. The urban infrastructure to be developed in the plan would have a place only in relation to the proposed development of the agricultural and manufacturing activity in the region. Development of infrastructure all by itself may not be a sufficient (through a necessary) condition to stimule economic development.

To sum up, the strategy of development emphasizes:

(i) Scientific management of resources and providing adequate work to the mass of workers in the region, whereby increase the internal potential rate of growth.

(ii) The retaining of growth impulse in the region by ensuring backward and forward linkages in the non-agricultural sector of the regional economy. The organization of the development process must ensure that the levels of productivity, and consequently the incomes of the mass of workers, in the region experience steady increase over successive periods, for which initially investments from outside in the form of basic infrastructure in agriculture and in industry may be necessary, but the priorities in such investments need be so arranged that these investments help release the potentialities of growth in the region, so that over the years the region will be on the path of self-propelled and self-sustained economic development.

Integrated development of the national economy will be possible only if we formulate development plans for the different regions in the country, where the examination of the process of economic development and technical and structural factors responsible for the growth, or better still the non-growth, of the regional economy will be the point of departure for the planning of each regional economy, which analysis will provide the base upon which the entire structure of the regional plans will be built taking into consideration the natural endowments, the structural peculiarities and the development potential of the region. "The regional plans so formulated to cover the entire national space, national resources and total population of the country will have to be integrated to operate within a national frame which will direct itself to national level policy issues such as fiscal, monetary and price policies and the organization of core industry and transport and communication network etc."[9] Only when such a regional planning methodology is adopted that the acceleration in the rate of growth and the reduction in the inter-regional disparities in levels of living can be made complementary objectives, rather than conflicting goals in the exercise of planning for development.

VII. SOME IMPLICATIONS

Based on her experience at drawing up the Marathwada Plan, Sulabh Brahme mentions certain re-orientation for Maharashtra but they are true in several other parts of the country even today. It would, therefore, be worthwhile quickly reviewing what she had to say.[10]

Development of agriculture under dry conditions is critical in regional economy and where irrigation facilities are limited improved methods of dry cultivation have been developed and attempts are being made to propagate these methods for several decades. Improvements in the yields to the extent of 30 to 50 percent were observed on the experimental farms as a result of the adoption of measures like contour ploughing, strip cropping, proper crop rotation, mulching etc. However, these methods are hardly adopted in actual cultivation and the inter-year yields in dry agriculture continue to fluctuate violently. The basic difficulty in the adoption of improved methods in dry cultivation is that many of these practices are not easily applicable under the conditions of small and fragmented land-holding and in the absence of proper preservation and augmentation of the community resources like the pasture and the forest. The problem of development has been so far considered largely as a technical problem, but experience clearly indicates that it is scarcely enough to enact land legislation or to develop improved techniques of production and leave their implementation in the hands of inefficient bureaucracy and entrenchment of power in the hands of local big land-owners and the Kulaks.

Obviously the best laws passed will remain dead letters in the Statute Books if they are in conflict with the interest of the local power groups and the techniques profitable to the rural rich will only find their way into practice.

Indeed yield improvements have been achieved during the last decade mainly through adoption of improved seeds along with the application of water and chemical fertilizers in controlled measures. The adoption of new technology is feasible in irrigated areas on individual holdings and is mainly accessible to the bigger land-owners. For those wealthy farmers who can afford to buy all the complementary inputs, the change can be very profitable as the average differential in cash profit between the traditional and the new methods is quite large, but the bulk of the cultivators, particularly the dry cultivators continue to operate the land with traditional methods and are still left at the mercy of the vagaries of nature in general and of the monsoon in particular. The adoption of "building on the best" approach has in effect meant bestowing the benefit of agricultural development on the regions which are already the most developed regions, neglecting the less developed areas.

Additionally, the adoption of new technology can hardly be considered appropriate for extension to a substantial proportion of agriculture because of its heavy dependence on imported or import-based inputs. The new technology warrants the use of heavy doses of fertilizers, without which the yields may, at times, be lower than even those under the traditional technology, and apart from the fact that the HY (High Yielding) Varieties are delicate and highly susceptible to pest. Further, the over-simplification of the ecosystem through concentrating on only a few varieties creates a highly vulnerable target for pests and disease, and adoption of new technology, therefore, implies use of large quantities of pesticides. The short size of the HY varieties, particularly in the case of wheat and rice, creates new problems of weeding and an inducement to use chemical herbicides, which makes the new technology to have a heavy dependence on imported inputs. In view of the level of development and the factor endowment in the country the adoption of big farmer-oriented approach cannot be considered to be either feasible or desirable.

The development programmes in agriculture, particularly the introduction of new technology, have basically followed the 'production target' approach, and the basic logic underlying has been that of a technician aiming at higher and higher levels of total production. On the basis of experimental results in relation to a particular crop or a particular breed of livestock, specific varieties, breed, etc., have been propagated with a view to attaining specific targets in relation to individual crops. The basic objective being the physical production target, the small farmer tends to be neglected, because the potential for increase in production from an individual farm is relatively low due to the basic resource constraint, and the small size of the resources implicitly indicates that the costs involved in reaching a small farmer through institutionalized agencies are relatively high. Consequently, effort is concentrated on the developed areas and the large farms with capacity to cope with the substantial expenditure and other demands implied in the cultivation of new varieties. The approach to development is worked out on the basis of the individual farm ownership and naturally it is the 'project approach' and not the 'overall agricultural development approach' that gets accepted. Consequently, the problems of conservation and augmentation of the resources of the region remain totally neglected, and therefore, a majority of the farmers remain out of the purview of development process. Unless a possibility of a different form of the organizational set up is considered, a comprehensive development approach cannot be meaningfully incorporated in the development plan.

Had the improved dry cultivational practices and water conservation methods been adopted on a wide scale, the agrarian situation could have improved considerably over the last two decades, and experience has demonstrated that what is lacking is not so much the technical knowledge but the appropriate changes in the institutional patterns so that the technical knowledge can be applied fruitfully in the organization of farm business. For example, one need not labour the point that if all the garbage including animal and human waste scattered all over the place in the villages are collected, a good source of fertilizer could become readily available and a major source of disease would be largely checked. It is far better to make operations of this kind to succeed than to import tonnes of chemical fertilizers and antibiotics. Similarly, the need for conservation of soil and proper harvesting of the water resources is stressed time and again. The technicians draw blueprints of these measures, the economists formulate plans and the Legislature legislates, but how the millions of peasants will abandon their present practices and change over to these new ones and the reasons why they are not affecting such a change, are not taken into consideration. Actually they are constrained in this respect simply by their poor asset positions, and under the Indian conditions, where the man-land ratio is adverse,[11] efficient management of resources as a whole is far more important, but well-nigh impossible, under the present peasant-proprietorship situation with a hectare or so of holding per cultivating family. What Indian planning lacks is not either the knowledge of new technology or the knowledge planning techniques, but the proper approach and the appropriate institutional set-up which will promote the adoption of the scientific methods for resource development in the interest of the people of the region.

The approach has to be an integrated and comprehensive one. The land use pattern, the choice of crops, the livestock management, the forest development, and the rest of it, all have to be worked out as an *integrated* activity network so that optimum production potential of the resources of the region is realized; and it has to be *comprehensive* in that all the aspects, viz., technical, financial, organizational, storage, marketing, and processing, are dealt with in their totality and not attended to in a piecemeal manner by different agencies, disparate and largely uncoordinated, as it is being done today.

Adoption of scientific measures for soil and water conservation and in cultivation implies large inputs in terms of technical know-how, particularly agronomic know-how, and involves complex decision making. The incremental variations in the inputs in terms of technical expertise as well as the need to consider sizeable areas of land for proper resource management necessitates increase in the scale of operations, and for that purpose, farm co-operatives will have to be established, which will facilitate area-specific experimentation in new crops and new methods of cultivation. Pooling of labour power will also make feasible a variety of labour intensive practices like desolating of water reservoirs and spreading of silt, collection and composting of dung, mulching, small irrigation work, and the like. Co-operatives can also organize programmes of pisciculture, pasture and forest development, but emphasis will have to be placed on labour intensive technique in organizing all these works. While employment will be generated in asset building activity and in the maintenance of these assets, the indirect effects of such capital formation will be reflected in additional work generated in agriculture due to increase in production potential. The subsequent increase in the rural incomes will create new demand for consumer goods. The co-operatives will have to promote household industry and small industry also, so that work could be generated in diverse economic activities. The underemployment of thousands of cultivating families and artisan families in the rural areas can thus be mitigated only by actively promoting the village co-operatives.

The initiative for building up the village co-operatives has to come from below, that is, from the peasants and the agricultural workers themselves, because the co-operatives, in the true sense of the term, cannot be delivered as a ready made package from above. A host of problems will have to be faced in the formation as well as in the operation of the village co-operatives. Production plans for the co-operatives will have to be drawn up taking into account the overall requirements of foodgrains and the need to diversify agricultural activity with a view to providing adequate work and earnings to the members of the village co-operative. The plan for the distribution of work and the criteria for work evaluation will have to be worked out carefully. Special efforts will have to be made to elicit involvement of all the members in decision making as well as in the day-to-day work on the farm and in the related activities. The operational inter-relationship of the village co-operatives *inter se* and with co-operative industrial units will have to be worked out.

The adoption of co-operative form of organization on a comprehensive scale at the regional level will be difficult in the absence of a consistent policy regarding industrialization, taxation, pricing, etc. at the national level. Otherwise it would be necessary to take some measures akin to protectionism to facilitate adoption of appropriate technique of production and proper utilization and disposal of production at the regional level.

The re-organization and re-orientation of education will be of vital importance in the promotion of co-operative agriculture and industry, with highest priority being accorded to the spread of the improvement in the primary education. Primary education must be universalized among the school-going age-group (6-14) and special efforts will have to be made for imparting elementary education to the middle age groups. The course in primary education should be a self-contained one, oriented to prepare the educated to take up the responsibilities involved in the scientific conduct of agriculture and other primary activities. Besides ensuring proficiency in reading, writing and arithmetic, the courses in general science, geography, etc. at this level will have to be so designed as to inculcate a spirit of inquiry among the students. At the secondary level, the teaching of sciences, both natural and social, will have to be oriented to integrated understanding of the development of science, society and civilization, and in all these subjects the emphasis will have to be placed all along on experimentation, innovations and improvements in agriculture and related activities through continuous interaction between the educational institutions, the experimental and research centres and the experience in the field, which alone will lead to development of appropriate technology and make education and research dynamic. And the education so imparted will have to be combined to certain work responsibility at every level. There is also a need for inculcation of a new set of values such as replacing the competitive attitude by co-operative spirit, and egalitarianism has to be accepted as the highest social value, and these social interests can serve as the chief motivation for work if it is realized that the development of an individual can be furthered only through the development of the society as a whole.[12] Thus education can act as a major lever for preparing the people for taking up the various responsibilities, technical, financial and organizational, implied in the co-operativisation of the production activities in the region. The people committed to the co-operative endeavour, working towards the building up of a new co-operative system, can become a force which will set the pace for the growth of the co-operatives in the region. Such reorganization of production activity will facilitate utilization of the resources of the region in an integrated manner and adoption of appropriate techniques of production. This is imperative for ensuring self-sustained development of a backward region like Marathwada.

VIII. SOME OBSERVATIONS

This methodology, is in the tradition of what was being developed at Poona (Gokhale Institute of Economics and Politics) and therefore, the imprint of the thoughts and work of Prof. D.R. Gadgil is clearly discernible in this work. Much of this methodology, has been influenced by the pioneering work of Prof. Gadgil discussed elsewhere in this book.

Generally, the methodology laid considerable stress on providing adequate employment to the mass of workers in the region and in the process cause incremental variations in the potential rate of growth of the regional economy being planned for. This may seem to be the area that no planning methodology at or below the sub-state level can ill-afford to avoid. Nevertheless, there are three distinguishing features in this methodology to which we shall presently turn. *First*, the stress is on the judicious use of natural resources, and their scientific management.[13] For full benefits of improved productivity to accrue to the agricultural worker management of productive resources is sought to be passed on to the worker himself, and to strengthen the resource base for providing adequate work for a large number of agricultural workers, conservation, augmentation and enrichment of the natural resource. That is, the issue of "assetless" of the poorer sections of society[14] and the danger to ecology and environment were identified and sought to be taken care of.

Incidentally, the methodology did not leave it at that, but made an attempt at prescribing an institutional arrangement through co-operativisation of the rural landscape. But the co-operatives suggested is not the "supply side co-operative" variety that have collapsed all over the place, but co-operatives built on the initiatives from the peasants and agricultural workers themselves, and the problems in so organizing the co-operatives have been discussed quite competently.[15] Given the era when this methodology was evolving and the crucible in which it was maturating (namely, the Marathwada region) stress on co-operatives was a most natural phenomenon. It was logical and appropriate then, irrespective of what it would be now, because the success or otherwise of the co-operative movement elsewhere in the country is another matter.

Secondly the methodology interprets the problem of linkages from the right perspective. The organic link of any plan of industrialization with the area under plan, at the sub-state level is beautifully worked out. That the methodology envisaged the accessing of the "activity—interaction potential" of each of the industrial unit proposed in the form of "backward" and "forward linkages", and explicitly stated that to the extent that the loci of these linkages lie outside the area under the instant planning exercise, the impact of the multiplier within the aforesaid area will be reduced, were significant progress in the thinking on this issue. To maximize the "activity-interaction potential" of a given increase in manufacturing activity, therefore, the methodology correctly envisaged the extension of the chain as much as possible within the planning area itself. Additionally, planned development of resource-based industries were taken to be the most appropriate instrument for initiating a process of sustained industrial development in a backward region.

In the agricultural sector as well the methodology has a lot to commend itself. The approach to agricultural development suggested an integrated and comprehensive approach: the land-use pattern; choice of crops to be cultivated; livestock management and forest development, have to be worked out in what is called an "integrated activity network", for realization of the full production potential.

In one sense, this methodology is a challenge to the methodology propounded by Prof. K.N. Raj: while Prof. K.N. Raj suggested that the approach to district planning can partake the nature of planning at the national and state level, but on a miniscule scale, this methodology led a frontal attack on what is called here "econometrics of growth" and the growth models approach to planning at the national level. This methodology, therefore, mounted a very strong plea to capture, instead, the "unmeasurable socio-economic and political inter-relationship" as mirrored by the institutional set up and pattern of asset ownership of the poor, which is left uncared for by the neat growth models. Whether one agrees with this track of reasoning or not, is another matter but the neatness and internal consistency in the approach is beyond question.

Notes and References

1. Basic Source: Brahme Sulabh: "Approach to Planning", *Artha Vijiana* Vol. 17, Nos. 1 & 2, 1975.
2. For a very competent treatment of the various planning models, see Gupta, S.P.: *Planning and Development in India: A Critique* (New Delhi: Allied Publishers) 1989.
3. See Mukherjee, Amitava: *Foundations of Decentralisation* (New Delhi: Heritage) 1990, Chapter II for a quick review of regionalisation techniques.
4. This has subsequently been called the improvements in the quality of life, or what A.K. Sen has re-christened as the 'right to live long and well'.
5. This is the crux of the great nutrition debate in this country. See Rao, V.K.R.V.: *Food, Nutrition & Poverty in India* (New Delhi: Vikas Publishing House) 1983.
6. Brahme, Sulabh: *loc. cit.*, p. 27.
7. This has subsequently been corroborated in material particulars by serious research. See for example: C.H. Hanumantha Rao:" Changes in Rural Poverty in India: Implications for Agricultural Growth", *IASSI Quarterly News Letter*, Vol. 4, December 1985, Nos. 3-4, pp. 7 to 14. Dhanagre, D.N.: "Green Revolution and Social Inequalities in Rural India", *Economic & Political Weekly*, Volume XXII, Nos. 19, 20 and 21, Annual Number, May, 1987, pp. AN-137 to AN-144.
8. The terms of trade debate is far from over even now. The classic work of Mitra, Ashok: *Terms of Trade and Class Relations* (London: Frank Cass) 1977 is worth reading. See also Tyagi, D.S.: "Domestic Terms of Trade and their Effect on Supply and Demand for the Agricultural Sector", *Economic & Political Weekly*, Review of Agriculture, 28th March 1987.
9. Brahme, Sulabh: *Op. cit.*, p. 27.
10. *Idem.*, p. 163.
11. The position obtains even today. Land records are in shadules everywhere. Even the system of records-of-right we have is inefficient. See Wadhwa, D.C.: "Guaranteeing Title to Land", *Economic & Political Weekly*, 14th October 1989, pp. 2323 to 2334.
12. See Mukherjee, Amitava: *Economics Redefined* (New Delhi: Concept Publishing Co.) forthcoming for an elaboration of this point, though in a slightly more involved context.
13.. These are issue that are agitating experts now: See for example Hanumantha Rao, C.H.: "Agricultural Development and Ecological Degradation", in *Economic & Political Weekly*, December 24-31, 1988.
14. See the issue discussed now in Mukherjee, Neela : "Lessons of Poverty Alleviation Programmes", *Yojana*, 15th August, 1990 and the reference to the terminology used in this regard by the General Editor of this book.
15. This partook the nature of organization of the poor, though in a different framework, which found forceful articulation in the *Report of the Working Group on Block-Level Planning* (New Delhi: Planning Commission) 1978, and in subsequent several documents including the brilliant analysis in Saxena, K.B.: *Organizing the Rural Poor: A Paper of Discussion*, Manuscript (for restricted readership) a copy of which is available with the District Planning Unit, L.B.S. National Academy of Administration, Mussoorie.

CHAPTER V

DISTRICT DEVELOPMENT PLANNING

(K.N. RAJ METHODOLOGY)

I. INTRODUCTION[1]

If institutions of local government are to serve as active instruments for decentralized planning and not merely as allocating mechanisms, or distributing agencies, within an organizational framework which is otherwise highly centralized, determining the kind of developmental work (including mobilization of resources for development) that can be best planned, and best administered most effectively at what level in the administrative or planning hierarchy, is inescapable. A decision with regard to how the responsibilities and powers in respect of developmental activities should be allocated between the Centre, the States, and these institutions of local government can only then be arrived at.[2] The issue pertaining to the extent of autonomy and of flexibility at these different levels of decision-making and execution in the planning hierarchy, which can be built into the system easily needs to be resolved first, despite the fact that the scope for more effective planning from below is closely linked with the total structure of the organization for planning and with the distribution of functions and powers at each of these different levels of administration.

On the general question of the division of developmental responsibilities as between the Centre and the States, Professor Raj referred to what Prof. D.R. Gadgil had deduced as a guiding principle from "the actual operation of the planning process" as Prof. Gadgil saw it in 1960:

> "The fields of action of the Centre and the States are, to a large extent distinct. The Centre builds up and maintains the overall instrumentalities of national economic life such as the credit and the monetary system, the railways and ports. It also acts in relation to the basic requirements of long-term plan of industrialization, with emphasis on large industry and exploitation of mineral resources. The States are concerned, on the other hand, with acting on the total life of all the people in their charge and on all the diffused, dispersed small-scale units and activities. The Centre is concerned with the most generalized features of the national frame and with highly concentrated action at a few strategic points; the States must affect all areas and localities, all the relevant fields and all units. The Centre is concerned with the strategy of the long-term plan and with initiating the crucial movements; the States have to engage themselves in transmitting the forces impelling economic development in all activities and sectors, and areas and

localities, and protecting the standard of living and improving and ameliorating the situation, social and economic, of all individuals within their territories."[3]

Subsequently, when district authorities with specific planning powers were set up in several States, Professor Gadgil modified this formulation by adding that "the objectives and fields of State Planning activities as described in the extract quoted above may be taken generally to apply to the existing situation in relation to District Development Planning",[4] but this, according to Professor K.N. Raj, was very vague with regard to the basis on which responsibilities and powers were to be distributed between the State Governments and the new authorities constituted at the District Level.

One need not labour the point that the State Governments should have, within the framework of national planning, greater scope for framing development programmes appropriate to the particular conditions of their States, and for exercising initiative in mobilizing resources for the purpose. And then it is necessary, to determine what developmental functions and responsibilities the State Governments would carry out within a system of decentralized multi-level planning and what could be entrusted to the lower levels of planning (more particularly at the District level). The following considerations are relevant in this connection:

(a) Granted the widely "divergent" resource endowments and the specific objectives of planning that different States may have, there are certain developmental policies and programmes that require to be formulated and executed at the level of the respective State Governments, which may be the development of communications, transport and power; the supply of water through irrigation projects having a large command area; the exploitation of mineral resources; forest or marine resources where wider considerations (such as the need for conservation of such resources) are involved or the development of industrial complexes which require organization of financial and other resources on an extensive scale.

(b) In several other areas of development, such as social services, there exists no compelling reasons for centralized control and management, and indeed in States which have gone farthest in decentralisation, like Maharashtra and Gujarat, (at the time of outlining this methodology) the responsibility and powers in respect of both administration and development in these areas have been largely transferred to Zilla Parishads and/or Panchayati Samitis, but how much has been gained in the process, from a functional point of view is still not very clear.[5] It is a matter for consideration whether the gains of decentralisation in some of these areas outweigh the disadvantages.

(c) In respect of the necessary local infrastructure for the development of agriculture and small and medium-scale industry, the scope for, and the advantages of, planning at the grass-roots level are likely to be the greatest. The case for transferring to Panchayati Raj Institutions or other local level bodies, wide areas of responsibility and power in important spheres of development is, therefore, prima facie very strong.

(d) The balance of social and political forces at this level has to be carefully judged and it has to be ensured that the powers so transferred to lower levels of governance and planning are not likely to be used in practice by the upper strata of rural society to appropriate to themselves most of the benefits of development. At the same time one has to recognize that broad based social or economic transformation in the countryside is impossible without the balance of power being changed in favour of the less privileged social groups, which is necessarily a political process where institutions of local government could play an important role, and that changes in the balance of forces should not only get reflected in but be promoted, to the extent possible, by the means adopted for mobilizing resources and the use to which they are put. The transfer of developmental functions and powers to Panchayati Raj Institutions in the spheres of agriculture and small and medium-scale industry needs to be effected in phases with reference to the circumstances of each State.

These differing considerations taken together suggest that, in correcting the bias towards centralization which is so evident in Indian Planning hitherto, care has to be taken in working out the precise manner in which decentralisation is effected, which would warrant, apart from the changes in Centre-State financial arrangements, improvements in the methodology of planning at this level and efforts to frame realistic development programmes suited to State-specific needs in the light of the resources likely to be available to it. The experiments attempted in District Development Planning have to be viewed as a part of the effort for framing meaningful and realistic programmes related to the conditions of each area within a State.

II. DEVELOPMENT STRATEGY

Several States such as Maharashtra, Gujarat, and Andhra Pradesh have conceived the phenomenon of "Planning from Below" and transfer, to Zilla Parishads and/or Panchayati Samitis, the executive powers and developmental responsibilities with regard to certain broad developmental heads like education, health, and sanitation, where grants from the State government support the development activities under these heads (the Zilla Parishads having no power to tax or borrow), and therefore, in these States it would be impossible to reverse the changes already effected, but in States where no such steps have been taken so far, it may be worthwhile experimenting with "Planning from Below" along somewhat different lines.

It seems logical to confine developmental activities and planning in the initial years at the District, Taluk (or Block), and Village level, on a few areas, which would strengthen the production base for agriculture and small and medium-scale industry, help in making better and fuller use of unemployed and under-employed manpower and indirectly encourage methods of domestic resource mobilization which would be more equitous than those resorted to before. It would be in order to first examine briefly the logic of the more specific proposals set forth subsequently in this chapter.

Evidently the kind and class of development that has been experienced in India thus far has raised land values both in rural and urban areas at a much faster rate than the rate at which growth of income in general has taken place, so much so that in urban areas land values have increased between five hundred to one thousand per cent in many cities between 1950 and 1965 and even more in some others, and the rise in land values in the rural areas, where the potentialities for rapid agricultural growth have been demonstrated, has been as pronounced as in the urban areas. For instance:

> "Land values in Punjab have been rising over the years, but it is the steady penetration of the green revolution that has pushed them upto new peaks... Land sold five years ago at Rs. 2,000 to 3,000 per acre sells presently at Rs. 10,000 to 12,000 or 15,000. Instances are not lacking of prices doubling within the last two years".[6]

This sharp rise in land values has in part been a reflection of actual increase in rental value, and in part due to speculation in anticipation of the rise in value. Generally, a rise in land values of this magnitude mirrors the external economies created by the larger developmental process and can be attributed only in a limited way to the investment undertaken by those in possession of the property in each case, which provides the justification for considering the gains in capital value as mostly "unearned".

Considerable difficulty has been experienced in working out a system of taxation of urban (or rural) property which while containing speculation, would help significantly to raise resources from those who have had "unearned" gains in capital value from development, to finance further developmental efforts. The nature of the problem has been described by writers in the context of the need to control the hike in urban property values,[7] and such considerations apply in relation to taxation of rural income as well.

Professor K.N. Raj saw only one way of meeting this problem effectively and that is, by direct intervention in the market for land such as the one suggested below:

> "Land values could be fully controlled and speculated once land completely avoided only through public ownership of land... Several ways can be ...suggested for public acquisition of land paying compensation

which is both within the means of public authorities and acceptable to the public in general.... Ideally speaking, public authorities could acquire land in urban areas by simply extending the jurisdiction of the Estate Acquisition Acts which were passed in the fifties by the different States in order to abolish the Zamindari System.... If the Estates Acquisition Act is suitably amended, the control of urban land by public authorities will not be a problem.... By paying the market value of land to private sellers on the one hand and by imposing a stiff capital gains tax on all realized gains on transfer of real properties on the other hand, public authorities will be able to cut down the net cost of public acquisition of land to make large-scale acquisition relatively easy. The Centre does impose a tax now on capital gains from transfer of real properties but the rate is not enough to bring down the net cost of land acquisition. Second, the revenue from this tax goes to the Central Government as it is a tax on the Central List....If the tax on real estate properties is transferred to the State List, the States can impose this tax to their advantage not only as a means to yield revenue and appropriate part of the 'unearned increment' but also to cut down the total cost of land acquisition. Since the taxes will be on all sales, no one will be discriminated against".[8]

Other variants within this overall approach which is worth one's consideration also exists.[9]

What is being driven at in the present context is the desirability of initially establishing a public authority at the State level having powers to acquire land in rural and urban areas and for generally undertaking operations in the land market.[10] Programmes can then be framed deploying unemployed and under-employed manpower for the intensive development of acquired land and for the related construction activities, and additionally arrangements can also be made for redistributing the land so acquired and developed, in part, at concessional rates to the poorer sections of the society (so that they can have a homestead or a work place of their own) and in part to others at market prices through public auctioneering. If acquisition of land for these purposes is supported by legislative measures to expedite the process, and backed by a capital gains tax levied by State Governments, the land acquisition and "operations" programme can be expanded rapidly and perhaps become largely self-supporting in due course with the progress of planning.

In the subsequent stages, it would be relatively easy to work out, within the framework of such a land-acquisition-development-cum-employment programme, an important role for the Panchayati Raj Institutions or the institutions of local government set up at the District, or Sub-district levels, who all could be expected to identify, and recommend to the proposed State level public authority having powers to acquire land, such land that might be acquired by the latter; take the initiative in working out programmes of development-cum-employment that would enhance the value of such land;

devise ways and means for mobilizing idle man-power for executing the programmes of development for enhancing land value (say through labour cooperatives, who might undertake construction work on a piece-rate basis) and defray, if necessary, a part of the expenditures involved from its own sources.

The impact of such programmes would naturally be substantially enlarged if these local level institutions have sources of revenue in order to finance the employment of labour and other related expenditures. One possible source of such revenue which may be earmarked for the local level institutions could be the capital gains tax itself, which would additionally provide them some incentive in promoting the acquisition of land for developmental purposes. The revenue from capital gains tax may, however, be inadequate to support a large enough employment programme, particularly so, where the local level institutions have to expend a part of their revenue towards assisting the poorer and weaker sections of the society through alternative channels, such as through acquisition of developed land at concessional rates for, or for building houses (or workshops) of, the poorer and weaker sections of society. Alternative sources of finance, therefore, needs to be explored and found if the programmes devised and executed by the local level institutions are to have a significant employment impact.

Additional finance which may be made available by the Central Government in support of employment programmes organized by local level institutions would not all by itself be very useful unless there are clear cut indications about how this additional finance could be raised by the local level institutions invested with the responsibility of devising ways and means for, and executing, development-cum-employment programmes. A re-structuring of the taxation of wealth such that it covers a larger tax paying public, concurrently with an across the board reduction in the rates of tax, is a possibility worth considering in this regard.[11]

The current statutory rates of wealth tax are steeply progressive but several permissible tax deductions and exemptions that exists, and the various legally valid methods of evasion such as through formation of companies and trusts, declaration of individual property as the property of Hindu Undivided Families, etc., reduces substantially the efficacy of the tax as a source of revenue, and in consequence, in addition to the premium on illegal evasion placed by steeply progressive rates of taxation, when incidence of such high rates of taxation falls on only one category of assesses, namely individuals, it leads to only some changes in the forms of organization (particularly in the legal forms of property ownership) for taking advantage of the lower tax rates applicable to some other categories of land owners, namely, companies and trusts. In the case of high rates of income-tax, the increase in respect of resources raised will be only marginal from wealth tax.

Should the exemption limit for wealth tax be lowered to widen its coverage, should agricultural property brought within its purview (by amendment of the

Constitution if necessary), and should the *rates* of wealth tax net be lowered sufficiently, it would become so compulsive that to resort to various forms of evasion would on the balance be disadvantageous, and the yield from wealth tax could exceed what is expected from it currently. No injury is likely to ensue if extension in the coverage of the wealth tax (along the lines indicated) is accompanied by similar reform of income tax.[12] This could possibly lead to a huge administrative work load of return checking and assessment, but the problem is, nevertheless not as formidable as it may look at first sight, because in the lower ranges of wealth and income, the checking of the returns filed by assessees may be based on random samples but it should be intensive, and accompanied by deterrent penalties in cases of evasion or under-reporting. The potential revenue from wealth-tax, when re-structured along the foregoing lines, was estimated to work out at approximately Rs. 275 crores per annum,[13] which can be earmarked for projects with a high employment potential undertaken by local level institutions.

III. DISTRICT ECONOMY VIS-A-VIS NATIONAL ECONOMY

The approach to developmental planning at the district and sub-district levels outlined above is based on schemes that would largely involve non-recurring expenditure,[14] which to begin with, ensures that as decentralisation proceeds, activities involving a larger element of recurring expenditure having the potency of leading to proliferation of staff and loss of efficiency is thoroughly discouraged. Nevertheless, this approach would not be adequate to exploit all the potentialities for district development planning in particular, or for "planning from below" in general and therefore, it can be regarded as only a convenient point of departure, with the intention to widen the scope of activity with the flux of time.

This brings us to the most crucial question of how planning of a district can be developed such that the full potentialities of "planning from below" can be realized over a period of time. *"There is no reason why the planning of a district should not be conceived of in the same way as the planning of a national economy"* (emphasis ours).[15] Notwithstanding that several elements in the organization and functioning of a national economy which admits of change by policy-makers have to be taken as given within the framework of district or sub-district planning, and even granted that the functions and powers of policy-makers within the districts will be limited, there is nothing unrealistic in assuming that the basic variables in terms of which the operation of an economy is usually judged, and to which consequently most of the planning targets and policies are directed at (for instance production, prices, income, distribution, consumption levels, rate of saving and size and composition of the capital stock) are no different whether one looks at the economy of a district, or of a State, or of a country.

Moreover, there is no reason to believe that because several elements which admit of change at the national level may have to be taken as given at the district level, district planning is necessarily subject to more serious constraints than planning at the national level. With no legal or administrative restrictions on the mobility of labour as between districts; with the 'domestic' market for a district's products not limited to their own boundaries, and with the existence of a common currency and banking system make possible free movements of capital unchecked by balance of payments considerations of the usual kind, the constraints of development planning at the district level are less serious, than it appears at first inspection, if full potential of district planning is exploited through appropriate policies and programmes. Thus, just as in case of national level or even State-level planning, an appropriate set of macro-estimates for each district has to be constructed, on the basis of which the implications of setting alternative targets in respect of income, consumption, etc. could be quantitatively assessed. The data requirements for such an exercise at the district level, however, are likely to be very large and difficult by all accounts.

The estimation of a district's "income" (corresponding to the national income) as distinct from the "domestic product" of the district (the value added by production within the district), would be difficult because this would imply quantifying the factor incomes that flow out of the district, and the factor incomes that flow into the district from outside the district ("rest of the world" in an "Input-Output Table"), after locating the permanent residence of those to whom such factor incomes accrue out of the value added both within and outside the territory of each district, a difficult task by any standard. The problem will be worse confounded when unrestricted mobility of factors of production between districts exists and there are no political or administrative system for recording systematically inter-district transfer of income. Determination of the comparative levels of productivity, and measurement of variations or changes in them, over time, is possible through estimates of the domestic product, but if the the estimates are to measure the relative levels of welfare of the different districts or to assess their saving potential, the relevant estimates are of district income, which is difficult to come by as stated above.

Similarly the construction of a set of accounts relating to what may be called, "its balance of payments" of the district with "the rest of the world" would be very difficult, and where both the magnitude and the sources of saving for the investment outlay within a district is not quantifiable, with a reasonable degree of precision, construction of macro-estimates for individual districts as a tool for planning, loses much of its validity.

At the district level use of proxies or "indicators" of the relevant macro-magnitude has to be resorted to. Though estimates of district 'domestic product' (of the value added by production in each district) have limitations, nevertheless they could be used as indices of the relative levels of productivity in different districts; and, if it is possible to judge the direction and rough magnitude of the net transfer to factor incomes, their use even as indices of their respective levels of income is possible. The district-wise domestic product estimates by Andhra Pradesh, (Bureau of Economics and Statistics),[16] indicate the kind of use that can be made of them though the results are tentative and are rough approximations. These estimates of productivity levels in different districts, together with other information such as on the extent of the agricultural land in the district owned by the residents outside the district and on the amount of the revenue collected and expenditure incurred in each region by the Government,[17] would provide some clues about the root causes for grievances emanating from regional imbalances and help in working out a plan to remove the grievances, to the extent possible within the scope of a district planning framework.

Attempts at collecting systematic "data for each district relating to the industry-wise distribution of the labour force, the literacy rate and levels of educational attainment, the scale of marketing operations (derived from, say, sales tax collections in the district), the wage-rates paid to casual agricultural labourers for different farm operations, the wages paid to workers in small artisan enterprises in rural areas, and the monthly or weekly incomes of those engaged in services such as transport (separately for human-drawn, animal-drawn and mechanized transport), loading operations, assistance in shops and restaurants, and clerical work in moderate-sized private establishments".[18] Data on the deposits received and the loans advanced by the branches of banks in each district;[19] the amounts received and paid by the government treasuries at the district and taluk levels; and the remittances made to and from each district through post-offices can be collected and collated. Household with a certain income level can be found out. On a sample basis, sample surveys conducted from time to time on the composition and quantity of consumption among different strata of the population; on the percentage of "employees" among those who are employed (and of the proportion of women among such "employees"), on the percentage of the population in the rural areas with less than 4 hours work on an average a day but would be willing to work more, if available at the current wage rates, etc., would provide a good idea of the essential economic characteristics, the comparative level of development, and the more important problems of the district, which would need particular attention in district development planning.

The foregoing identification of problems district-wise, if not taluk-wise, would be aids in working out the strategy and content of the local development programmes directed at, wherever possible, tackling the more urgent needs of each area. The data collected towards this end, and their statistical analysis would also help in assessing the relevant trends in each district over a period. Thus plan formulation and evaluation, warrants the collection and collation of such information.

It is important that concurrently with the generation of data and information, the resource endowments of each district and the possibility of their exploitation and development be closely examined which would essentially be techno-economic analysis where the costs and returns of the available alternatives are analyzed together with the exploration of the various possibilities open from a purely technical perspective.

These aspects of district development planning were also emphasized by Professor Gadgil.[20] The preparatory work is considerable and, even though it can be taken up in stages, there is no cause to assume that the informational and data base for district development planning will be adequate to begin with. Nonetheless a beginning can be made on the basis of available data and informed judgments and the balance of the necessary knowledge and information may be collected as development planning at the district level takes root, which will also need planning and, granted that there is no surfeit of technical personnel available at the district level, it will have to be organized at the State level.

The mode of organization of the available administrative and technical personnel necessary for the formulation and execution of programmes initiated at the district level deserve serious consideration, with extensive changes in the existing pattern and structure of district administration. This is particularly important in order to strengthen the technical staff available at the district level, and for providing them with greater autonomy in taking initiative, drive and action, without unnecessary control over them either from the State headquarters or from the non-technical bureaucracy within the districts. A minimum of change in these directions is considered a pre-condition for any significant progress towards planning from below at the district or sub-district levels.

Prof. Raj deliberately left several loose ends to be tied up later, since

(a) the working out of the details is a time-consuming exercise and require contribution of subject matter specialists with different backgrounds, and

(b) the important thing was to first agree on some of the basic considerations in the approach to "planning from below". The analysis and the suggestions made here are, therefore, according to Professor K.N. Raj, to be regarded as "agent provocateur".

IV. SOME COMMENTS

K.N. Raj by training a macro-planner and an economist, articulated his ideas on district planning methodology as far back as in 1971, while at the Centre for Development Studies Trivandrum.[21] This methodology enjoins that district planning is tantamount to reduced form of national planning and, therefore, the approach to district planning can partake the nature of national planning as, the methodology envisages, the basic variables in terms of which the operation of the economy is generally judged and to which planning targets and policies are generally related, (both directly and indirectly) such as output, employment, prices, income distribution consumption level savings rate, size and composition of stock of capital, are the same irrespective of whether the issues appertain to the local economy of a district or the national economy of a country. In one sense this is a more radical view than it appears at first inspection.

The methodology was based on a full and realistic assessment of the "State of Art" with regard to district development planning. Therefore, while advocating delegation and devolution of planning and plan implementation functions to district levels a "stage-approach was advocated". Initially only *three* areas were proposed to be earmarked for local level institutions: *one,* those that strengthen the base for agriculture, *two,* those that encourage small industry and *three,* those that make a better and fuller use of "surplus" manpower. Very wisely the methodology wanted a begining to be made on agricultural development front and on the unemployment front (which term includes under-employment), first and then as planning at the lower level gets entrenched, more areas could be brought under district planning.

The advocacy of public ownership of land, and then generating income and employment opportunities through land development, is strikingly refreshing. What was bordering on land nationalization, through extension of the provisions of the Zamindari abolition laws, sought to keep the poor in the forefront of development effort by making arrangements for redistributing the land so acquired (and developed in part) at concessional rates to the poorer sections of society to provide them with either a hearth or a work-place and in part to the relatively affluent sections of society at market prices through public auctioneering.

The basic strategy advocated in the methodology is "land acquisition—development–cum–employment" programmes to combat unemployment, and tax those who have unearned income from autonomous increase in land valuation. Thus resources are being sought to be raised by exactions from the relatively rich for the employment of the poor, by (implicity) adhering to the principle of heaviest burden on the broadest back. This approach, in one sense saw the flow of development forces to be generated in the urban areas first, which would then move on into the semi-urban and rural areas.

The methodology was radically different from most other methodologies, in so far as it sought to empower lower tiers of government with powers to tax –an idea which is still fraught with great dangers.[22] The methodology even identified Capital Gains Tax as the one genre of taxation that could be entrusted to the local level institutions. The possibility that this source may not yield enough revenue to sustain this developmental activity, was clearly anticipated and hence a plea was mounted for restructuring of the wealth tax system and lowering the rates of tax, to raise a higher revenue in the balance.[23] As a corollary, the methodology also favoured a cut in the tax rates, to raise the yield from Income Tax. And the increased yield in Income Tax and Wealth Tax emanating from these tax cuts, could than be passed on to the local level institutions involved in planning at the district level.

The methodology (as stated above) was clear with regard to sources of taxation, namely capital gains tax, agricutural property tax and lowering the rates of taxation of income and wealth. The proposal for reducing taxes on wealth and income (and more so of imposing tax on agricultural property) in an age when a leaning towards the "left" was quite fashionable, was bold and, as events have subsequently revealed, full of farsightedness: what the Government did in the late eighties with regard to Income Tax and Wealth Tax rates, was outlined in the early seventies in this methodology.

The emphasis on the local level institutions suggesting acceptable ways and means for raising additional resources, whenever they ask for additional grants-in-aid from higher tiers of government was germane to attempting at developing self reliance among the local level institutions, and to containing within acceptable limits the submission of "charter of demands" for more funding from the State or the Central Government by local level institutions. Lot of public resources (time and money) could be thus saved, which have alternative uses.

Clearly Raj Methodology was thinking ahead of his time, and despite the fact that public ownership of land is common in progressive countries like Sweden, Norway, Holland and Denmark, it was too radical a view to have many takers here in this country, where despite forty years of hectic efforts, land reforms to the extent of even recording the tenants could not touch the periphery of the problem:[24] public ownership of land was a far cry. In any event, the methodology, implicitly, was woven around the assumption that probably legislative support would be forthcoming to support the land acquisition methods endorsed in the methodology, to expedite the process, and with capital gains tax, would impart a self-supporting texture to the scheme. Unfortunately the political fall-out of such a course of action would be too large, even now, to be acceptable to the political executive then. In one sense, the methodology was overly ambitious.

Secondly conceptually, with the existing level of competence, data base and administrative arrangement, failure of an attempt at an estimation of "exports" from and "imports" to, a district is a foregone conclusion. There has been some attempts at building a regional Input-Output Model, but a district-wise Input-Output Model, even of the Leontief static variety, which is sustainable is yet to be seen. In hindsight, so it seems, thinking the district economy as a reduced form of the national economy is a false premise to start with.

In an age intensely environment conscious, any prescription of mere exploitation of the resources (whatever the end) with no indication of how to conserve, scientifically manage and (whenever possible) renew these resources, may not be an acceptable position.

Notes and References

1. Basic Source: Raj, K.N.: *Planning from Below with Reference to District Development and State Planning* (Trivandrum: Centre for Development Studies) July, 1971.

2. This is one of the principles of planning. See. Food and Agriculture Organization of the U.N.: *Towards Improved Multi-level Planning* (Rome : FAO) 1987.
3. Gadgil D.R.: *District Development Planning* (Poona: Gokhale Institute of Economics and Politics) p. 4.
4. *Ibid.*
5. In Karnataka, till 1987-88, the Zilla Parishads were only implementing schemes at the district level framed at the State headquarters.
6. Ladejinsky Wolf,: "The Green Revolution in Punjab: A field Trip", *Economic and Political Weekly*, June 28 1969, Review of Agriculture as quoted in Raj, K.N. : *op. cit.* 1971.
7. Madhab Jayanta,: "Controlling Urban Land Values", *Economic & Political Weekly*, Special Number, July 1969 as quoted in Raj, K.N.: *op. cit.* 1971.
8. Madhab Jayanta,: *op. cit.* as quoted in Raj, K.N. : *op. cit.* 1971
9. Jayanta Madhab has himself several alternative suggestions to offer. The cost of acquisition of land could also be reduced, in appropriate cases, by amendment of the provisions in the Constitution regarding compensation for property acquired.
10. Countries like Sweden, Norway, Holland and Denmark have had a long tradition of public ownership of land. In India the Delhi Development Authority has been able to show significant result under the Delhi Development Act of 1957 for acquiring land and re-selling it after development.
11. This was the underlying philosophy of Reagan's Economic Policy and also substantially influenced the Long-Term Fiscal Policy of the Rajiv Gandhi, Government of India. See Mukherjee, Amitava: "Supply Side Economics-I : Relevance to Indian Economy", *Business Standard*, January 15,1983, p. 5. See Mukherjee, Amitava: "Supply Side Economics-II : Tax Cuts & Revenue in India", *Business Standard*, February 25, 1983, p. 5 and "Supply Side Economics-III : No Cure for Developing Nations' Ills", *Business Standard*, February 26, 1983, p. 5.
12. This approach to wealth and income taxation looks, Prof. Raj mentioned, much like the suggestions made by Professor Lord Nicholas Kaldor. It may be argued that the approach suggested here would go against the policies for reducing the range of economic inequalities by setting ceilings on income and wealth, but such ceilings can be made effective only through more fundamental changes in the economic system and in the role of the private sector within the economy. Fiscal devices alone within a system which is expected to function as a mixed economy with a large component of productive activity based on private ownership of property can not be effective in this regard.
13. For details of this estimate, and the assumptions on which it is based, Prof. Raj refers to the paper by Professor T.N. Krishnan on taxation of wealth (Working paper No. 2, Centre for Development Studies, Trivandrum).
14. They could, however, include schemes for minor irrigation, soil conservation, construction of godowns, warehouses, residential houses, roads, workshops, market-centres and buildings for providing community facilities, etc.
15. Raj K.N. : *Loc. cit.* p. 34.
16. Prof. Raj refers to S. Sasirekha, "Regional Income Estimation -- a Study", paper presented at the Seventh Indian Conference on Research in National Income held at Hyderabad in January 1970.
17. Prof. Raj refers to C.H. Hanumantha Rao, "Budgetary Surpluses of Telengana", *Economic and Political Weekly*, October 18, 1969.
18. Raj K.N.: *loc. cit.* p. 41.

19. The data available on bank deposits and the credits advanced by banks as at the end of 1967, Dr. Raj mentions, that "the ratio of the deposits collected to credits advanced was much lower in some of the less commercially-advanced districts of Kerala than in the other districts–reflecting an outflow of funds through the banking system. For instance, it was as low as 24.2 in the Palghat District compared to 69.3 for the country as a whole)." Cf. *Economic and Political Weekly*, November 8, 1969. Such data reflect of course only a part of the total picture and need to be interpreted with caution. There seems to be some confusion here between deposit-credit ratio and and credit-deposit ratio. A low deposit-credit ratio is likely to "prima facie" indicate an inflow of funds, and a low credit-deposit ratio would "prima facie" indicate an "outflow of funds". See Mukherjee, Amitava: "Low Credit-Deposit Ratio - Does It Restrict Growth"? *Economic Times*, July 27, 1987, page 5.

20. "Planning in its technical and economic aspect is closely related to relevant knowledge and information. Unless there is a minimum base of such knowledge and information, a plan of development for an area like the district cannot be built up". *Op. cit. District Development Planning*, p. 16.

21. This is based on (as stated above) Raj, K.N.: *Planning From Below With Reference to District Development and State Planning* (Trivandrum: Centre for Development Studies) July 1971, Working Paper No. 1. It does not incorporate Prof. Raj's Ideas as reflected in *Thoughts on Decentralisation of Development Planning and Implementation in Administrative Arrangements for Rural Development —A Perspective* (Hyderabad: National Institute of Rural Development) December 1985.

22. See *Recommendations* of the International Expert Group Meeting on Decentralized Planning (Mussoorie: L.B.S. National Academy of Administration, Government of India) June, 1990.

23. This was the philosophy of "Supply-Side Economists" and incorporated in the Long-Term Fiscal Policy of the Government of Indian enumerated in 1985.

24. See *Land Reforms in India: An Empirical Study: 1989-90, Report of the First Year*, of the Project Sponsored by Ministry of Rural Development, Government of India, (Mussoorie: Land Reforms Unit, L.B.S. National Academy of Administration) no date mentioned. Even States ruled by political parties with left ideology have not made much headway. See Ghosh, Tushar Kanti : *Operation Barga and Land Reforms : An Indian Experiment* (Delhi: B.R. Publishing Co.) 1986 and Ghosh, Arun : "Decentralised Planning: West-Bengal Experience", *Economic & Political Weekly*, Review of Agriculture, March 26th, 1988.

CHAPTER VI

PLANNING METHODOLOGY FOR A SUB-DISTRICT SUB-STATE REGION COINCIDING WITH ECONOMIC REGIONALISATION

RAYALASEEMA METHODOLOGY

I. INTRODUCTION

The Rayalaseema is methodology is based on the preparation of the regional development plan for Rayalaseema Region (Andhra Pradesh, India)[1], which is an important exercise in the theory and practice of the regional planning in this country because it denotes a comprehensive development plan prepared with a view to implementation, associated with the process of which is the political will with authority to help arrive at appropriate decisions in planning, and the administrative element which is expected to translate these decisions appertaining to planning into action.

The methodology here summarizes

(a) the background of the region,

(b) the steps involved in regional development plan,

(c) the methodology per se,

(d) and problems of the regional planning in terms of — (i) preparation of resource inventory, (ii) choice of techniques of analysis, and (iii) identification of strategy, and expressions of the strategy in terms of plan frame.

II. BACKGROUND

In the work relating to the regionalisation of the country, Rayalaseema finds a place as a distinct homogeneous region. For instance, according to the work undertaken by the Registrar General, Census of India, for identifying inter-state regions, sub-regions and division of India, the four districts of Rayalaseema are considered as a division.[2] In the study made by the Town and Country Planning Organization of the Government of India, on delineation of planning regions of India, districts in Rayalaseema and Nellore district constitute a group of component districts.[3] In the analysis of Bhat, Kurnool, Cuddapah and Chittoor are treated as one category and Anantapur as another category[4], but these are grouped together into a broader common region. According to the work on "Economic Regionalisation of India" by Sen Gupta and Galina Sadasyuk,[5] the

Rayalaseema Plateau is taken as a micro-region for resource planning. Though Rayalaseema was thus delineated as a district region in the academic exercises on the regionalization of the country, it did not figure as a region with regard to policies in any national policy of accelerated development of a region, except periodic attention being paid to problems of the famine.

III. STEP IN PREPARATION OF PLAN

If there exists no well-established methodology for such a work, a number of studies have to be initiated concurrently and these had be rearranged and fresh avenues of study explored. The steps involved in the plan preparation could be summarized follows:

A Resource Inventory has to be prepared, based on an analysis of the on-going government schemes for development and the physical resource potential particularly those related to agriculture, irrigation, forests, soil, land-use, urban structure and industrial structure etc., which will enable the planner with indications to work out an over-all strategy of development for the region as a whole, basically in terms of agricultural development. An attempt can then be made to sub-divide the region, be it the district or any sub-district entity, into homogeneous sub-regions and indicate a primary and secondary activity appropriate to the resource potential, which can be discussed in a seminar where the heads of departments of the districts, the elected representative of the people and experts in various fields, could examine facts, deliberate and then arrive at the alternative strategies of development of the districts.

An attempt has to be made to indicate the hierarchy of settlement pattern, and the locational aspects of social and certain economic services (like, education, health, sanitation and marketing), to enable the planners to decide upon an appropriate area development approach.

It is at this stage that the objective of a long-term plan for the region, or the districts can be enunciated in the light of the overall studies made. An attempt has to be made to estimate broadly the investment-income implications of the development programme for the region, but in working out the investment-income implications, the activities in the district sectors for which the plan is being worked out have to be clearly demarcated from the aetivities that are deemed as being outside the district sector, which are only to be mentioned to the extent that they complement the district sectors.

Having arrived at the broad investment-income assumptions and projections, the investment possibilities have to be broken up into various district segments. The financial resource constraint (to avoid an unmanageable list of demands) and the physical resource possibilities are to be carefully considered by the *district* authorities, and then they may consider working out the details of the possible priorities and pattern of schemes that could be incorporated in the district plan on the basis of:

(i) the objectives and physical resource potential for each sub-region within a *district*;

(ii) the primary and secondary activity to be developed within each sub-region of the *district*;

(iii) the market places to be developed and the areas to be integrated into markets; and

(iv) the overall policy constraints that are defined by the Planning and Development Board or whatever institutional arrangement established for approving plans.

The *district* plan thus obtained are to be scrutinized, its consistency checked and the plan has to be again discussed by the technical, administrative and popular representatives. The Perspective Plan for fifteen years may then be approved. After approval of the Perspective Plan in these broad terms an Annual Plan for the *district* for every year has to be drafted by the district authorities within the overall framework of the perspective plan.

The studies undertaken relating to the on-going schemes and the resource inventory done for this work is likely to prove useful in making ad hoc suggestions for a re-orientation of the broad priorities with regard to concrete programmes.

IV. METHODOLOGY

In preparing the Plan a number of alternative approaches may have to be considered. Firstly, it could be based on demand projections of important commodities for the *district* similar to the approach adopted for the national plan. This may not be very appropriate always, primarily because for a comparatively small region like a *district*, the aim cannot be self-sufficiency: the aim should be to achieve the development of the *district* by identifying activities which would provide the maximum regional income within the overall policy framework. The second possible approach is by studying the current income distribution and thereby, work out the programme for income redistribution as an objective, which may not also be deemed appropriate on the consideration that income redistribution is to be brought about mainly through appropriate institutional structure and appropriate techniques of production. Such an approach is an unexplored field even at the national level, apart from the fact that, at the district level it is impossible to assume an institutional framework very different from the state or nation as a whole. The third approach could be to indicate specific objectives of the levels of income that should be reached, then arrive at the investment requirements on the basis of broad investment-income ratio and then disaggregate to various sectors through appropriate strategies adopted for the area. This last approach may be adopted with one change, namely, keeping investment as a constraint.

The approach to the preparation of a plan based on the last approach will have to take into account the need for realism and hence the overall financial constraint has to be kept in view. Secondly, to be operationally relevant the existence of an institutional frame has to be taken for granted. Thirdly, it has to fit into the overall value framework of the members of the district planning team rather than a single optimization model. Fourthly, due to data gaps emphasis may have to be more on the method of successive approximations and sound judgement than technical perfection. Fifthly, since the spill-over commitments are already substantial in the plan, (that is, the fact of on-going schemes that cannot be abandoned) the manoeuvrability in the short-run is limited and very specific and detailed suggestion in the long-run may not be desirable, and therefore, in a number of areas a deliberate amount of flexibility may have necessarily to be built in by expressing the overall direction and purpose rather than providing the minutest of the details. Finally, though the expression of the plan into financial outlays, is not necessarily warranted, yet financial outlays are to be spelt out in order that the relative priorities are appreciated by the plan implementing agencies or departments and the people at large.

An initial step in the preparation of the plan is collection of data and analysis of the data which have to undertaken with a view to:

(a) review the economic and social situation of the *district;*

(b) compare the performance and the structure of the economy with the rest of the state;

(c) analyze the distinguishing social, economic and physical characteristics of the *districts;*

(d) study from the village level itself the activities which have significance at the level in order to appreciate the economy of areas within the *district;* and

(e) understanding certain basic socio-economic activities in terms of their location and functioning such as influence zones of secondary classes, trends in population village-wise and so on.

Having obtained the data particularly in regard to primary sector at the village level, an attempt has to be made to regionalize the economy as far as agriculture is concerned. The broad regions would be meant to serve as a frame for appreciating the agricultural economy of the component parts of the *district* and to enable appreciation of external economies that can be created such as the level of processing units.

In order to enable meaningful formulation of *district* plan, there is need for sub-regionalization of the *district*, which may be done keeping the boundaries of *blocks or taluks* intact. It would be evident that the method adopted in regionalization and sub-regionalization is basically one of identifying homogeneous regions on the basis of agricultural characteristics. The possibility of using factor analysis may be explored but it in quite possible that data with different areal units as a base (such as the *village or the block* may be more amenable for mapping, and identification of homogeneity through a simple "map overlay" leading to sub-regionalization may be resorted to.

While the regionalization and sub-regionalization of the area has to be done on homogeneity criteria, the spatial units in terms of hierarchy of settlements is also to be analyzed, which may be done on the basis of the analysis of urban structure, the availability of social service functions at various settlements and their influence zones, and the direction of the movement of commodities and passenger traffic as between different settlements and the type of activities undertaken in more important settlements, which will enable an appreciation of the principle of polarization as against the principle of homogeneity which is applied in the regionalization and sub-regionalization that may be done to the *district*.[5]

An important aspect of the preparation of a such a plan, particularly when the area is small, relates to the delineation of strategy in terms of primary and secondary activities to be developed. In case of a particularly small region, by virtue of its resource endowment and present knowledge of the technology, broad directions in which the development could occur may be laid down. Quantitative techniques of relevance in respect of the resource of this region vis-a-vis the rest of the country, and the quantitative implications of alternative starategies as between different sub-regions may or may not be undertaken, because this would be dependent upon availability of techno-economic coefficients on these aspects. Under such circumstances, the delineation of strategy for the *district* as a whole as well as for the *sub-regions* has to be based on an appreciation of all the relevant data and informed judgement.

While the *broad framework* of development for the *district* is likely to evolve more easily, in regard to the sub-regions, say blocks or panchayats, substantial work has to be undertaken for delineating *strategies* since it is at the *sub-district* level that the strategy has to be converted into activity. For this purpose the method adopted can be threefold. *One*, on the basis of agro-climatic conditions, the primary and secondary activities in terms of agriculture and allied activities could be delineated. *Two*, the primary activity in agriculture and allied activities are normally related to or linked with activities of processing through select centres for which the socio-economic survey will give an indication of hierarchy of settlements. *Three*, to enable area development approach, the level of availability of social service has to be obtained and the area gaps and locational gaps in the social service have to be identified and filled up involving growth centre approach.

An important aspect of planning methodology in this regard is the preparation of a macro framework, which enjoins the need for regional input output tables and information on more important projects in the field which is not, however, available, and the overall investment-employment implications are possible at macro-level if dependable data are available. Thus the major emphasis has to be laid on indicating the direction in which development would take place and the activities on which to focus attention on, despite the need to impose certain resource constraints so as to ensure that the plan is kept within manageable limits which require a rough indication of the investment possibility and the income levels likely to be achieved. To this end, therefore, a frame of perspective has to drawn up, even if very tentative.

For the purposes of sectoral disaggregation, sectoral capital-output ratio may or may not be used depending on the availability and the limitations of the data. One approach be could be of delineating a lead sector for a region and assuming that the other sectors would grow at the same rate as the lead sector if sectoral capital-output ratio cannot be worked out for any reason. The lead sector mentioned here connotes a sector that is capable of generating an exportable surplus.

In terms of spatial expression of these activities, the sub-regionalization and the socio-economic surveys have to be undertaken to indicate certain relevant aspects, though, a comparative cost of the activities as between different regions need not be worked out in detail. In regard to projects, however, a shelf of projects may be obtained but depending on the details, a decision has to be taken about their use in the planning process for the *district*. In any event, the shelf of projects is more relevant at the operation stage of conversion of Perspective Plan into Medium Term Plan from time to time than at the Perspective Plan formulation stage itself. In terms of phasing, in case of activities, consistency must be ensured and linkages identified in only principle, leaving the detailed working out to the stage of operationalising the plans.

An important aspect in the methodology of the such plan is the final preparation of *district* plans. The results of studies including an indication of the primary and secondary activity to be developed and the infrastructural requirements are looked into, which information coupled with differentiation between state sector and district sector is made available. The ***district authorities*** are expected to prepare the plan keeping in view:

(a) the physical strategies worked out and
(b) financial resource constraints indicated.

The *district* authorities are to prepare the plan only for the sectors identified as being relevant to the district and to indicate the district plan's linkages for the state and national level. The more important activities for which detailed plans need be worked out relate to agriculture, irrigation and animal husbandry. For these three activities detailed proposals indicating input requirements and output possibilities as also avenues for agri-processing units have to be obtained, which provides a mass of valuable information.

V. PROBLEMS

A preliminary task in regard to any sub-national planning exercise relates to the collection of data regarding the economic and technical factors relevant to the region. The sources from which this information has to be gathered are varied. There may be published material like District Gazetteers, Census Publications and periodical publications such as those by Bureau of Economics and Statistics; there may be old records such as the population of the various villages from 1890 in order to study the growth of settlement pattern; there may be unpublished material such as the list of factories and number of workers covered by the Factories Act in the area or even the figure of the district incomes and regional incomes[6] the results of certain special studies undertaken earlier, relevant to the region may be available;[7] yet, even then it may be necessary to conduct specialized (though improvized) surveys in order to gather data at a disaggregated level;[8] and it may be necessary to organize the collection of technical data and material already available with technical departments to specially orient it to the needs of the planning exercise.[9] And after identifying the crucial gaps in the data to provide the framework of the plan, certain technical studies have to be commissioned or undertaken. For instance, the functional linkages as between the various settlements and the hierarchy of settlements could not be identified with the available data resulting in a specially conducted socio-economic survey of all the villages in the region.

There is need for a careful choice of the techniques of analysis that have to be undertaken. Since a sub-national planning exercise would present innumerable possibilities for analysis, to be in the realm of manageable magnitudes, it is necessary to keep three elements in view, namely, the cost of *collecting* data, particularly fresh surveys; the cost of adequately *analyzing* such data; and the *time* involved for these. These elements should be set off against the possible value and relevance of results. Secondly, to justify planning at the sub-state, district and sub-district levels there would be need for disaggregated data and a more disaggregated analysis of the various factors in the economy of the area for which the plan is prepared. Then, a careful choice has to be made about the level at which data would be dependable. For instance while a study of population, emigration and immigration would be useful, it need not be and cannot be appropriately collected at the village level. In other words, every aspect of the economy has to be viewed with reference to the available data; the relevance of the data for various spatial levels such as village, taluk, block, or district; the dependability at various levels; the cost of collecting data; the use to which this could be made and its unique relevance to the economy of the area under reference for the planning exercise. That is, information on different aspects is best collected with reference to different spatial levels and as such any standard spatial unit for all purposes may be discarded. Thirdly, sophisticated analysis on the basis of data available may prove to be quite misleading unless the way in which this data is collected or computed is understood. For instance, given the incomes of the district, it is natural that an analysis is sought to be made about the sectoral composition of the income and the trend thereon, but such an analysis would be most misleading, because except with regard to the primary sector, the figures of income are mostly imputed on a pro-rata basis of the population to various districts. Factor analysis, again, in regard to regionalization would be a very sophisticated and interesting analysis but would result only in giving a picture on the basis of present data. It is seldom that we have quantifiable information on potential for smaller areas.

Thus, the whole analysis would be built on:

(a) an overall appreciation of the economy of the region and

(b) as in-depth analysis of the region in regard to the physical characteristics of the various parts of the region.

The homogeneity aspects is best served, in foregoing background, by the map overlay method. In order to understand and appreciate functional linkages and the way the economy has been functioning at a micro-level in terms of settlement pattern, in-depth studies have to be conducted regarding the growth of population in each settlement (number of settlements could be very large over a span of several decades); the village-wise endowments of various socio-economic functions (including agricultural workshops, petrol pumps, barber shops and tailoring shops); an analysis of flow of passengers in various directions; the functional characteristics of the urban areas and such other dimensions will provide a deeper understanding of the economy of the region. At this stage fitting these various observations regarding characteristics of settlements, and the behaviour of the various factors relevant to the economy into a model which admits of simultaneous solution would be difficult, if not impossible, and therefore, in keeping with the general tenor of the methodology, appreciation and sound judgement will have to be invoked at some stage, and the effort would be for analyses of greater comprehension but not necessarily of direction leading to solutions.

The basic strategy of development has to, in a way, flow from the objectives of the plan and the conditions or the factors available in the area being planned for. For working out the strategy an important consideration pertains to the position of the regional economy under consideration (be it a district, a sub-district or supra-district at the sub-State level) vis-a-vis the other regions and the rest of the economy. The information available on other regions, or the role of this region in the national perspective, will in most cases be practically not available and to obtain such information will be too expensive and too time consuming a process to be expedient. Therefore, the economy of the area being planned for has to be viewed either as a national economy in which case it would be unrealistic, or some rough estimates have to be made regarding the position of the sub-state economy under reference vis-a-vis the national economy. The latter has been done for various exercises. Additionally, for a comparatively small region, the strategy would be in terms of identifying a lead sector, which phrase implies the sector whose growth really determines the growth of the sub-state region, again is to be carried out more on the basis of well worked-out comparative cost consideration. Thirdly, there could be a conflict between priorities arrived at based purely on techno-economic consideration and priorities as is expected by the people's representatives at whose instance and for whose approval the plan is being prepared. For instance the energisation of the wells may not be an important element in the plan if only techno-economic considerations are taken into account but due to the insistence of the Planning Board this may had become a priority activity. Fourthly, in working out the strategy to translate the objectives into reality certain technical problems may emerge, resulting in a mere mention of statements of desirable changes, rather than a clear action plan with investment implications. For instance, relief against drought, it is clear, cannot conceivably be provided completely by dry farming alone, and the limitations of dry farming in the context of the drought areas would be clearly thrown up but there may be no technical alternative to it. Similarly water saving techniques may be attempted at but their relevance in terms of the farmer's economy are yet to be established beyond the shadows of all reasonable doubts. In a particularly poor resource endowed area (like Rayalaseema) the techno-economic changes required to make the economy prosperous are so many that they cannot be easily comprehended. Therefore, these have to be only indicated. Fifthly, there may be institutional bottlenecks which makes enunciation of strategy incomplete. If we take an objective, viz., the provision of a minimum level of income to the people, it would require substantial institutional changes which are not within the competence of planning at the sub-state level, like a district or block planning exercise.

VI. LESSONS FROM EXPERIENCE

Some important lessons of general interest derived from the Rayalaseema exercise could be mentioned. *One*, in spite of accepting the four districts as a policy region, it was impossible to get over the significance of district as a unit: the district a crucial unit apart from the State and the nation for any planning in view of the data availability, the institutional structure and institutions of peoples representative.

Two, where technical capabilities do not afford the preparation of the district plan at the district level the need was to build up a system which will involve greater and greater analysis of the district position by the State level authorities, posing questions specifically to the district level authorities in fixing objectives, defining constraints and instruments and making them come forward with alternatives, reflecting the local situation and the locally felt needs of the people. Therefore, district planning under such circumstances are to be treated as a process of planning for the district by the State level authorities (or planning at the district level with intense guidance from state).

Three, the preparation of plan for one level in a multi-level frame requires full appreciation and cognizance of the relevant functions at the other levels and the complementarities between them. The question of complementarities between the district sector, state sector and national sector prove to be crucial in the actual process of planning for essential social service provided for every area. It would also be viewed as an infrastructure for development and could be integrated with the possibilities of ground water potential. In each case there would be a different set of priorities. Further, the regional sector would concentrate on rural electrification. Its linkage in terms of making available the generation capacity would impose another complementarity. In short the whole process has to be iterative.

Four, there is generally a tendency to opt for cataloguing of projects. No doubt, the physical elements and the project phase are most crucial at the lower order spatial levels but in terms of the plan frame in a perspective, a shelf of projects would not be very relevant, that is, the concept of the "project off the shelf" over a period of 10-15 years would mean investigation of an enormous number of schemes, and these projects would cease to be of much significance except in a plan frame. The details of minor schemes are better worked out for a shorter, say a medium term plan or annual plan, within the Perspective Plan frame, and priorities worked in the regional planning exercise than over a perspective of ten or fifteen years.

Five, it is undeniable that a sub-national planning exercise of a district or a group of districts would provide for a system wherein the felt needs of the people are more readily reflected than at higher levels. There may be no better illustrations than the Rayalaseema plan itself. The reading of objectives which were framed and approved as far back as 1970 in the Rayalaseema exercise would show that there were four important ingredients of the whole plan, viz., the mitigation of drought, the need for growth, the provision of minimum facilities and problem of minimum levels of consumptions. The third aspect relates to the provision of socio-service facilities such as roads, drinking water and rural electrification. The plan insisted that these facilities are essential for civilized existence and that providing these should be the right approach, which subsequently found place in the Minimum Needs Programme of the Fifth Five Year Plan. The fourth problem relates to the need for the levels of consumption of the masses of poor people and attempts to quantify the permissible inequalities in the perspective. These two elements really constituted the core of Fifth Five Year Plan.

VII. SOME OBSERVATIONS

The Rayalaseema Methodology is the case of planning for a region whose administrative or political boundary was co-terminus with economic regionalisation in successive experiments.[10] This uniqueness makes planning for Rayalaseema and its methodology very important for those attempting at sub-state and district level planning. By conception, it can apply as much to district as to supra-district planning at the sub-state level should the need arise as was advocated by the Economic Advisory Council in 1983:[11] in the former event the district may be conceived of as the region, and it may be sub-regionalised by the application of any conventional techniques of regionalisation, particularly the homogeneity criterion.

The methodology emphasizes the importance of a Perspective Plan and the Annual Plans. The Perspective would provide the long term view and targets to be pursued through the Annual Plans as instrumentability of affecting the ctirical variables. It provides for continuity in long term approach and a system of change within that framework.

The data requirements, and the constraints to their obtention have been appreciated in the right perspective. The corrective steps indicated here are different from what the normal prescriptions are, in that the methodology enjoins successive approximations, in each round nearing the reality all the more, and then exercise sound judgement to perceive the reality: this is much more than trying to achieve technical perfection.

The methodology correctly advocates that in all classes of regional planning where no well established methodology exists, one big go at it can unleash a plethora of problems. Therefore, the best course is to initiate "almost simultaneously and from time to time these" have "to be rearranged and fresh avenues of study explored." Once the Resource Inventory is prepared and the hierarchy of settlements is indicated, the long-term plan for the area under reference is to be enunciated in the light of the overall studies made, and then an attempt at working out the investment income implications of the development programme of the area, is to be made.

From the foregoing it is apparent that the methodology by and large, accepted the growth centre strategy and pinned considerable faith in building up an hierarchy of settlements. Implications and appropriateness of this acceptance have been discussed at other places in this book[12] and is, therefore, not dealt here in detail, except to indicate that this was in keeping with the Hyderabad-Mysore nexus of growth centre approach to district planning that was established by the pioneering contributions of Lalit Sen[13] and R.P. Misra[14] at Hyderabad and Mysore respectively. Though there has been several criticisms of the growth centre approach,[15] it still has considerable elements of promise for micro-level planning.[16]

The methodology is likely to succeed in a developing community because the usual confusion between objective strategy, and framework has been circumvented: it clearly distinguishes the three, and then the strategy component is itself delineated as "primary" and "secondary". Then the methodology enjoins that "in the preparation of plan for one level in a multi-level frame requires full appreciation and cognizance of the relevant functions at the other levels and the complementarities between them".[17] Thus there is a clear indication of conforming to the Principle of Nesting and Integration of Plans,[18] and an appreciation of function of sharing between different levels of planning.[19]

In one sense the methodology outlined here partakes the nature of the "Trial & Error" approach of the Reduced Planning Methodology,[20] in the sense that it has encouraged experimentation with and examined several option before choosing the final strategy but unlike the Reduced Planning methodology it is based on systematic regional analysis and without reposing faith on large project.

This is perhaps the only, among the earlier methodologies to lay down what are the pre-requisites of decentralised planning, which imparts it pragmatism and brings it nearer to ground conditions. Indeed the realism of the planning methodology is further bolstered by its "advise" as discussed above that technical perfection may not be achieved (and may not be achievable given the data base and expertise of planning personnel) but must not flounder on informed sound judgement. If income levels to be reached are worked out, and if the allocation is based on broad investment-income-ratio, this seems to be one of the better ways, otherwise accurately working out first the warranted income levels and then matching it with exact (or nearly so) allocation of resources will both be too lengthy and too long a process for a district or sub-district planning exercise.

Notes and References

1. Basic Source: Reddy, Venugopal Y.: "Regional Development Plan for Rayalaseema India: A Case Study", in Mishra, R.P. et al. (eds.) : *Regional Planning and National Development* (New Delhi: Vikas) 1978.
2. Sen Gupta, P.: "Framework of Economic Regions", in *Economic Regionalisation of India : Problems and Approaches* (New Delhi : Census of India 1961) Monograph series No. 8, Vol. I. This work is still highly regarded. See Alagh, Y.K.: "Guidelines for Agro-Climatic Planning—A Draft for Discussion", *Journal of Land Development*, Lucknow, Revenue Board, Vol. I, No. I, 1988.
3. Mitra, Asok: *Levels of Regional Development in Indian Regional Planning: Concepts, Techniques, Policies and Case Studies* (New Delhi: Government of India) 1965. This is another classic work. See also his "Levels of Regional Development in India", in Sadasyuk, Galina and Sen Gupta, P.: *Economic Regionalisation in India Problems & Approaches* (New Delhi: Census of India) 1961. Monograph series No. 8, Vol. I.
4. Sadasyuk, G.V.: "Urbanisation and the Spatial Structure of the Indian Economy", in *Economic and Socio-Cultural Dimensions of Regionalisation* (Census of India, 1971) Centenary Monograph 1971.
5. See for techniques of regionalisation the classic work of Friedman J. and Alonso, W.: *Regional Development Planning: A Reader* (Cambridge, Mass.: M.I.T. Press) 1964. For a summary see Mukherjee, Amitava: *Foundations of Decentralisation* (New Delhi: Heritage Publishers) 1990, Chapter II.
6. An example relates to the goods traffic originating at different stations of the railways in terms of quantities and categories.
7. Examples are the special study on Road Transport of Andhra Pradesh as also the Study of Small Industry in the unorganized sectors in the urban segment of the area under study.
8. For instance, while the broad classification of the soils, taluk-wise, may be available, the soil differs as between the various tracks requiring fresh gathering of data at the disaggregated level. Such data at the disaggregated level would only provide the raison-ditre for any regional planning exercise at the sub-state, district and sub-district levels.

9. For example, the mineral potential and irrigation potential had to be estimated by the respective technical organizations based on the material available with them.
10. Sen Gupta, P. and Sadasyuk, Galina: *Economic Regionalisation of India: Problems and Approaches,* Census of India, Monograph, Series No.8, Volume No. 1, 1961. Mitra, Asok: *Levels of Regional Development in India, Regional Planning: Concepts, Techniques Policies and Cases Studies* (New Delhi: Government of India) 1965.
11. Economic Advisory Council of the Prime Minister: *First Report of Decentralisation of Development and Implementation in the State,* 4th October 1983, text published in *Economic Times,* New Delhi, 14th January 1984.
12. See the observations on Gadgil Methodology and NIRD Methodology.
13. See Sen, Lalit: *Readings on Micro-Level Planning and Rural Growth Centres* (Hyderabad: National Institute of Community Development, Since renamed National Institute of Rural Development) 1972 for a contemporaneous view of Sen's work.
14. See Misra, R.P.: "Growth Pole Strategy for Rural Development in India", *Journal of the Institute of Economic Geography,* 1970, pp. 33-38, for a contemporaneous view of Misra's work as well. Incidentally Misra et al. has propounded subsequently the Growth–Foci approach.
15. See for instance Wanmali, Sudhir: Service Centre in Rural India (New Delhi : B.R. Publications) 1983 and Shah, S. M.: *Growth Centres and Rural Urban Development* (New Delhi: Abhinav Publications) 1985.
16. The N.I.R.D. approach followed in the Pilot Project district Plan for Nashik sponsored by the Planning Commission follow this approach. See *Pilot Project on District Planning Perspective Plan 1990-95* (Nashik: Office of the Collector) 1989, pp.5.
17. Venugopal Reddy, Y.: Loc. cit., p. 432.
18. Sundaram, K.V.: "Multi-Level Planning; Concept, Principles and Some Aspects of Its Application to Sectoral Planning", in Sundaram, K.V. et al. (eds.) *Regional Planning and Development,* Vol. I (New Delhi: Heritage Publishers) 1989 p. 103.
19. F.A.O.: *Toward Improved Multi-Level Planning for Agricultural and Rural Development in Asia and the Pacific* (Rome: Food & Agriculture Organization of the U.N.) 1985, p. 94.
20. Waller, P.: "The Reduced Planning Approach for Regional Development Programmes in Lagging Regions", in Bendavid-val, Avrom and Watter, Peter P. (eds.): *Action Oriented Approaches to Regional Development Planning* (New York: Praeger Publishers) 1975.

CHAPTER VII

ASSOCIATION FOR VOLUNTARY ASSOCIATION FOR RURAL DEVELOPMENT METHODOLOGY[1]

I. INTRODUCTION

The concept of decentralized local planning has been accepted in principle by policy-makers and planners in the country, but its application requires to be carefully watched, for past experience of district and sub-district level planning, in most cases is that the local people were almost completely excluded from the exercise. The reason lies in the old and outdated attitude of officials and experts who consider the people as mere beneficiaries and not partners in the adventure of development.

One of the major objectives of micro-level planning is not just the growth of society but the improvement of the economic conditions of the poorer sections by involving the people both to diagnose their own problems and to resolve them and to have a greater control over their own affairs. If the people have known how to master their political destiny, there is no basis in logic and no great probability in practice as to why they should not be allowed to determine their economic destiny. Judging by this criterion, past planning efforts by the administrative agencies have by and large failed.

Ideally, the people themselves should come forward and take over the planning effort, which, however, is not easy, particularly so in a country like India, because the people are not organized,[2] which is why the role of non-official voluntary agencies in this context becomes extremely important. The absence of bureaucratic delays and official insensitivity in the functioning of voluntary organizations and their ability to provide professional services and offer necessary expertise for solving local problems with the help of their intimate knowledge of the local situation, make the voluntary agencies good institutions for being encompassed in the planning process and given a definite role therein. While professional competence in planning is required for the efficiency of a development programme, this will not carry us very far without an intimate knowledge of local problems, without the involvement of the people and without a certain amount of dedication to the cause of the poor to complement professional planning. It is here that the role of the voluntary agencies far outstrips that of official bodies.

It is well known that the upliftment of the poor is a difficult task, and it involves provision of services from outside for fulfilling their needs, and at once, the development of a feeling of self-reliance in them.[3] One must have full knowledge of human resources and human problems, of the village power status structure, of the exploitation of one class by another, of the factional politics and of the value system of the local people. The established relationships based on feudal, class and caste hierarchy may be too well entrenched for any plan to succeed. The development of special groups and minorities such as women, scheduled castes and tribes, the small and marginal farmers and the landless labourers requires special attention and knowledge on the part of the planners. People's involvement in planning could complement the knowledge of the planners and, therefore, may be carefully promoted nurtured and sustained.

Judged against the backdrop of the foregoing, micro-level planning should have the following objectives which may have to be elaborated, modified or changed, in terms of each local situation.

Social Objectives

(1) Progressive elimination of exploitation of, and injustice meted out to, the poor and the oppressed.

(2) Removal of disparities.

(3) Encouragement and increase in people's initiative and participation and inculcation in the common people the spirit of self-reliance and "swadeshi" in the Gandhian sense.[4]

(4) Fostering community feeling and sense of mutual help, cooperation and sharing, among the masses instead of the desire to pursue one's own self-interest,[5] particularly through appropriate institutions of the youth, the women and other groups.

Economic Objectives

(1) Provision of opportunities for full and gainful employment to every person in the community, starting from the poorest.

(2) Bringing in local resources and the means of production progressively within the control and direction of the local community in order to make equality a reality.

(3) Increasing use of local resources both material and human supplemented by outside inputs only where necessary.

(4) Production of goods and services oriented towards the meeting of basic and minimum needs of the masses with surplus available for capital formation and further development.

(5) Planning infrastructural facilities, such as roads, markets, energy sources, warehouses, agricultural inputs, distribution and cooperatives.

II. METHODOLOGY FOR THE FORMULATION OF BLOCK-LEVEL PLANS

An integrated area development plan for a block should fully take cognizance of people's needs and potentialities. Though the preparation of the plan will have to be a professional exercise, nevertheless, people's involvement in its formulation will not only make it realistic but will also impart it greater acceptability for the common man. The following steps are suggested as guidelines for the formulation of a block plan.

Step I

Launching a survey for collecting detailed information on the various facets of life in the block, must necessarily be preceded by the survey team (consisting of subject specialists like an agronomist, irrigation expert, animal husbandry specialist, economist, sociologist and industry expert) meeting as many people and groups as possible in the relevant planning area, including those below the poverty line, scheduled castes, scheduled tribes, women and youth groups. Discussions with these groups regarding their problems and prospects and of the area under consideration for planning, would provide a reasonably complete and balanced picture of the task at hand. The importance of the fact that detailed records should be kept of these discussions, and facts, to be verified later, should be clearly underlined. In preparing their appraisal reports, the subject specialists will technically examine the suggestions given by the people and include those found feasible, after giving technical appraisal to the common sense approach of the people of the locality.

These discussions should be followed by a meeting with local officials at the panchayat, block and district levels for collection of secondary data,verification of facts and discussion of issues raised by the people. Particular stress should be laid on information regarding all development programmes which have been implemented in the past and/ or are currently under implementation in each of the sectors under study. Details about programmes which are being considered for the current plan should also be gathered.

On conclusion of these series of discussions, a profile of the area being planned for should be prepared giving a complete picture of the block including agro-climatic, typographical, techno-economic and socio-cultural dimensions. Some of the pertinent data to be collected could be through the questionnaire method, (a Questionnaire is at Appendix-II) to be used by the subject specialists to prepare their separate appraisal reports giving contours of development for the block.

Step II

At this stage a widely representative meeting of the block leaders including the elected representatives of the Panchayati Raj Institutions and other representatives of various Gram Panchyats, representatives of voluntary organizations (since rechristened as Non-Government Organizations) and social service institutions working in the area, should be convened and the findings of the Planning Team should be presented to them, with regard to at least the following:

(a) The importance of furnishing full and correct information by families and individuals who will be approached by the Planning Team should be stressed.

(b) Suggestions, based on considered opinion of the leaders of the area regarding the problems which need immediate attention, and problems which are of comparatively lesser urgency and whose solution can be spread over a period of time should also be discussed threadbare and their opinion should be solicited about how these problems should be approached and solved.

(c) The leaders may be asked to name volunteers to join the Study Team for collecting information, taking care that the new recruits must enjoy the confidence and respect of the local people, are well-educated to understand and carry on the task entrusted to their care, including a brief report-writing.

(d) Broadly the nature and content of the information to be gathered through the questionnaire should be discussed at the meeting and comments invited.

Step III

The Study Team should now formulate a questionnaire, which while eliciting standard items of information required for professional planning and physiographic, techno-economic, socio-cultural and other data, should have the flexibility to include elements suggested by the local people during earlier discussions. That explains why the questionnaire should be provisionally drawn up and the format should be amenable to both manual tabulation as well as computerization according to the needs of the planning mechanics.

Simultaneously, thematic maps should be prepared, highlighting the characteristics of the area, for analysis of data and for planning purposes. These maps could be:

(i) Location map.
(ii) Relief and drainage map.
(iii) Soil map of the block.
(iv) Settlement pattern & administrative divisions map.
(v) Infrastructure map.
(vi) Density of population map.
(vii) Map of Central Villages along with their command areas.
(viii) Existing and proposed irrigation facilities map.
(ix) Electric transmission lines map.

Step IV

After preparing the questionnaire it should be pre-tested in a few villages and on a few households, which would constitute the "control group", for assessing the lucidity of the items and questions. The reaction and responses of the respondents of this control group should be carefully noted and tabulated. Frequency counts should be made of these reactions to observe the distribution of responses against each item which would form the basis of revision or elimination of items that may turn out to be redundant.

The newly recruited members from the local area should be trained during this period of "questionnaire pre-testing". After each day's work the Study Team should discuss the filled-in questionnaires with the new recruits and point out the errors if any and educate the new recruits about the correct way of interviewing and recording the relevant responses from the interviewees.

On the basis of this "pre-testing", the questionnaire ought to be finalized.

Step V

One of the major difficulties faced in a detailed survey of this nature is the preparation of a sampling design because no area in the country has uniform characterizations. A careful *selection of villages* representing socio-political and regional variations in the block and problems arising out of such variations should serve the purpose. A random sampling of villages after stratification by broad characteristics may cover notable diversities. Considering the constraints of both time and resources, stratification of villages can be done with the help of local leaders and knowledgeable officials rather than basing it on the outcome of a pilot survey.

From experience in a number of situations in the country a minimum of ten villages in a block consisting of about 100 villages, or 10 percent, (the standard practice) may serve the purpose, but the actual number would of course depend on the heterogeneity of the population. This method of selection of the villages will help statistical estimation of a number of variables and draw a socio-economic base line. For *selection of households* within each village, either a complete coverage of all households in a village can be achieved provided the number of villages in the overall sample design is reasonably small, or alternatively, if the number of villages is high, a careful stratified random sampling method should be adopted, which should reflect all groups, with higher weightage given to the poorer sections of society.

Step VI

The distribution of problems amongst the blocks may not be uniform, in as much as some blocks will have concentration of problems and special problems at that. Such Blocks with special problems may require special in-depth case studies in addition to a socio-economic survey, and so is the case with the problems of women, scheduled castes and scheduled tribes, landless agricultural workers and village artisans in every case.

Step VII

On completion of the tabulation of the survey data an interim plan should be prepared on the basis of these tabulations, the Block Profile, the appraisal reports given by the experts, the discussion notes made earlier during discussion with the common people, government functionaries and elected representatives of the people on the Panchayati Raj Institutions, and the case studies commissioned, both generally and with regard to blocks with special problems. The outer limits and priorities of the plan should be set forth along the lines suggested by local people, elected representatives and opinion leaders in the meeting referred to in Step II above. The plan ought to contain and provide detailed analysis of the various choices possible within these outer limits and priorities under reference, and should include the identification of priority problems and long-term potentialities of the area; the role of the existing planned programmes; methods of introducing the development programmes including the formation of local groups to influence them; the impact of the programmes, services and institutions according to the overall financial implications. It would be expedient to have Maps prepared to visually illustrate the recommendations made in the plan for better appreciation by a wider spectrum of the people.

Step VIII

The draft plan should then be presented to a widely represented meeting as described in Step II, and their reactions carefully noted. The local leaders and institutions should also be asked at this meeting to provide full support in implementing the plan, form organizations necessary for the purposes of implementation, which ought additionally ensure local level participation and availability of local resources (material, financial and human) in the implementation of the plan at every stage.

The plan ought additionally be invariably presented before a meeting of officials at the block and district levels for better coordination with official efforts and possible financial assistance.

III. CRITERIA FOR CHOICE OF SCHEMES

While selecting specific schemes for inclusion in the block plan it is essential to have certain overall criteria which may have to be applied in this regard. The following could be in the nature of a checklist against which the project has to be judged as meriting inclusion in the block plan.

(1) *Inter-block consistency*: Some schemes or projects existing or coming up for location in the block may have interlinks with areas falling outside the boundaries of the block, and which schemes or projects have to be appraised and decided at the district, supra-district or State level. A block plan while it may mention the various possibilities about such schemes but it should not include them in the definitive pattern of investments, irrespective of the nature of projects, whether related to either production or social service.

(2) *Local resource and market based:* In order to be block-specific the proposed schemes or projects (an industrial scheme, for example) must ensure that it has sufficient supply of the raw material locally available and preferably its product should be dependant upon the local market for sales.

(3) *Priority group:* The schemes or projects should be relevant to the needs and capabilities of the weaker sections of society, such as those below the poverty line, especially scheduled castes and scheduled tribes, and particularly women and children amongst them.

It is important to ensure that the existing form of social organization, for example in tribal areas, are not tampered with and social systems which are based on community ownership and growth are not affected. The special economic roles of women in society must be taken cognizance of so that they are neither displaced nor neglected in manpower planning.

(4) *Employment expansion:* The schemes and projects should expand job opportunities in the block, giving priority to self-employment, and with special reference to the employment needs of the priority groups. Preference ought to be given to improving the durability and income of the under-employed.

(5) *Technological choices*: In the context of employment generation, technologies may have to be built into the schemes or projects may have to be chosen, which use labour intensive technologies, but in the event of a conflict arising between productivity and employment, the scales should ordinarily be weighed in favour of the latter. Keeping in view that the objectives of planning at the block level are full employment and eradication of poverty, suitable technologies might be recommended and concurrently the infrastructure needed to make those technologies operational should be identified, planned and provided for. Innovations should attempt to enhance productivity in the existing sources of employment rather than displace them, and because male and female activities in the economic sphere are different, technology choices should identify male and female specific activity separately.

(6) *Utilization of existing capacities:* On-going schemes and spill over projects from the previous period should be scrutinized to check whether they can be made fruitful, bearing the priorities in mind, before going in for new schemes and fresh projects. Acceleration of the utilization of, say, irrigation facilities provided in specific programmes, like the Command Area Development Programme, through the provision of field channels and crop planning, inputs and extension support, is possible under the plan for the block being currently prepared.

(7) *Form of Organisation, Self-employment, etc.*: Keeping in view the objectives of planning at the block level the prioritisation of schemes and projects in relation to their form of organisation should be self-employment, village industry, and small-scale industry, the latter two preferable under the relevant community ownership.

Subject to the foregoing one can form an idea about the kind of socio-economic activities that can be taken up, with a limited perspective of a block, from the general guidelines given below, which are subject to such modifications as may be warranted by local requirement, conditions peculiarities:

(i) Agricultural development should be attempted at, having due regard for, inter alia, the soil characteristics, climate, irrigation potential, traditional cropping patterns, employment situation, land-man ratio, land-holding pattern, accessibility to market, and human element. Agricultural planning would additionally consider ways and means to raise productivity through extension work and land-shaping and water management, including horticultural development.

(ii) Minor irrigation.

(iii) Occupations allied to agriculture such as dairying, poultry, piggery, sericulture, pisciculture and bee-keeping.

(iv) Social forestry and forest crops, with specific preferences. Tree planting could include minor forest produce, firewood, fodder and house construction materials.

(v) Increasing the productivity of agricultural and minor forest produce, including horticulture and sericulture, and their processing.

(vi) Cottage and small industries including artisan, trades and handicrafts and programmes of skill formation and upgrading.

(vii) Social services, including and particularly drinking water, health-care and sanitation, education, housing, child-care centres, and eradication of social evils.

(viii) Local infrastructure, including village roads and electrification, community centres, local museums to instill identification and integration among groups, formation of interest-based groups and social education.

(ix) Spatial planning, especially location of growth centres and central villages along with link roads.

IV. PLANNING FOR IRRIGATION

Having discussed the overall objectives, steps, and methodology of planning, it would now be appropriate to discuss methodology for sectoral planning because micro-planning implies a more intensive sectoral planning together with spatial planning. The sectors discussed here are irrigation, agriculture, livestock, micro industry, tertiary sector, social services and household sector. We take up irrigation first.

Objective

The general objective of irrigation planning at the sub-district level is to extend the facility of irrigation to as large a cultivable area as possible, subject to the availability of water from various sources, the environmental considerations of efficient drainage, and cost of irrigation.

For micro-level area planning, only minor irrigation schemes are particularly relevant because major and medium irrigation works stretch the relevant areas beyond the boundary circumscribed for micro-level planning, say up to one community development block in the Indian context.

Among the specific objectives, consideration of social justice has to be a dominant consideration while choosing means of irrigation, whether a tank or a tubewell or a masonary well, and priorities in the delivery system have to be decided upon, with small and marginal farmers receiving higher priority. And to enable small land holders to own, operate, manage and maintain their minor irrigation schemes some organizational arrangement ought to be devised along with sufficient provision of credit. A system of community ownership of assets is one method that has been mentioned, which can be successfully tried in areas where social mobilization work has been in vogue for some time.

Data Needs

Data will have to be collected to work out the contours of the existing position of irrigation, to cull out the relevant information and technical details for estimating water supply, and to assimilate agro-ecological information to estimate the maximum area that can be brought under cultivation and to ascertain the category of cultivators who will benefit from the scheme. Information on the ownership pattern of irrigation assets can be gathered separately either by the subject specialist or by the socio economic investigators. The inter-relationship between irrigation and landholding size is indeed a matter of great interest.

It is necessary to collect month-wise and year-wise distribution of rainfall over the past ten years or so, for which the local records of the nearest meteorological office have to be consulted. At times, irrigation or agriculture department at the district headquarters or local block or tehsil office may help, and in certain cases private sources, for example tea estates, can also be tapped. The maximum rainfall in the area in a day in known history, if available, will help in designing surface water schemes. It is absolutely essential to collect information on existing means of irrigation, where Block officials can be of considerable assistance. Information on state tubewells and canals is usually available with Irrigation Departments.

Information on land use is of critical importance. The possible sources of information is the District Census Handbook and the local block office, but comparable figure from the revenue department can at times bring out interesting differences needing a lot of discussion and judgement in the selection or reconciliation of all the available data and such reconciliation of data emerging from several sources may lead to the healthy practice of making midway correction of faulty data bases.

The other technical data of interest would be geo-hydrological survey of the area, which may include any remote sensing exercise, geo-chemical data and information, strata charts and working of the existing tubewells, spring-level or water-table and standing water in wells by seasons, level of water in tanks and other surface water sources by seasons or months, recharging capacity in case of ground water sources, flow of water in streams and rivers, and capacity of natural springs and the possibilities of storage of rain water. Information pertaining to the present position of electrification availability in villages, future electrification programmes in the villages keeping in view the matching availability of credit, maps showing low tension (LT) transmission lines and distance of unelectrified villages from LT transmission lines, will all be necessary, which should normally be available with the Sub-Divisional Office of the State Electricity Board, and the Rural Electrification Corporation.

For preparing project proposals for the future within the framework of the block plan for irrigation, it is very important that, information is sought on prices of materials and wages, the availability of local labour, unskilled as well as skilled, during seasons and the supply of equipment like rigs, drilling sets, air compressors, on hire from various agencies. The source of supply of construction materials, like steel tubes, pumping sets, hume pipes, stone boulders, chips, bricks, cement, sand, and lime, along with their prices should be ascertained. Finally up-to-date information regarding the government or non-official plans like the District Credit Plan or the Watershed Management Plan for the sector in the next five to ten years, is very crucial and should be taken cognizance of will finalizing schemes under the irrigation plan for a block.

Procedural Steps

Acquisition of a thorough knowledge of the existing state of irrigation in villages, including the sources of water, is the foremost step. More often than not, to complete the inventory of possible source of information, primary investigation involving a tour round the villages and discussions with local officials and non-officials may become absolutely necessary. Secondly, after concluding sufficient discussions at all levels, the maximal limit of cultivation in the micro-region should be worked out. The selection of suitable schemes for inclusion in the plan would require technical appraisal of suggested schemes in respect of water resources, irrigation need and other relevant factors. Topo-sheets of the area along with base-line map would help identify probable sites in respect of surface water irrigation schemes.

In certain difficult cases, a detailed geo-hydrological investigation for the delineation of potential ground water zones within the block perimeter may appear to be necessary, for which without entailing sizeable expenditure, assistance can be sought of the geo-physics departments of Universities or technical institutions functioning at or near about the block. Though the geo-hydrological and geo-chemical position is usually not known for most micro-regions, yet it would be worth while checking it up with the local offices and the ground water investigation departments of the State and Central Governments, and with offices of the Geological Survey of India as well.

Plan Proposals

While drawing up plan proposals, in addition to the "engineering" input of scientific survey of the terrain and catchment area, and the rainfall data, a good deal of social mobilization work is necessary, which includes:

(i) specifying the project details, implications and likely impact on the village community;
(ii) formating of local advisory committees;
(iii) determining the potential beneficiaries and their involvement or organisation for implementation or use and maintenance of facilities;
(iv) rehabilitating the displaced owners or cultivators of farms to be submerged in case of irrigation projects which entail such sub-merging; and
(v) employment surveying and planning to adjust work plan to periods of labour availability.

Voluntary agencies operating in the area, if any, may also, given their experiences, provide suggestions, which may lead to good feasible irrigation schemes, but not necessarily so. Where the foregoing does not generate good irrigation schemes, the planner should use his knowledge, experience and perception, and attempt to comprehend, articulate and decide the issues emerging out of discussions with local people, including beneficiaries, and examine them against the touchstone of his and his colleagues' technical knowledge and experience.

Once the issues relating to the means of irrigation for different areas have been settled, the planner should prepare broad cost estimates, which must relate to the local conditions. In case of certain schemes, like tubewells, it would, for all practical purposes, be sufficient if estimates of a couple of typical model schemes are provided for in the plan document.

Cost-Benefit Analysis

The inclusion of any scheme or project for irrigation purposes, should be preceded by a cost-benefit analysis, particularly so, where the project is likely to inundate cultivable or homestead land. For the purposes of cost-benefit analysis, assessment is necessary of the total cost of a scheme, the annual incremental income due to it, the number of years during which the scheme will pay for itself, and the increase in production due to irrigation alone which leads to the traditional problem of economics posed by the Law of Variable Proportions. The increase in annual production of food grains exclusively as a result of irrigation is usually taken as 0.25 tonne per acre, which may be evaluated in money terms and set against per acre cost of irrigation to judge the economic worth of an irrigation programme being examined.

The social benefits of the programme can be estimated in terms of employment of workers from priority households, namely, the weaker sections of society, including the scheduled castes, scheduled tribes, the landless and women labour. Gain in production of the small or marginal farmers should be given a higher weight in evaluation vis-a-vis production by the big farmers. The terms on which either water is provided to the poor, or employment is provided to the unemployed, should receive close attention.

Employment generation is an important goal of every micro-level planning, which objective is achieved through irrigation schemes and projects, because substantial temporary ,employment is generated through them, and additionally, increased crop intensity due to irrigation transforms, for example, mono-crop lands into double cropping lands and so on, all of which in turn lead to increase in permanent employment in agriculture. Employment opportunities may also expand in the secondary and tertiary sectors. The number of mandays generated in the construction of irrigation works is not difficult to estimate and yardsticks are available to measure additional employment in irrigated agriculture, but only intelligent guesses can be attempted at with regard to employment generated in consequence of irrigation in other sectors of the economy.

Detailed Plans and Estimates

Despite all efforts and all wanderings through the detailed exercise enunciated above, the Plan for irrigation in a block would only be indicative, and it is only at the implementation stage that *detailed* plans and estimates for each of the schemes will have to be worked out, and the decision to drop, or substitute a few schemes suggested in the indicative plan by new ones have to be taken. It may be mentioned here that subsequent techno-economic non-feasibility, non-availability of land, apathy of beneficiaries towards the scheme, etc., provide obstacles to implementation of the plan for irrigation.

V. AGRICULTURAL PLAN

As a general objective, agricultural planning would aim at increasing productivity of land and of the peasant or labour in conjunction with irrigation. A decision with regard to specific goals for an agricultural plan for a given area at the micro-level can be decided only after reviewing the present position and studying the potentials for growth. The targets for average crop yields, rational land use, socially-oriented cropping pattern and employment of human resources together with considerations of, social justice and employment promotion, can be pre-determined.

Data Base

The data required for agricultural planning belong to the genre of physical features, like terrain and soils, climatic features like sunlight, rainfall, temperature, humidity, extremes of heat and cold, winds, proximity to sea, hills or desert, land-use features like cropping pattern, horticultural and forest crops, agricultural practices including shift cultivation (also called Jhum Cultivation), and institutional features like land ownership, fragmentation of holdings and the like. The human factors, specially education, skills, work capacity, habits, traditions and role of incentives are other points to be kept in view, which are all needed to ascertain the base-line as also the potentials for growth.

The block questionnaire and household questionnaire referred to earlier elicit most of the required information, but certain very technical data like soil texture, minerals in it, salinity, pH value, and so on, and data on institutional factors and the human element need to be collected by the agricultural expert. The relevant data about institutional factors and human elements have to be generated, the latter two through the method of unstructured interviewing of a cross-section of the local informed population.

Detailed information on the present infrastructure of agricultural development, extension services, special government and/or non-official programmes, the future plans to strengthen services and increase supplies, land reforms including ceiling on holdings, legislation concerning sub-division and fragmentation of holdings, farmer or cultivator organizations, fixation of minimum wages, welfare schemes for the landless (like allotment of homestead) and the progress of implementation of all these, variations in the infrastructural environment through opening up of the area by rail and roads, setting up of a good grain and/or agricultural produce market, increased facility of credit by banks and establishment of godowns, seed and fertilizer depots, and processing units, all have considerable bearing on agricultural development in the area. The relevant information about these issues and elements will have to be collected, without too much delay and too much expenditure.

Some of the elements that play a critical role in determining the future of agriculture in a block are the extent of culturable waste land, the present status and the likely claims on it by pastures, forests, horticultural crops and non-agricultural uses. A good knowledge in these areas is absolutely essential. Keeping in view the ecological considerations, the planner in consultation with the local, both technical and non-technical, people would need to work out the extent of cultivable waste that can be brought under agriculture. Barring few exceptions here and there, nearly all blocks in the country today need increase in area under forests,[6] and hence the agricultural expert should in all fairness discuss this issue with the Divisional Forest Officer concerned. An agricultural plan might include some outlay on the rehabilitation of the existing forest lands and social forestry, including planting of trees on roadsides, along ponds and canals, which might be a necessary component of a people's plan for block development whose success would in subsequent periods provide a good index of the social action that has taken place.

As a principle, all villages must have a conveniently located and sufficient forest growth to meet fuel requirements of the population as has been successfully tried in Jhargram in the District of Midnapore in West Bengal. Maintenance of such forests stocked with selected trees and managed for long term use of every household ought to be an area of major concern: the shift could be from forest protection to forest management. Due cognizance must be taken of community rights on forests, particularly so in the tribal areas,[7] and wherever such rights on forests exist, they should be used as signposts to guide the planning and use of social forestry.

The cropping pattern of any micro-region should *ceteris paribus* include cultivation of vegetables, pulses, oilseeds and horticultural crops, supported with social and health education by extension workers, and in areas lying in proximity to urban centres, truck cultivation is of good economic value even otherwise. Though heavy initial investment on inputs and proper marketing arrangement for outputs would be the two constraints to reckon with, the plan should be indicative of the implications of such constraints and attempt at circumventing them. The Plan for a block additionally should also aim at the employment of priority groups in the services emerging from the altered pattern of production.

Procedural Steps

Step One: The planner attempting at agricultural block planning should have available with him a cafeteria of information and statistics as indicated below:

(i) Land use pattern of the block and in the villages falling within the territorial jurisdiction of the block. (Source: Revenue Development and District Census Handbook).

(ii) Distribution of land holdings by size in the block (Source: Household Survey, Revenue Department and latest Agricultural Census).

(iii) Average yields of different crops (Source: RDO Office, District Statistical Officer, District Agricultural Officer, Primary Investigation).

(iv) Cropping pattern (Same sources as indicated in iii above).

(v) Labour use separately for males and females (Source: informed local people and Gram Panchayats).

(vi) Sowing and harvesting seasons of principal crops (Source: BDO Office, District Agricultural Officer, Gram Panchayat).

(vii) Area irrigated in village (Source: BDO Office, District Agricultural Officer, Irrigation Department Office concerned and Panchayats).

(viii) Distribution of irrigated areas by crops (same sources as indicated in vi above).

(ix) Crop rotations (Source: BDO Office and Agricultural Extension Officer).

(x) Current seed rates and cultivation practices for different crops (Source: BDO Office, and Agricultural Extension Officer).

(xi) Current supply of improved variety of seeds and fertilizers in the block (Source: BDO Office, Gram Panchayats and Agricultural Extension Officer).

(xii) Distribution of different improved agricultural as also traditional implements in use (Source: Latest Agricultural Census Reports and BDO Office).

(xiii) Current practices regarding marketing of agricultural produce; distance from market; nearness to towns (Source: BDO Office).

(xiv) Current practices regarding storage of food grains (Source: BDO Office).

(xv) Present agricultural credit facilities in the block (Source: BDO Office, Lead Bank Office, Co-operative Banks and local lending institutions).

(xvi) Soil map of the area (Source: District Agricultural Officer).

Step Two: It is quite likely that some of the data like soil map and labour use by sexes and seasons may not be available readily at all, in which event the planner has to go by informed views, but subsequently advise the implementing agency to make appropriate arrangements to test representative soil samples for filling in the possible information gap on soil and household sample data for labour use. This same rule of the thumb applies in respect of the other information sets enumerated above.

Step Three: This is the stage where the agricultural planner has to firm up his estimation of the maximal limit of cultivation, and while deciding the maximal limit of cultivation, all considerations bearing upon the current and future needs, long-term considerations of ecology and economics of permanence should be weighed. Each time the rising curve of employment meets the rising curve of production, it should be indicative of the point of introspection and in most cases a position of halt. Assistance of the irrigation plan of the area should be availed of in recommending a suitable cropping pattern, use of high yielding variety seeds and of fertilizers in agriculture in the block.

Step Four: It is essential that the quality of present agricultural extension services be appraised to pinpoint the scope for improvement, and wherever required a programme of strengthening these services should be incorporated in the plan. Special programmes of agricultural development for the area including flow of credit to agriculture should be taken note of while suggesting the agricultural plan for the block.

Plan Proposal

The agricultural plan, broadly speaking, will suggest:

a) a revised land use pattern for the subject area if needed, and

b) a statement of recommended cropping pattern framed having due regard for self reliance in food requirements of the subject area, namely, the block. The present cropping intensity and proposed intensity of cropping will be indicated, together with a suitable cropping pattern for marginal and small farmers to make their holdings economically viable. It follows almost axiomatically that the estimated requirements of seeds, fertilizers, insecticides and pesticides to support the new cropping pattern will be provided for, after taking cognizance of proper utilization in the block, of organic manurial resource in the plan. Suitable improved agricultural implements to eliminate drudgery and improve productivity of human labour and animal power may be worked out and suggested wherever necessary.

The requirement of supporting measures, like plant protection, storage and agro-services ought to be ascertained and their implication, together with estimated costs of such measures, should form part of the block plan.

Credit is an important input in economic development and it has been observed that sadly enough not much attention is focused on this element of planning. The need for a detailed estimate of credit requirements according to their end use, cannot be over emphasized. Financial requirements for improved seeds, fertilizers, tree saplings, plant protection, storage, marketing etc., ought to be separately estimated and their impact on the plan fully worked.

The plan has to be so worked out that it spells out the details of intensive extension service, the role of motivation of extension workers in agricultural development of the block, and budgetary provisions made in the plan, with grants and loans shown separately.

At the round-up stage, the cost-benefit analysis and the extent of increased employment generated through agricultural development schemes ought to be enumerated. It is difficult to give a break-up of the total benefit indicating the part attributable to irrigation and that to other measures, but in the absence of detailed paired sampling studies, reliance on informed judgements or estimates should be resorted to.

VI. LIVESTOCK DEVELOPMENT PROGRAMMES

Objectives

Livestock development constitutes an important element in any agricultural development strategy and hence deserves careful consideration in the context of block level planning. A livestock development programme should aim at improving the production and productive ability of animals and birds, given the management requirements, keeping-capacity and veterinary care-capabilities of the owners thereof. Supplementary support in terms of advice in scientific management, ensuring the availability of health care facilities for birds and animals and the supply of proper and sufficient feed for such of the animals and birds which constitute the livestock should be imperative components of an animal husbandry development plan. In terms of aims, livestock development plan should augment the supply, or attempt at augmenting the supply, of milk and other livestock products, besides leading the village working population towards the goal of fuller employment. And for ecological reasons, to inculcate the sense of self-reliance amongst the masses, particularly the weaker sections of society and for facing the impending energy crisis, steps should be taken in any block level planning excercise to encourage, facilitate and assist in the setting up of bio-gas plants in villages which would concurrently deal with problems of sanitation, manure and sources of energy for cooking and, to a limited extent, illumination.

Data Needs

A "Prelude" to a plan for livestock development, would most certainly be an assessment made of the existing position. From the government office records and/or the periodic livestock census reports, it should be possible to make a detailed, village-wise inventory of the livestock wealth. Time series dàta in this regard can indicate conditions of popularity or otherwise, of certain types of birds and animals, amongst the people. The existing veterinary services at the block level and schemes for their expansion and proposed developments can be fairly accurately ascertained from the concerned officers in the block and district administration and several other agencies working in the area under consideration.

Basic Considerations and Procedural Steps

The planners and those responsible for implementing block plans, will obviously enough like to ensure that the availability of common cattle sheds for safe-keeping of animals and common pasture grounds for feeding of animals in villages is catered to in the plan. As the market for animal products expands, the need to apply scientific methods to management of livestock will increase appreciably, and the output of livestock products could be greatly increased by simply resorting to better care of the existing types of animal. Genetic improvements in the quality of livestock may not often lead to improved results, unless the standard of management of livestock is improved.

As a procedural step, an analysis would be rewarding of the current animal feed, and the quality elements in it. Animal needs are different in varying conditions of ecology, and the work expected from them vary widely from place to place. Scientific feeding demands that the right amount of nourishment for a given level of production and work expectation from animals is prescribed at the most economical cost, which should be an integral part of planning at the sub-district level.

For ruminants, pasture is usually the best source for the major part of feed, and therefore, any plan for the block should have provisions with regard to the present and future pasture lands and should spell out where such pasture land ought to be located. Pasture lands may be ploughed, sown with productive grasses and leguminous plants and watered to get better results. Under ideal conditions, the time and intensity of grazing should be controlled, and at once grasses should not be allowed to grow too long, as they then turn coarse and of lower nutritive value, all of which should go into, as far as possible, the making of the plan proposals for livestock development in block level planning.

Scientific management of livestock product would mean matching supply of animal products to the present and future demands thereof. Thus if the demands of the market for liquid milk, for example, are met even in periods of lean supply, the probability of generating a surplus at the time when development is accelerated becomes very high, notwithstanding that development may also be expected to result in increased local use of milk and higher demands thereof. After weighing these and such other factors, plans for production of articles like butter, ghee and cheese ("channa" type) to provide an outlet for surplus milk has to be drawn up.

In this connection, it is important to emphasize that an animal husbandry development programme must include the care of calves in its scheme. In the interest of producing milk for sale and of producing milk products, calves are weaned away from their mothers early, leading to the young animals not receiving colostrum, which occurs in mother's milk after calving, and the young stock become susceptible to diseases generated by lack of cleanliness.

Improving Animal Quality

Piggery, goatry, sheep-rearing and poultry stand almost on a separate footing than bovine livestock. It is true that these activities need much less effort and resources to start with, than even 2 to 3 head cattle units, yet much more care is needed as regards ensuring adequate marketing channels and work acceptability of the operators. The need for scientific management, health care and supply of feed to such units cannot be ignored as has been generally done so far in this country except in a few cases where such activities were financed by commercial banks. The plan proposals at the micro-level should spell out measures pertaining to health care and supply of feed to piggery, goatry, sheep rearing and poultry and take into account matters related to their scientific management.

The low return poultry farming at present is mainly due to poor productivity of non-descript birds and short supply of good poultry feed. While preparing a plan for a backyard unit, the number of birds per unit may be decided after discussions with the prospective keepers and local experienced breeders and subject specialists. Additionally, arrangements should be suggested for a balanced feed system, which utilizes kitchen and agricultural wastes. For the success of these schemes, veterinary attention through a common service station at the block headquarters with sub-centre in one of the interior villages may be planned. To help the very poor, loans and working capital needs of the new entrants into this line of activity must be met either out of plan funds or arrangements for tying up subsidy with credit from commercial banks may be made. Arrangements for continuous consultation and refresher training for the bird keepers are necessary, which should be provided for in the plan.[8]

Pig Farming

For development of piggery along efficient lines it might be necessary to provide institutional credit facilities to pig farmers, ensure them incentive prices and organize training programmes for all those engaged in piggery and related activities: field extension staff, pig farmers, butchers and processors.

Pisciculture

In areas where a significant proportion of population depend upon fishing for their livelihood, a detailed study of their present economic activities need be made, which should provide information and data about the approximate length of their work periods (in man-days), seasonality in the work period, the capital employed (nets, boats, gears, etc.), and storage and market facilities available for their catch. Sources of credit and organizational arrangements in production (catch), marketing and processing, if any, are to be noted to identify all relevant problems or difficulties they face or are likely to encounter in the near future. With regard to inland fishing, the resource position can be described in terms of number of ponds, separately for the privately owned and for the community owned ponds, their depth, surface area and qualities and quantities of water.

Fisheries in their tiny sector can help the landless or the unemployed persons find a new job opportunity in view of the fact that villages with small ponds is quite common, and in villages where none exists now, new ponds can be developed for this purpose. The rights on these newly developed ponds can be vested in such landless or unemployed persons on a long lease (10 to 15 year duration) basis, who can then be given proper training by the Fisheries Department. Basic knowledge about feed, knowledge about aeration, age mix of stock, proneness to disease, suitable breeds, and the like need be imparted to the trainees. Depending upon the need, financial help, partly as grant (subsidy) and partly as loan on personal security can be provided for: the subsidy component may be provided for in the plan and the loan component may be arranged from banks under the Credit Plan and even as part of IRDP targets. Anticipating surplus production over local demand, the minimum arrangements may be planned for at least marketing of the prime fish when the need arises.

Plan Proposals

Keeping in view the specific resource position, potentials and needs of the area, a number of projects can be developed. Since under the livestock development programme there is concerted effort to help the poorest of the poor families, as a *first* step a careful count of the target groups and interested families in villages should be made; as a *second* step, the number of livestock of all types to be supplied to them is to be estimated, for which local prices have to be used; and finally as a *third* step, the need and cost of mounting extension services during the next five years should be estimated. As far as possible, the recurring expenditure should be within the paying capacity of the local population after they have started receiving benefits from the programme. A detailed scheme about the sale of surplus produce must be worked out, and the supply of milk and milk product should be integrated with the chilling plant wherever possible, within the area or in the vicinity of the area being planned for. And finally, a project-wise total cost may be struck to indicate financial needs of the programme, with grants and loans indicated separately. Cost-benefit analysis and additional employment potential of the suggested programme would, of course, be a part of the plan.

VII. MICRO REGIONAL INDUSTRIAL PLANNING

Industrial development in the rural areas cannot be treated in isolation from other development tasks and should be taken as a part of the broader infrastructural development. The aim of industrial development at the block level will be:

(a) to provide locally gainful employment opportunities in fields other than agriculture;

(b) optimum utilization of locally available material and human resource;

(c) to meet internal demands in particular and external demands in general;

(d) to reduce the out-flow of raw-material and financial resources of the area to the minimum by setting up processing industries locally;

(e) to minimize the out migration of human resources to urban areas by providing social and financial security in the rural areas.

The specific goals for the subject area can be determined only after its thorough study, but some information can be collected through the questionnaire used for collecting secondary data for the block, though the task of collecting and collating more specific information should be left to the subject specialist.

Step I

A detailed inventory of resources, needs and supporting infrastructural facilities for industrial planning for the block will cover the following:

(1) Occupational distribution of population to assess the existing pattern of employment/unemployment; qualitative and quantitative standards of different sectors and social and communal constraints to development; information about the number and size of settlements, educational standards, seasonal rotation of employment and unemployment, and related issues.

(2) Information about the availability transportation and communication channel; electrification; existence of financial and commercial institutions like banks, cooperatives, voluntary agencies, administrative and political structure, scientific and technical institutions; ease in obtaining raw material, and existence or proximity of the product markets; and the state of the distribution system, linkages with external markets and resource bases, and such other matters.

(3) Actual and projected material and human resources, covering the quantitative and qualitative information on agricultural and forest produce, mineral resources of significant local use, live and fallen cattle population and extent of technological change and mechanization in the field of agriculture which will help evaluate the extent to which available resources are exploited and indicate potentials for development, is indispensable. The evaluation of human resources in addition to quality and quantity of available skills and

talents will cover entrepreneurial and organizational capabilities. In rural areas the traditional skills are generally either too underdeveloped to meet the changing needs of a dynamic society or are stagnating because of various socio-economic constraints. A careful assessment should be made of the situation keeping in view that a cooperative habit of executing community tasks or otherwise, in certain communities needs special mention.

(4) The current as well as projected demand of the community needs to be determined because the success of an industrial plan largely depends upon the market for the end product, both local and otherwise. In estimating demand for industrial end product and assessing local consumer preferences, note should be taken of the primary objectives of promoting the use of locally produced goods though proper social education or intervention popularizing use of local produce.

(5) Village-wise distribution of artisan-craftsmen and number of cottage and small industrial units, number of persons employed, income and profit margin, wage pattern, production and consumption, surplus over local demand, mode of marketing, available financial assistance, technological co-efficients are other items of information necessary, because a survey on these counts will bring out the strength and weakness of the working industrial units.

Step II

The next step in micro regional industrial planning is to identify the growth factors, which might include population growth; changing consumer tastes and functional needs; changing per capita income and saving; investment capabilities; expansion and improvements contemplated in the existing and incoming new units and the technologies they propose to use; demand for the locally produced goods; availability of raw material and financial resources, technological and managerial skills.

The need to investigate the existence or otherwise of an organizational pattern to suit the area under reference and the situation obtaining therein as also to ensure distributive justice in such a planning exercise, can hardly be overemphasized.

Step III

All the foregoing information needs to be documented in detail, item-wise, but the aims of industrial development must be kept in mind before deciding to recommend a particular industry for the subject area, and the collective wisdom of the people must be given due regard in so far a prospects for different industries are concerned, weigh the same against positive and negative factors relating to each suggestion and then come to a final conclusion.

Step IV

The final step will be to prepare the industry plans which should involve, inter alia, the following:

(1) identifying the products which suggest themselves for development;
(2) determining the quantities and qualities of industrial goods to be produced;
(3) locating the sector which may be called "self-employed artisan, small, cottage" sector in which production will take place;
(4) ascertaining of the market for the goods to be produced whether wholly local or otherwise;
(5) examining the position with regard to raw materials and labour including skills;
(6) determining the form of organisation that appears most appropriate; whether self-employed, factory-based or dispersed factory system;
(7) assessing such a programme from within;
(8) calculating cost and benefit (social as well as private) and an investigation of the possibilities of diversion of labour from agriculture to industry and the possible influence on out migration of labour to cities;
(9) assessing managerial capabilities, the management structure, availability of managerial skills locally, ways and means to develop entrepreneurship; recommendations regarding managerial and organizational structures;
(10) working out the financial and technical implications of the recommendations, the sources of finance; extent of loans and/or subsidies; the pattern of financial assistance, terms of loans, repayment schedule, etc.;
(11) investigating the availability of the technical know-how in the village; investigating whether it needs improvement, and where know–how is not available ascertaining how such know-how can be made available;
(12) ascertaining the need for technical training;
(13) phasing, and sequencing of the plan and priorities; and
(14) framing proposals for stabilizing and improving marketing networks, procurement of raw materials, market intelligence about designs, quantities and qualities of products and giving out infrastructural, technical and financial implications of the same.

The report should also state the extent to which the industrial plan enmeshes with, or is coordinated with, the overall development plan of the area covering development of agriculture, education, health, transportation and communication. Care should be taken to make full use of the activities of the District Industries Centre and the Rural Marketing Centre; and avoid duplication of effort as far as possible.

VIII. EMPLOYMENT OPPORTUNITIES IN THE TERTIARY SECTOR

As a consequence of development, need for services will arise in the transport and construction sectors, many of which will call for new skills and many others can be attended to by the resurgence of lost and/or attenuated skills. Certain services can be classified as falling in the domain of artisan trades while others would partake the nature of personalized services, and the planner will need to classify them under economic sectors, but their general philosophy and conceptual importance under an anti-poverty programme continues to be undiminished.

It has to be remembered that in the normal course many of these employment opportunities in these sectors are absorbed by the entrenched entrepreneurial classes, and many services will continue to be utilized only by those with higher levels of purchasing power, unless special efforts are made to bring them within the orbit of a larger majority by modification, both in terms of items or basket of services and in terms of costs.

Step I

As a first step, those who supply traditional services to the community must be identified, who usually are the blacksmiths, potters, cobblers, masons, sweepers, domestic servants, barbers, grain cleaners and grinders, and tailors, and all those who are employed in the sale of self-made goods in the weekly village markets which traditionally dominate rural retailing. One need not labour the point that, these classes of people can be strengthened in their respective roles, through both training and organisation. For example, blacksmiths can repair ploughs and other agricultural implements; potter can become brick makers. It is a common sight to see that cobblers go out of business as plastic mass-made shoes are dumped as substitutes for leather shoes in rural markets which explains why protective laws may be necessary all along, at the block level, district level, state level and at the national level. Finally, there are services in the category of community facility centres: grain cleaning and grinding, repair and laundering of clothes, creche services, "Balwadi" etc., which can be organized by institutions like the Panchayats and the Mahila Mandals.

Step II

To safeguard the interests of the poorest of the poor, amongst whom, so often, the process of production and distribution are both moulded in one, the preservation of weekly markets or "Hats" may be essential, which requires limiting the emergence of daily market places of regular shopkeepers (who are merely traders) though admittedly, this may be possible in only some areas as it may be too late in others. The self-employed street or pavement-vendors like vegetable sellers and sellers of other homemade artifacts are usually outside the orbit of protective laws as well as social support, whose economic roles are pre-empted by, organized built-up shops and shopkeepers. Additionally, it may be especially beneficial to promote associations of such self-employed persons and they may be provided with credit support from banks and financial institutions, and other inputs, apart from the licenses and market areas for open-air vending.

Some new trading and service avenues that emerge in this context relate to agricultural tools and chemicals, grain storage and plant nurseries (for forestry, horticulture, sericulture). For the development of pisciculture, poultry and also plant nurseries, both with regard to production and distribution, the block planner should provide for training of the deserving sections of the population in skills required in these areas or activities, and ensure their self-employment through provision of work places because left to themselves, these services will be usurped by urban entrepreneurs confounding the problems of the rural masses even more. Currently even saplings, fish-seed and poultry are "imported" into the villages from established trades in nearby urban centres.

Step III

The role of the women in the expansion of the tertiary sector is very critical, and they usually dominate professions like nursing, teaching and domestic service but apart from nursing and teaching, their remuneration in domestic and other services are usually low, even though requiring skills. Special arrangements, both with regard to institutional support and training, should be made to upgrade these occupations and professionalise them, and attempts through training and organisation has to be made at absorbing the women in the newly opened avenues like forestry, fishery, poultry, and cattle breeding services.

Commonly owned women's cooperatives could sell fish, poultry and poultry product, forest seedlings to Government and other agencies, like banks, seeking to develop self-employment. For instance, domestic service, grain cleaning and grinding; dried food and vegetable preparations etc. can be made into a skilled professional service, which has been done by many social welfare organizations in their attempts at strengthening the destitute women (like "SEWA" and "Jyoti Sang" in Ahmedabad) which is why the scheme for "community facility centres" could be a women's scheme, where women offer these manifold services, including specific domestic tasks.

The grain golas can be linked to women's centres, where grain is cleaned or cleaned grain is processed, bagged, labelled and so on, and indeed the grain golas themselves can be built, maintained and managed by women. Training and organisation have to become the pivotal points if this sector's expansion is to benefit the poor, both from the point of view of employment and the availability of services.

Step IV

While preparing the manpower budget for the block, employment possibilities through the tertiary sector should be estimated and adequate facilities for training, investment and credit planned for in the planning exercise. As opposed to food-for-work programme and construction works programme on irrigation, the jobs in the tertiary sector is likely to generate enduring year-long employment.

IX. PLANNING SOCIAL SERVICES

Social services have a wide connotation, but in our current context social services include health, maternity and child care, creche facilities, family planning services, education (both social education and non-formal education), special services to handicapped sections of the population whether physically or socially handicapped, drinking water and roads.[9]

Step I

In undertaking a social development plan for a block it is necessary to scan the area for the existing available services, as well as for glaring intra-block inequalities in health, education, etc. of the population, which should be based on collection of quantitative and qualitative data. While qualitative data base could be provided by visits to areas within the block, discussion with local population, especially the less privileged groups, an analysis of the mortality rate, morbidity pattern and literacy profile of individual sub-block areas, such as villages, would generate a true and fair account of the intra-block disparities in crucial social indicators.

Maps may be designed to depict the data so collected and information so generated about disparities and existing location of facilities, and to picturise the density of population and availability of roads, dispersal of voluntary agencies engaged in social services, and the distribution of the sources of drinking water.

Step II

The strategy to be evolved for implementation of the plan for social service is the next step in this regard.

One such strategy would be the identification of central village or focal points and then operationalisation of the distribution of the social services listed above from those identified central villages, which necessitates the identification of the central villages and graphic presentation of their location. Size of population, junction of roads, existence of facilities like Block Development Offices or other government offices, post offices, banks, high schools and colleges, hospitals or primary health centres or sub-centres, markets, bazars, veterinary hospitals, bus stops, railway stations, warehouses, agro-service stations, milk collection centres, cinema houses and power lines are the critical factors that ought to enter the determination of the central village. It is important to note that, each of the socio-economic infrastructure catalogued above has a hierarchy of functions and norms of distance from the service population which will be followed for their distribution or location in villages and higher level places.[10] It goes without saying that, the standard given in these documents may be modified in view the physical features and other characteristics of the area to make the plan more realistic and operationally pragmatic. A block plan should include a map showing location of central villages, and their command areas and an attempt ought to be made that in the process of planning, certain infrastructures provided at the relative central villages are indicated.

While in the selection of a central village, the centrality and accessibility by roads would be important, but in a few cases the need to suggest new road links to enable them to perform the expected functions cannot be ruled out. Possibilities for developing altogether new centres or townships in a few cases, particularly so in cases where a new industrial unit or new industrial estate is coming up, or where institutions or model village experiment is under way (which are very important consideration for integrated development of the infrastructure of the area), have to be given a careful consideration and looked into very thoroughly.

Atomized location of services and building up the related facilities, whether they are roads or bridges, building or personnel, is the other alternative approach, where the planners response will be determined by the critical need of, say a village, or a priority social group within the village.

Overall "economic" considerations of the cost of delivery or spreading the structure may be weighed carefully against considerations such as dispersal of services to avoid making certain villages too attractive because of concentration of facilities, which may cause population inflows to the village with all attendant problems of congestion, over-stress on infrastructure and social tensions.

Step III

A deepening of the impact of existing programmes is the third step in this direction. Revised Minimum Needs Programme of the Government of India (RMNP) had already incorporated many of these services as basic to human development, which have been underwritten by Central and State budgets. The package of services in the RMNP includes roads, potable drinking water in every village, access to to a primary school by all children in age group 6-14, primary health centre for every 50,000 population, locally recruited health motivators for every village, adult education centres in every village with a teacher from the village and so on. It is, thus, important for the planner at the block level to consider the extent of RMNP implementation in the block, the constraints faced by the administrator, official and non-official in such implementation of the programme, and include in the block plan such items which will facilitate delivery of, and be complementary to, the RMNP.

An important issue to be resolved in the planning and implementation of social services at the block level is the question of a levy, for it is often maintained that a service is better appreciated, better used and better maintained by local people, especially the poorest, when it is rendered for a fee or charge. Additionally, it is argued that self-reliance will be strengthened if these facilities can be supported by the local community (rather than wholly from grants from government) which generates the culture of dependency on the Government for everything that has to be solved where for every case of market failure the Government is looked upon as "Mai-Baap".[11] In taking a decision in this regard the past history of services in the area, the views of the relevant population on this issue, the capacity of the local social workers and mobilisers to develop the methodologies for self-supported services, are all very relevant and must be carefully borne in mind, examined and acted upon.

Step IV

A programme of social development with special emphasis on weaker and neglected sections of society could work successfully only if these groups have strong institutional or organizational support. If experience is any guide, it has been found, for instance, that the existing structures which represent women, youth, or Harijans, apart from other non-official elected bodies, like the Panchayats and the Cooperatives, have generally not been able to represent in full measure the interests of the assetless, the poor, the socially neglected sections of society. To correct this shortcoming several changes in the methodology of institutional development would become necessary which are briefly summarized below:

(a) The people living below the poverty line would have to be mobilized into organizations and these organizations will have to be devised as instruments for the development of the various social services.

(b) It is necessary to identify the entry-point for involvement if the organizations of those living below the poverty line, is to be mobilized, which may vary according as the socio-economic situation of the group. Simple door to door enquiries, for identifying the critical immediate concerns of these households or persons would be useful, which would help in identifying the priority areas concern, and develop the necessary service or policy (it could be a legal issue) to arouse the interest of the group and ensure that such interest is roused.

(c) In order to develop and press into operation these mobilization techniques, social mobilisers will have to be trained and pressed into service. As part of social education, non-formal education and adult education, the socially neglected, the poor and the assetless should be encouraged to discuss their common problems and develop in them the desire to unite, and to exercise their collective strength in the community for the women, for the assetless, and for groups otherwise alienated, training should therefore, be provided for as part of the social development plan.

Social services are particularly relevant for the weaker and neglected sections of society, but in many parts of our country their "absorption" by local population has been distorted because their choice and location have not been related to the actual needs and capabilities of these vulnerable sections of society. Where an assessment of their actual needs and capabilities are correctly made, the introduction of a new service in this sector becomes the most powerful entry point for the mobilization of these priority groups, which ought to be remembered while drawing up any plan at the micro-level.

X. SUPPORT TO PRIORITY HOUSEHOLDS

Introduction

Planning at every level so far, has largely been an exercise in sectoral development with increase in production of goods and services, and in creating new employment opportunities as its dominant goals; and indeed there can be no plan for economic development which does not take increase in output and employment as its pillars. In block planning, as outlined above, a qualitative change in the plan has to be embodied (in addition to the foregoing quantitative dimensions) with emphasis on social objectives of eliminating exploitation, injustice, poverty and disparities, by attempting at providing full and gainful employment opportunities to the people in the area, particularly the weakest and poorest sections of society. It is obvious that in order to achieve these qualitative and quantitative goals, the planner for micro-level planning will have to take into consideration the household or family as the basic unit of planning, and be justified in according a high priority to the upliftment of the poorest families, but one needs to be reminded that integration of the specific needs of the poor neglected families in the block plan would be, by all accounts, a challenging task. Assuming that the whole plan would be oriented towards the poorer sections of society, even then the welfare of such "Antyodaya" families may need immediate and specific attention. What follows may serve as a convenient point of departure in evolving the methodologies for making the block plan serve the interests of the poorest-Antyodaya families.

Rajasthan has been the pioneer in Antyodaya programme whose aim was to plan for the economic rehabilitation of the poorest families. Five such families in each of the villages were selected by the Patwari in consultation with the village council to be made the focus of effort for their upliftment above the poverty line. Once they have been helped to come above the poverty line, the next five poorest were picked up for similar assistance, and then the third round would commence and so on. In five years it was expected that one-fourth of the population in villages in Rajasthan will be covered by the Antyodaya Programme.

Irrespective of whether the Antyodaya Programme succeeded or not, the fact remains that Antyodaya Programme signified the importance which planning should attach to the needs of the poorest of the poor.[12] It may be added that the identification of the Antyodaya families left much to be desired, and though provided with certain guidelines, the Patwari and the Village Councils operated largely in terms of subjective considerations.

Drawing lessons from the Antyodaya experiment of Rajasthan, it is maintained that in identifying the poorest of the poor, it is seemingly advisable for the planner, to prepare in open consultation with the local community, a panel of average 25 households in a village. A simple questionnaire may be canvassed to them bearing upon their (i) traditional occupation, (ii) current occupation, (iii) assets, (iv) degree of employment, (v) reasons for penury and (vi) the size of the family. If the above questionnaire is canvassed and information collected over an average of 100 villages in a Community Development Block, the planner would gather vital information for 2,500 families having about 5,000 adult workers. As estimated in over one dozen surveys by AVARD, there are on an average 6,000 (when the methodology was being evolved) chronically unemployed persons in a block, without including the disabled and the "too-old-to-work" persons as they are deemed to be out of the purview of the work force, but as the society has to bear their responsibility through pensions, and other transfer payments, the Antyodaya programme must take care of them as well.

The data thus collected would re-validate the aggregative data collected through the questionnaire used for manpower planning. To draw a base line for the selected five Antyodaya families, it is deemed advisable that a household schedule be filled in for each of the family members by one of them and kept by the planner for record and future reference.

Procedural Steps

The first step is to chalk out carefully a list of 25 poorest of the poor families in each village as suggested by the village assembly, and then fill in the questionnaire as suggested in the foregoing paragraph for each of the families. Specific questions to answer are: the estimated monthly household income, the number of persons male-female (in the 5 to 9, 10 to 14, and 15 to 59 age groups) seeking employment or are in the employment market, the main bread-winner, source of his/her income, the traditional skills possessed and new training as being imparted or desired to be imparted for future, the land holdings and other assets that the family can mobilize and the past debts and obligations either to private individuals or to institutions.

Five families are to be selected who are to be given immediate help, whose names are to be announced after re-consultation with the Village Assembly or Gram Sabha.

The new job opportunities, anticipated and planned, under the comprehensive block plan that suit some of the workers in the selected Antyodaya families are to be taken careful note of in the planning.

The available training facilities as envisaged in the block plan against what are requested for by certain workers in Antyodaya families have to be carefully checked.

The implications of operationalising employment and training facilities as identified, which may contain quantum of grants, subsidies, loans, supplies of tools and equipment and raw materials, marketing support and sustained training of workers and consultancy service, if required, have to be fully worked out.

That the individual schemes of assistance have to be prepared in detail need not be reiterated once again.

One supervisor in the block who would monitor the progress of each sector of the plan and the utilization of funds for purposes as indicated in each of the family-help schemes, ensuring that each of the recommended assistance schemes help the Antyodaya family to attain an income above the poverty level, has to be provided for. A broad survey of the programme may be given in a statement showing name of the benefactor (head of the household), his or her present income and anticipated income after the assistance has been fully made use of.

Plan Proposal

The total outlay on the Antyodaya programme will have basically two components: *one*, schemes for employment generation together with training that have already been included in the comprehensive block plan, and *two*, special self-employment schemes, which are in the nature of emergency relief and which may or may not survive in the long-run under dynamic conditions.

The components of both grant or subsidy, and loan would be separately shown for immediate reference to financing institutions and for the release of grants.

XI. INTEGRATED AREA PLAN

Our wanderings have brought us to the stage where we need to net the various elements. The steps needed for formulating the block level plans as indicated in earlier sections can be summarized as under:

> "To prepare a resource inventory for the block; to identify the less privileged, poorer sections of the society including priority/Antyodaya families; to survey development potential and needs in different economic sectors based on available information, both technical and the local population's awareness; to draw a socio-economic base line for the block including incomes and manpower disposition; to identify appropriate technologies to promote employment, to prepare indicative plans for all the sectors and feasibility reports for selected schemes considered desirable for immediate implementation especially for the priority groups of households and to identify service centres/central village along with their service areas for recommending location of package of infrastructure."[13]

On completion of the exercise as detailed above, it will be necessary to reconcile various sectoral recommendations, because the possibility lurks round the corner that the needs and demands of competing and/or complementary sectors may be missed by a subject specialist, or the subject specialist may overlook through inadvertance to take note of the wider implications of a programme he is contemplating to operationalise, like ecological effects and socio-economic fall outs. Under the circumstances, co-ordination of different appraisal reports warranting enlargement, pruning or amendment (as the case may be) of project proposals and/or programmes in the light of comprehensive, long-term needs of the area is imperative. A manpower budget has to be prepared at this stage for matching the projected manpower and available employment opportunities in the course of implementation of the plan, which would reflect the need or otherwise, for re-look at the project proposals in various sectors to ensure attainment of the employment targets.

In contrast to the subject specialists, who attempts at saturating the area sectoral development and services (for example irrigation saturation, link roads for all villages) which would be his concern, the function of th. coordinator remains in the domain of reviewing the various projects given the time horizon (say five years or so), the available resources, the capability of the local implementing agency, possibility of an emotional shock with backward/tribal communities and the paying capacity of beneficiaries in respect of productive schemes where the issue of repayment is significantly large. The co-ordinator would be required to assign priorities given the urgencies of the situation and the possibilities of mobilizing or motivating people for planned tasks. Above all, in every micro-level planning exercise, the co-ordinator ought to take cognizance of the fact that considerations of social justice should inform all decisions made by him in this regard.

It needs to be clearly underscored that location of new infrastructure in places other than those suggested by the block planner could generate difference of opinion, which explains why the co-ordinator should convince the people at large, either directly or through their elected representatives, about the rationality of a particular choice made in the plan with regard to location of facilities or infrastructure. Controversies could possibly be contained within tolerable limits, if the choice of location of infrastructure reflects objectivity, collective wisdom and felt needs of the common people.

The cost of implementing proposals will have to be worked out at this stage and the priorities set forth in terms of the importance and phasing within each sector described. Employment (mandays to be generated) in each case and the sources of funding (namely, subsidies, loans, or credit and self-contribution) will have to be clearly spelt out and the sub-totals for each sector will will have to be aggregated in order to arrive at the grand total.

Overheads is an expenditure that would require a serious look now. The project officer will have administrative staff, social workers, financial adviser or consultants and other personnel, common to more than one sector, all of which entail recurring expenditure. Financial provision, should additionally be made to enable the staff to make continuous monitoring and evaluation of the whole project for securing necessary feed-back and effecting corrective action. While every effort should be made to contain expenditure on this account to the minimum, overdoing such economy drive can be counter-productive and defeat the very purpose of having the structure per se.

The rounding up section of the report ought to contain an "impact sheet" indicating, inter alia, the possible outcomes upon implementation of the suggested schemes and programmes; the areas that would be needing special attention; the number of new employment that could be so provided; the number of households who will be lifted above the poverty line; the possible rate of growth of the economy of the area under consideration; the rate of growth of per capita income; the attainable level of consumption of certain essential items like milk, and food grains; the probable social change, relating to say the release and rehabilitation of bonded labour, reduction of unproductive indebtedness in the rural sector and so on.

If possible a chapter on the "Perspective of Development" at the beginning of the report would be particularly worthwhile. A strategy of development should in all probability emerge from such an analysis which makes it worth while, even if decidedly difficult.

XII. CRITICAL OBSERVATION

The detailed methodology outlined above is the outcome of extensive experience of planning at the sub-district level and has been presumably used as well in planning at the sub-district level. The Mushari Block Plan and the Imphal East Block Plan out of scores of plan prepared by AVARD have been referred to in several places.[14]

The methodology is marked by pragmatism and down to earth approach. It follows the general pattern envisaged in the work of Roy and Patil[15] on block planning, but it stresses voluntary organisation, (since renamed non-government organizations) in the formulation of the plan. Given that planning by the government departments, agencies and planning teams have churned up plans which, except for some exceptions, are no more than collection of a bunch of schemes with outlays jacked up by a margin of about 15 percent or so over the average outlay per year over the last five years proposed outlay, it would be worthwhile involving in greater measure the non-government organisations in the preparation of plans at the sub-district (and district) level.[16]

The clarity of the methodology is apparent from the following features:

(a) There is clarity about the nature of data to be collected and the interviews to be held. The questionnaire prepared for the purpose is well structured and can be used under a wide variety of circumstances. The method to be adopted for selecting the field investigators and for conduct of the interviews as laid down in the methodology remain valid till date. Not much progress has been achieved in this direction, as indeed in district planning per se.

(b) The sectors to be covered and for which the plan should make provision have been identified and clearly laid down. To that extent there is no overlap and the methodology has taken due care to see non-violation of the Principle of Functional Decentralisation and Non-concurrency.[17]

(c) It is among the earliest of the methodologies to emphasize the need for cost-benefit analysis, and every sector for which planning is attempted ought to include a cost-benefit analysis under this methodology.

(d) The choice of schemes have been given appropriate weightage, because the entire planning exercise and its efficacy can be made or marred by how good or how bad the schemes chosen are. The criteria to be applied in such choice have been laid down in considerable detail and very systematically.

(e) The emphasis on protecting the interest of weaker sections of society, particularly the Scheduled Castes and Scheduled Tribes, the Women, the landless and the children is quite striking because reference to these were not fashionable, at least not quite so dramatically, during those days. It is just possible that the inherent characteristic of the organization propounding the methodology could have imparted this pro-poor flavour,[18] nonetheless the explicit mention and emphasis throughout on these dimensions deserve cheer.

(f) Naturally from (e) above and for the reason, amongst others, mentioned in (e) above, there is ingrained in the methodology of "Antyodayas" and its modification to develop a vehicle for diffusion of the fruits of planning to the poor.[19] The criticality of support to Priority Households has been very well brought out in the methodology.

(g) The final stage of preparation of Integrated Area Plan is crucial in the methodology, involving reconciliation of differences among sectoral plans as well as between the sectoral plans and the manpower budget and summarizing all major planning proposals for affecting additions and deletions, as the circumstances may warrant, in the light of the long-term needs of the area.

The methodology enjoins detailed programmes for agriculture and irrigation works and also indications of the conceivable non-agricultural activities and the extent of social overheads required. The methodology, as a starting point, requires a broad picturisation of the development potential as well as developmental status of the area on the basis of secondary information available and then resort to comprehensive primary investigation, using a well structured questionnaire. The primary investigation will be both at the village level and at the household level, based on stratified sampling procedures.

While preparing the inventory of resources the information gaps have to be identified. No special attempts are prescribed for enlarging the information base by in-depth investigation in critical areas of data gap. However, the services of specialists have been recommended whenever required. Primary investigation to collect data on income, expenditure, savings and investments are implicitly advised, particularly so, when viewed against the backdrop of the Questionnaire prescribed.

The methodology lays down the need to provide project recommendations within the framework of the overall strategy for development of the block, and project feasibility including cost-benefit analysis and a prima facie evidence of their feasibility. The basic thrust of the methodology is employment generation.

The dominance of faith in the central place theory is quite apparent, particularly with regard to social service. The issues pertaining to hierarchy of functions and threshold distance as well as threshold population have been very precisely, though not exhaustively, dealt with in the methodology. The thought that has gone in, in proposing organisations of the poor is quite revealing.

While a review of the plans is clearly not a review of the methodology, nevertheless the former may shed light on the operational worthiness of the latter. The plans prepared (supposedly) in terms of this methodology have exhibited substantial variation in scope and content. For instance the block plan for Mushari Plan, in the district of Muzzaffarpur Bihar, the degrees of unemployment or under-employment in the block seemingly was left uninvestigated. In respect of works relating to irrigation and in some cases of road construction works, the generation of the number of man-days of employment has been estimated, but they have been left unmatched with the estimated number of idle man-hours.

Non-agricultural activities have been planned for but only to the extent of being indicative, except for Mushari block plan referred to above where detailed industrial development plan has been worked out. Project profiles of a group of twenty four industrial lines along with viable size, feasibility in the light of the availability of raw materials, plant and machinery, labour and other inputs, have been set out. The demand for the manufacturing products now and their market potential have been assessed. The Mushari Plan (along with the Meiti plan of Manipur) has attempted at figuring out the output structure of the economy and estimates of growth rates by economic sectors.

The emphasis is primarily on agricultural programmes and irrigation works but some plans have made attempts to solve the problems peculiar to the area. For instance, for the Adhara block in the district of Rohtas, where rural indebtedness had attained real crisis proportions, a plan was prepared where debt relief work by non-government organisation, motivation of the people, programme of social education and non-formal education, increasing productivity in agriculture through better irrigation, agricultural extension service and marketing facilities, received very high priority.

The socio-economic infrastructure to be provided and their location have been indicated in the plans, influenced by the concept of the "Central Village" which is emphasised in the methodology as already observed earlier. However, the analysis is sketchy and lacks in detail. Markets, godowns, collection centres, social education, non-formal education, drinking water, health services and the like have been provided for in the plans.

The Mushari plan has received very favourable review from the experts because of its designing of the pattern of investment for creating employment opportunities for the weaker sections of society in the rural area, so that they could attain a desirable minimum level of living in the area (which was Rs. 360 per annum per capita calculated at 1970-71 prices). The objectives in terms of increases in average private consumption and increase in the net output and expansion in employment opportunities, have been clearly set forth. And finally, the estimates of employment opportunities that will be created for unskilled worker, both in terms of seasonal and regular employment have been provided for.

It is hoped that with deeper faith in, and renewed enthusiasm for decentralized planning, and to a certain extent, disillusionment with the government departments and planning machinery, the role of the Voluntary Agencies (the Non-Governmental Organizations) would increase and this methodology would receive wide acceptance.

APPENDIX I

PROFORMA FOR BLOCK LEVEL PLANNING

NAME OF THE BLOCK ____________________

BLOCK/PROJECT AREA PROFILE

1. Identification Name of the State, Name of the District, Name of the Block, Date of Inception of Block, Present state of the Block.
2. Number of villages in the Block as per last two census
3. Number of uninhabited villages in the Block as per last two census.
4. (a) Number of Towns in the Block as per last two Census
   (b) Their names and distance (in kms) from the Block Headquarters town-wise separately.
5. (a) Number of towns adjacent to the Block boundaries
   (b) Their names and distance (in kms) from Block boundary, town-wise.
6.* Number of Panchayats/Gram Panchayats in the Block, and Number of V.L.W.'s Circles in the Block...
7. Whether the Block has been reorganized since last census
8. If yes specify in detail: Whether any area or village/or villages have been added or deleted.
9. Location of the Block: Location; Latitude & Longitude and Bounded by.
10. Topography of the Block
11. Drainage system
12. Type of Soils in the Block
    (a) Soil Testing Reports; (b) Soil Conservation Programmes/Progress

* Please give in detail the name of the village under each Gram Panchayat VLW Circle

13. Climate

(a) Type of climate (b) Monthwise distribution of rainfall for last 10 years and average annual rainfall (c) Monthwise temperature (d) Different seasons (e) Rainy seasons (f) Rainy days (g) Remarks.

14. POPULATION/CASTE/LITERACY

As per last two Censuses (Indicate Separately for the two)

Adminis-trative Unit	POPULATION			SCHEDULED CASTES			SCHEDULED TRIBES			LITERATES		
	Male	Female	Total	Male	Female	Total	Male	Female	Total	Male	Female	Total
* BLOCK												
DISTRICT												
STATE												

*Please collect village-wise information on separate pages.

15. MOST IMPORTANT CASTES/TRIBES IN THE BLOCK, INDICATING

Name of the Caste, approximate Number of Families and a qualitative note on Economic/Socio-cultural Conditions of each separately. Historical back-ground; whether immigrant and from where; occupation; any custom worth reporting; Personal habits; Constraints to development; leadership pattern; status of women; status of children and old people; any other, may be indicated here.

16. OCCUPATIONAL PATTERN, WORKERS AND NON-WORKERS* AS PER LAST TWO CENSUSES SEPARATELY FOR EACH CENSUS

	BLOCK			DISTRICT			STATES		
Sl. No. Classification of workers	Male	Female	Total	Male	Female	Total	Male	Female	Total
1. Cultivators									
2. Agricultural Labourers									
3. Mining Quarrying, Livestock etc									
4. Household Industry									
5. Other than Household Industry									
6. Construction									
7. Trade & Commerce									
8. Transportation									
9. Total Workers (1-9)									
10. Non-Workers									

*Please Collect Village-wise information for Block.

17. The major periods of seasonal unemployment or under-employment of major occupational groups:

Occupation	Months of Unemployment	Months of Under-employment	Average No. of days in month		Approximate No. of Persons
			unemployed	underemployed	
1. Cultivation Group					
2. Agricultural Labour					
3. Construction Labour					
4. Potter					
5. Smithy					
6. Carpentry					
7. Others					

18. Sex-wise unemployment

19. What occupations and/ or type of duties are (a) tailor to women and (b) exclusively reserved or considered suitable by custom by custom for women.

20. LAND UTILIZATION PATTERN

Sl.No.	Land Utilization	BLOCK AREA IN		DISTRICT		STATE
		5 Years age	Presently	5 Years age	Currently	
1.	Total Geographical Area (Sum 2-10)					
2.	Forests					
3.	Land put to non-agricultural uses					
4.	Barren and uncultivable land					
5.	Permanent Pastures and common grazing land					
6.	Miscellaneous tree crop and groves (not included in net area sown)					
7.	Culturable Waste					
8.	Fallow land other than current fallows					
9.	Current Fallows					
10.	Net Area sown					
11.	Area sown more than once					
12.	Total cropped area					
13.	Area Irrigated					

NOTE: Information for the Block should be collected village-wise.

21.DISTRIBUTION OF LANDHOLDERS BY SIZE OF HOLDING

Classification of size of holding	Number of Landholders	Area in Acres
Landless Labourers Upto-1 Acre		
1-1.25		
5.00-10.00		
10.00-20.00		
20 & above		

NOTE: Classification of size of holding may change. If possible, Village-wise or Panchayat-wise/ VLW Circle-wise data should be collected.

22. Average size of landholding, and the current price of agricultural land in the block; residential sites in villages, be indicated.

23. AREA UNDER MAIN CROPS

SEASON WISE CROPS	HYV/ LOCAL	YEAR				YEAR			
		Net area sown in	Production	Average price per quintal	Harvest Price	Net area sown in	Production	Average price per quintal	Harvest Prices
A. CROPS									
(name each)									
B.VEGETABLES									
C.PLANTATION									

NOTE: Please note down all crops for the latest year.

24. AVERAGE YIELD OF DIFFERENT CROPS IN THE BLOCK

Sl. No.	Name of the Crop	HYV/LOCAL	AVERAGE YIELD PER ACRE	
			Irrigated Area per acres (in Kg)	Un-irrigated Area per acres (in (kg.)
1.				
2.				
3.				
4.				
5.				

25. SEASON-WISE CROPS, MONTH OF SOWING, HARVESTING AND MARKETING

Seasons	Crops (name separately each crop)	Time Grown	Months of sowing	Months of harvesting	Months of marketing
RABI					
1.					
2.					
3.					
KHARIF					
1.					
2.					
3.					
ZAID					
1.					
2.					
3.					

26. The principal crops for which fertilizer is used and the average quantity used per acre/hectare be indicated in following format:

Sl. No.	NAME OF THE CROP (Use separate rows for each Crop)	Name of the fertilizer	Quantity per acre/hectare	Whether used for HYV only or local also
1.				
2.				
3.				
VEGETABLES (Use separate rows for each veg.)				
1.				
2.				
3.				
PLANTATION (Use separate rows for each plantation)				
1.				
2.				
3.				

27. Give below Seed Rates for different types of crops

Name of the crop (use separate row for each crop)	Type of seed HYV/Local	Average seed rate per acre
1.		
2.		
3.		
4.		
5.		

28. CONSUMPTION OF FERTILIZERS IN THE BLOCK

Sl. No.	Type of agency (distributional channel)	Type of Fertilizers	Quantity in quintals	Price per quintal
1.				
2.				
3.				
4.				

29. DISTRIBUTION OF SEEDS IN THE BLOCK

Sl. No.	Type of agency (distribution channel)	Type of seeds	Quantity in quintals	Price per unit
1.				
2.				
3.				
4.				

30. IRRIGATION FACILITIES

Type of Irrigation	No. in the Block	Area irrigated in acres				No. in the Block	Area irrigated in acres			
		Kharif	Rabi	Zaid	Total		Kharif	Rabi	Zaid	Total
Government tube wells										
Private tube wells										
Masonry wells										
Pumping sets										
Parsian wheels										
Government tanks (size)										
Pvt. tanks (size)										
Canals										
Rivers										
Springs										
Ahars Bundhis										
Others										

NOTE: In case of tanks, please also mention size.

Please collect this information village-wise.

31. Spriny level below ground level in feet in the month of June--------and October--------
32. Standing column of water in Masonry wells in the month of June-----(feet) and October----------(feet).
33. Ground water Survey Report.
34 Problems of irrigation--
35. Potentials and possibilities of extending irrigation facilities in the Block.

36. INVENTORY OF AGRICULTURAL IMPLEMENTS IN THE BLOCK

TYPE OF IMPLEMENTS	NUMBER IN THIS BLOCK		
	Year 1966 (15 years ago)	Year (ten years ago)	Year 1976 (present)
Tractors			
Trolley			
Threshers (simple)			
Threshers (multipurpose)			
Land lavalieres			
Power sprayers			
Power dusters			
Other (specify)			

37. LIVESTOCK WEALTH IN THE BLOCK

Type of animals	NUMBER (Last two livestock censuses)
Cows in milk	
Improved cows in milk	
Cows dry	
Buffaloes in milk	
Improved buffaloes in milk	
Buffaloes dry	
Poultry birds	
Pigs	
Others-	

Please collect this information village-wise/VLW circle-wise.

38. POSSIBILITIES FOR DEVELOPING

(a) Dairy farming (b) Poultry (c) Piggery, may be indicated separately. Problems if any may be indicated.

39. VETERINARY FACILITIES

Such as (a) Veterinary Dispensary (b) A.I. Centre (c) Stockmen Centre (d) Veterinary Mobile Units and (e) I.C.D. Programme.

40. TRANSPORTATION

(a) Villages connected by pucca road

(b) Villages connected by all weather kutcha road

(c) Villages connected by all weather road only

(d) Villages connected by footpath only

(e) Road length in the Block

(f) All roads

(g) Suggestions for construction of new roads and improvement of existing roads with distances and estimated cost.

41. IMPROVEMENT QF EXISTING ROADS

Improvement of existing linkage		Quality		Road length in m	Serving No. of villages	Serving population	Cost estimated	
From	To	Existing	proposed				Per m	Total cost
1.								
2.								
3.								
4.								

42. CONSTRUCTION OF NEW ROADS

Sl. No.	Desired linkage From	To	Proposed road length in m	Quality of proposed road	No. of villages to be benefited	Population to be benefited	Cost estimated Per m	Total cost
1.								
2.								
3.								
4.								

43. COMMUNICATION

NO. OF POST AND TELEGRAPH OFFICES IN THE BLOCK

Type of communication	Number in the Block
Post Office	
Sub-Post Office	
Telegraph Offices	
Telephone Exchange	
Telephone facility	

44. ELECTRICITY

(a) Number of villages electrified in the Block ______________________
(Please also specify names of villages)

(b) If some villages are not electrified, then village-wise distance to the nearest electric line ______________ Km.

45. DRINKING WATER FACILITIES IN THE BLOCK

Sl. No.	Type of water facility	Village having this facility in the Block: Number	Village having this facility in the Block: Name of the Villages
1.	Piped purified water		
2.	Piped water outlets		
3.	Tube wells with pump		
4.	Hand pumps		
5.	Masonry well/with hand pump		
6.	Open pucca well regularly chlorinated		
7.	Open kutcha well		
8.	Tanks		
9.	Rivers		
10.	Springs		
11.	Others (Specify)		

Please give below detailed notes on drinking water problem;
Village-wise facilities and need should be noted.

46. EDUCATION

Sl. No.	Type of schools	Number in the block	Number of children in schools		Number of teachers		Remarks
			Male	Female	Male	Female	
1.	Primary						
2.	Middle School						
3.	High School						
4.	Higher secondary school						
5.	Agriculture or technical school						
6.	Degree college						

Village-wise

47. HEALTH FACILITIES

Sl. No.	Type of facility	Number in the Block	Number of doctors & nurses	No. of beds
1.	Vaid/Hakim/Homeopath			
2.	Registered medical practitioners			
	(a) Government			
	(b) Private			
3.	Pharmacist			
4.	Family Planning Centres			
5.	Dispensary			
6.	Health Centres			
7.	Primary Health Centre			
8.	Hospital			

48. What are the important diseases in the Block and what can be done to improve the existing health problems.

49. Location of Medical Facilities.

50. INDUSTRIES

Sl. No.	Type of industries	Number of Units	No. of persons employed	Raw material	
				Local	Outside
1.	Small scale industries				
2.	Artisans & Cottage Industries				
	1. Blacksmithy				
	2. Carpentry				
	3. Pottery				
	4. Oil mills				
	5. Flour mills				
	6. Rice mills				
	7. Saw mills				
	8. Leather work				
	9. Printing press				
	10. Bidi making				
	11. Weaving				
	12. Bamboo/canework				
	13. Others				

51. What are the possibilities for developing small scale industries and cottage industries in the Block. Please specify the industries.

52. SHOPS

Sl. No.	Type of shops	Number in the Block	Number of persons working
1.	General merchant		
2.	Cloth merchant		
3.	Fertilizer and seed store		
4.	Bicycle repair shop		
5.	Agriculture implement		
6.	Pumping set repairs		
7.	Tractor repair		
8.	Chemists		
9.	Hardware store		
10.	Restaurant		
11.	Tailoring		
12.	Barber		
13.	Books, Stationery		
14.	Radio		
15.	Others		

53. FACILITIES IN THE BLOCK

Sl. No.	Type of facilities	Whether existing in the Block Check	If existing in the Block number of units	If No. Name of the nearest Place	Distance in Km.
1.	Post office				
2.	Sub-post office				
3.	Telegraph office				
4.	Telephone				
5.	Bus stop				
6.	Railway station				
7.	Guest house				
8.	Petrol pump				
9.	Cinema				
10.	Library				
11.	Community centre				
12.	Club				
13.	Police station				
14.	Cold storage				
15.	Daily market				
16.	Mandi				
17.	Warehouse				
18.	Collection centre				
19.	Others				

54. INDICATE FIVE IMPORTANT MARKET CENTRES

Sl. No.	Name	Location within or outside Block	Type of shops
1.			
2.			
3.			
4.			
5.			

55. SPECIAL PROBLEM OF THE BLOCK

Sl. No.	Problem	Name of the village in the Block	Remedies
1.	Waterlogging		
2.	Reclamation		
3.	Levelling		
4.	Water pollution		
5.	Wild animal		
6.	Others (Specify)		

56. CO-OPERATIVE SOCIETIES

Sl. No.	Name of co-operative society	Number of members	Depositor's share capital	Amount of loan advanced	Rate of Interest
1.					
2.					
3.					
4.					
5.					

57. COMMERCIAL BANKS

Sl. No.	Type of commercial banks	Amount of loan advanced as on		Remarks
		Agriculture amt., rate of interest	Industries amt., rate of interest	
1.				
2.				
3.				
4.				
5.				

58. PREVALENT AGRICULTURE & NON-AGRICULTURE WAGE RATES

Sl. No.	Occupation	Male		Female		Total	
		Maximum	Minimum	Maximum	Minimum	Maximum	Minimum
1.	Agriculture						
	(a) Ploughing						
	(b) Harvesting						
	(c) Others						
2.	Non-Agriculture						
	(a) Earth work						
	(b) Construction						
	(c) Masonry						
	(d) Carpentry						
	(e) Blacksmithy						
	(f) Shop assistance						
	(g) Driver						
3.	Others						
	(a)						
	(b)						
	(c)						

59. VOLUNTARY ASSOCIATIONS

List of Voluntary Associations operating in the Block such as for social welfare, education, development etc.

Sl. No.	Name of the Voluntary Agency	Number of members	Objective	Location
1.				
2.				
3.				
4.				
5.				

60. MAJOR EXPORTS OF THE BLOCK

Sl. No.	Name of the article	Unit	Quantity Exported	Important places of exports and distance in km
1.				
2.				
3.				
4.				
5.				

61. Most Important Development Needs of the Block or Project Area

What are the most important development needs of the Block/or Project Area (write in detail).

1.
2.
3.
4.
5.

62. Government Programmes/Progress

(1) S.F.D.A./M.F.A.L.
(2) I.T.D.A.
(3) I.C.D.P.
(4) D.P.A.P.
(5) C.A.D.P.

Appendix II

PRIMARY OCCUPATION ....
CLASSIFICATION ....

VILLAGE NUMBER

INTERVIEW NUMBER

SURVEY OF HOUSE HOLD EMPLOYMENT POSITION

QUESTIONNAIRE

REFERENCE PERIOD .... YEAR

HOUSEHOLD QUESTIONNAIRE

BLOCK -1

STANDARD IDENTIFICATION

1.1 State ....

1.2 District ....

1.3 Block ....

1.4 Name of the Village ....

1.5 Interview Number ....

1.6 Name of the Respondent ....

1.7 Is respondent economic and/or social head or neither of the family?

Economic Head ☐ Social Head ☐ Both ☐ Neither ☐

1.8 Respondent Sex Male ☐ Female ☐

1.9 Occupation of the Head of the Household:

Main Occupation ....
Subsidiary Occupation ....

1.10 Caste

Sub-Caste ....
Main Caste - Brahmin/Kshatriya/Vaish/S.C./S.T./Forward Caste.

1.11 If tribal, the name of the tribe to which household belongs ....

1.12 Religion

1. Hindu
2. Islam
3. Christian
4. Sikh
5. Jain
6. Baudh
7. Jew
8. Others (specify)

1.13 Are you a member of Co-operative Society? Yes ☐ No ☐

BLOCK II
MAN POWER

Q.2 HOUSEHOLD PARTICULARS
NUMBER OF FAMILY MEMBERS - Males (   ) Females   No of Earners -- Males (   )   Females (   ) Total (

								Occupation		Days Worked (Annual)				
Sl. No	Names	Relationship to the Head	Sex	Age (Completed years)	Marital	Education	Skil level	Main	Subs - idiary	Main Occupa - tion	Subs - idiary	Total	Activity status	Member temporarily working outside place
1	2	3	4	5	6	7	8	9	10	11	12	13	14	15
1														
2														
3														
4														
5														
6														
7														
8														
9														
10														
11														
12														
13														
14														
15														
16														
17														
18														
19														
20														

21														
22														
23														
24														
25														
26														
27														
28														
29														
30														
31														
32														

Note

Illiterete, litrerate, if educated,class completed, if student class studying

Please give occupation of each of members of household, and in case of unemployed house hold members give further details as given furtherdetails as given in Q. 2.1

(1) Earner - E (2) Dependent = d (3) Earning Dependent = Ed (4) House hold Worker = HW (5) Student = St (6) Infant = St (7) Retired = Rtd. (8) Non - student = N.St (9) Disable = Disd.

Q. 2.1 UNEMPLOYED HOUSEHOLD MEMBERS BETWEEN 16-60 YEARS OF AGE AND THOSE REPORTED WORKING LESS THAN

Sl No as Q.2	Sex	Age	Were you seeking or available for work/additional work Yes/No	How long were you seeking or available for work /additional work? **	How long were you seeking or available for work/ additional work? **	What type of work/additional work you would like to do? +	Status of work sought	Are you willing to accept wage/salaries employement within the village? Yes/No	If yes Q - 11 what is your acceptable? i. Daily wage(Rs/Ps) ii Monthly salary (Rs)	Are you willing to accept wage/salaries employement outside village Yes/No	If yes Q - 11 what is your acceptable? i. Daily wage (Rs/Ps) ii. Monthly salary (Rs)	What assistance you require to undertake that work?
1	2	3	4	5	6	7	8	9	10	11	12	
A. UNEMPLOYED												
1												
2												
3												
4												
B. LESS THAN 100 DAYS												
5												
6												
7												
8												

* 1 = Currently in the live register of employment exchange 2 = Made other efforts 3 = Made no other efforts

** 1 = Up to 3 Months 2 = 3 - 6 Months 3 = 6 - 12 Months 4 = More than 12 Months

1 = Both farm and non-farm work 2 = Farm work only 3 = Non-farm work 4 = Public work 5 Any other work

Wages/Salaries employent : 1 = full time 2 = Part time Contract/Piece Rate 3 = full time 4 = Part time Self employment 5 full time 6 = Part time

1 = No Assistance 2 = Initial Finance 3 = Working Finance 4 = Assured Marketing 5 = Training 6 = Help to find the job

Q. 2.2 FEMALES BETWEEN 16-60 YEARS OF AGE REPORTING HOUSEHOLD WORK AS PRIMARY OCCUPATION.

1. Sl. No as in Q. 2					
2. Occupation a. Primary					
b. Subsidiary					
3. Age completed years					
4. Do you spend most time on demostic duties? (Yes - 1, No - 2)					
If yes, average time spent,no of Hrs in a week.					
5. What is the reason for your usual Attachment to domestic duties? Primary need for domestic work - 1 Non availability of gainful work - 2					
6. Along with your domestic duties do you also regularly carryout: (i) *Free collection of fish, wild fruits,vegetables for domestic consumption ? (Yes - 1, No - 2)					
(ii)*Free collection of fire, cow dung,cattle feed,beedi patti, mahua patti,etc. (Yes - 1, No - 2)					
(iii)*Maintenance of kitchen garden, orchard etc. (Yes - 1, No - 2)					
(iv)*Work in household poultry dairy etc. (Yes - 1, No - 2)					
(v)*Sewing,tailoring,weaving, etc for household use. (Yes - 1, No - 2)					
(vi)*Tutoring children (Yes - 1, No - 2)					
(vii)*Bringing drinking water from outside the village. (Yes - 1, No - 2)					
If yes, approximate distance.					

*** If the answer is yes,note down average time spent, number of hours in a week.**

Q. 2.2 (Contd.)

7. Inspite of preoccupation in domes tic duties, are you willing to accept work , if made available at your household? (Yes - 1, No - 2)				
8. If yes, to Q. 7, the nature of work, acceptable to you: (1) Regular full time (2) Regular Part time (3) Occasional Full time (4) occasional Part time				
9. Type of work acceptable to you (refer code) (1) Dairy (2) Poultry (3) Spinning & weaving (4) Manu facturing wood and cane products (5) Tailoring (6) Leather (7) Ani mal Husbandry (8) Others - (spec ify).				
10. Do you have any skill/experience to undertake that work. (Yes - 1, No - 2)				
11. What type of assistance you re quire to undertake that work (1) No assistance (2) Initial fi nance on easy terms (3) Working finance facilities (4) Assured marketing (5) Training (6) Ac commodation (7) Creche				

Q. 2.3 FAMILY LABOUR

FAMILY MEMBERS ENGAGED IN OWN CULTIVATION

Sl. No as in Q.2	NUMBER OF DAYS WORKED			Total days worked
	Season - I Kharif	Season - II Rabi	Season III Summer	

Q. 2.4 INCOME FROM AGRICULTURAL AND NON- AGRICULTURAL WAGES

(Fill in for each wage earned separately and refer to work sheet if respondent finds it difficult to recall details

AGRICULTURAL WAGES									NON AGRICULTURAL WAGES								
		Number of days worked								Days Worked							
Sl No as in Q.2	Family Members Engaged in own cultivation (No of days)	Type of work (Occu pation)	First Season (Kharif)	Second season (Rabi)	Third season (Summer)	Total	Average wage per day Cash + Kind Rs	Total earning Cash / Kind Rs	Type of work (Occu Pation)	Kharif	Rabi	Sum mer	Total	Average wage per day Cash & Kind (Rs)	Total earnings (Cash & Kind) Rs	Days Worked	Income
1	2	3	4	5	6	7	8	9	10	11	12.	13	14	15	16	17	18
1																	
2																	
3																	
4																	
5																	
6																	
7																	
8																	
9																	
10																	
Total																	

1. If more than two types of works is done by a member for different periods in a year,note all one after the other
2. Average wage per day should include value of kind payments like MEALS etc

Q. 2.5 INCOME FROM SALARY

Sl. No as in Q.2	Occupation Nature of employment	Periodicty of payments Weekly/ Monthly	No of periods in employment during R.P Weeks / Months Rs	Salary (Gross) including allowances per period Weekly/ Monthly	Total salary including all allowances received during R.P Rs (col 4x5)	Employer contribution towards Provident Fund during the R.P Rs	Bonus,other receipts as commission, gifts, arrears, overtime payments, festival payments etc received during R.P	Gross income from salary during R.P	Income tax paid during R.P	Net Income	Government employment/ Private employment specify
1	2	3	4	5	6	7	8	9	10	11	12

Total income from salary Rs ....

Q. 2.6 TIME DISPOSITION OF LABOUR FORCE DURING THE WEEK ENDED........

Sl No as in Q.2	SEVENTH DAY		SIXTH DAY		FIFTH DAY		FOURTH DAY		THIRD DAY		SECOND DAY		FIRST DAY	
	Type of work	Hours spent	Type of work	Hours spent	Type of work	Hours spent	Type of work	Hours spent	Type of work	Hours spent	Type of work	Hours spent	Type of work	Hours spent
1	2	3	4	5	6	7	8	9	10	11	12	13	14	15

BLOCK - III
INCOME

Q.3. AGRICULTURAL AND ALLIED ACTIVITIES

Q.3.1 Do you or any member of your household cultivate any land ? YES NO
If yes, please give the following details:
(i) Land owned by all the members of the household (area in acres)
(ii) Number of pieces of land
(iii) Operational holding

Sl. No.	Details	Season I Kharif	Season 2 Rabi	Season 3 Summer	All Seasons
1.	Land Owned				
2.	Leased/Rented in				
3.	Leased /Rented out				
4.	Acquired throught Mortgage				
5.	Given on Mortgage				
6.	Total Holding (1+2-3+4-5)				
7.	Area cultivated				
8.	Of which Area Irrigated				
9.	Area under Plantation such as Tea ,Coaffee				
10.	Area under Orchards (Fruits)				
11.	Pastures & Fallow				
12.	Uncultivable Land				

NOTE: Land owned by the households means sum of the land owned by all the members of the saisd household.

Q. 3.2 IRRIGATION

Total area irrigated in acres
Source-wise and season-wise area irrigated

Sl No	Source	Number owned/ Points	AREA IRRIGATED IN ACRES			Total gross area irriga-ted in acres	If water is purchased then total amount paid as water Charges Rs
			Season I Kharif	Season II Rabi	Season III Summer		
1.	Masonry Well						
2.	Pump Set						
3.	Persian Wheel						
4.	Pvt. Tubewell						
5.	Govt. Tubewell						
6.	Tank						
7.	Spring						
8.	Canal						
9.	Others						

If season-wise area irrigated in not available,record total area irrigated by different sources.

Q. 3.3 INCOME FROM CROPS

Sl. No.	Name of the crop grown	HYV / Local	Irrigated Unirrigated	Area in Acres	Total quantity produced Kg	Total Quantity sold Kg	Total Quantity retained for consu-mption Kg	Quantity retained for kind wages Kg	Total Quantity retained for seeds Kg	Price per unit for quantity sold Kg	Harvest price per unit Rs	Value of total quantity produced Rs
1	2	3	4	5	6	7	8	9	10	11	12	13
	SEASON - I (Kharif)											
1												
2												
3												
4												
5												
6												
7												
	SEASON - II (RABI)											
8												
9												
10												
11												
12												

(1) In case of leased land,record total area, total production and other details;share of lessor in cash as well as in kind should be recorded in land rent paid column of oerating expenses.

(2) See that all crops grown during R.P are recorded properly.

Q. 3.3 Contd.

Sl. No.	Name of the crop grown	HYV / Local	Irrigated Unirrigated	Area in Acres	Total quantity produced Kg	Total Quantity sold Kg	Total Quantity retained for consumption Kg	Quantity retained for kind wages Kg	Total Quantity retained for seeds Kg	Price per unit for quantity sold Kg	Harvest price per unit Rs	Value of total quantity produced Rs
1	2	3	4	5	6	7	8	9	10	11	12	13
	SEASON - I (Kharif)											
1												
2												
3												
	SEASON - III (Summer)											
13												
14												
15												
16												
	Total Receipts from crops											
	Vegetables											
1												
2												
3												
4												
Total receipts from vegetables												

Q. 3.4 RECEIPTS FROM CROPS Rs...

Q. 3.5 RECEIPTS FROM VEGETABLES Rs...

Q. 3.6 INCOME FROM AGRICULTURAL BT-PRODUCTS

Sl. No	Name of the By-product	Unit	Quantity prodused Kg	Quantity consumed (retained) Kg	Quantity Sold Kg	Price per unit unit Rs	Harvest price per unit Rs	Value of quantity sold Rs	Value of quantity retained Rs	Total value of Bi-products produced Rs
1	2	3	4	5	6	7	8	9	10	11
1										
2										
3										
4										
5										
6										
7										
8										
9										
10										

Q. 3.6a Total Income from Agricultural By-products Rs..............

Q. 3.7 DO YOU OWN ANY ORCHARD OR PLANTATION? ☐ **YES** ☐ **NO**

If yes, give the following details:

Sl	Name of the Product	Number of trees	Area(acre) covered	Average yield/tree	
				Unit	Quantity
1.					
2.					
3.					
4.					
5.					
6.					
	Total				

Q. 3.8 IF YOU HARVEST THE ORCHARD/PLANTATION YOURSELF,WHAT WAS YOUR OUTPUT AND HOW DID YOU DISPOSED IT?PROVIDE THE FOLLOWING DETAILS:

Sl No	Name of the product	Unit Kg/ Nos.	Quantity produced Kg/Nos	Quantity sold Kg/ Nos.	Quantity consumed Kg/Nos	Price per unit Rs	Value of quantity sold Rs	Total value of output Rs
1.								
2.								
3.								
4.								
5.								
6.								
7.								
8.								
9.								
10.								

Q. 3.9 Gross receipts from orchards & plantations Rs...

Q. 3.10 Operating expenses on orchards & plantation Rs...

Q. 3.11 Net income from orchards and plantation Rs...

Q. 3.12 If the orchards/plantation was contracted out then net amount realised. Rs...

Q. 3.13 Total income from orchards /plantations (Q. 3.8 + Q . 3.9) Rs...

Q. 3.14 LIVESTOCK

Livestock	Number	Average yield of milk per day in Kg	Average lactation period (No of days in a year)	Average price per Kg	Total products
1. Local Cows					
2. Improved Cows					
3. Local Buffaloes					
4. Improved Buffaloes					

Q. 3.15 INCOME FROM LIVESTOCK

Product	Unit	Quantity Produced (unit)	Quantity Consumed (unit)	Quantity sold (unit)	*Price per unit Rs	Value of quantity sold Rs	Value of total product Rs
Milk							
Ghee							
Curd/butter/ cream							
Eggs							
Poultry bird							
Piggery							
Meat							
Hides & Skins							
Dung cake							
Others(specify)							
Total							

*Price per unit should be recorded even though the whole quantity is consumed.

Q. 3.16 INCOME FROM OTHER AGRICULTURE AND ALLIED ACTIVITIES

Sl No.	Activity	Gross Receipts Rs	Expenses Rs	Net Income Rs	No of persons working	Average No. of hours spent daily
1	2	3	4	5	6	7
1.	Bee keeping					
2.	Fishery					
3.	Sericulture					
4.	Forestry					
5.	Others (specify)					
6.	Total					

Q. 3.17 Total net income from other agriculture and allied activities.

Q. 3.18 INCOME FROM LAND LEASED / RENTED OUT

(i) Cash receipts Rs...

(ii) KIND RECEIPTS (for all crops)

	Commodity	Unit	Quantity	Price	Value in Rs.
1.					
2.					
3.					
4.					
5.					
Total					

Total income from land leased / rented out (cash + kind) Rs......................................

Q. 3.19 INCOME FROM HIRING OUT FARM ASSETS

Sl No	Details Type of equipment hired out	Receipts in Rs during			
		Kharif	Rabi	Summer	Total
1.	Tractor				
2.	Thresher				
3.	Tubewell (sale of water)				
4.	Pumpset (sale of water)				
5.	Bullock/Camel				
6.	Others				
	Total				

Total amount received Rs ....

Q. 3.20 ANNUAL INCOME OF PROFESSIONALS DURING REFERENCE PERIOD

Sl No.		Gross receipts Rs	Operating expenses* Rs	Net Income Rs
1.	Doctors			
2.	Vaids			
3.	Hakims			
4.	Engineers			
5.	Architects			
6.	Chartered Accountants			
7.	Lawyers			
8.	Others(specify)			
	Total			

Operating expenses include rent, staff salary, wages, electricity etc.

Q. 3.20a Annual Net Income of Professionals Rs ....

Q. 3.21 EXPENDITURE ON AGRICULTURE AND ALLIED ACTIVITIES
Crops and Vegetables (Work sheet)

Sl. No	Name of the crop	Home produced seeds value Rs	Purchased seeds value Rs	Value of manures purchased Rs	Value of fertiliser Rs	Total Pesticides Rs	Total material cost 3-7 Rs	CASUAL LABOUR DAYS HIRED								
								Ploughing		Sowing / Irrigation		Harvesting		Total days worked	Average wage per day cash/kind	Total wage for C.L
								No. of persons	Days worked	No. of persons	Days worked	No. of persons	Days worked			
1	2	3	4	5	6	7	8	9	10	11	12	13	14	15	16	17
1	Season I (Kharif)															
2																
3																
4																
5																
6																
7																
1	Season II (Rabi)															
2																
3																
4																
5																
1	Season III (Summer)															
2																
3																
	Total cost of inputs															

Q. 3.22 PERMANENT LABOUR (ATTECHED LABOUR)

Number of persons employed ....

Sl No.	Name of the Employee	Annual Cash payment Rs	Kind of payment*			Total payment Cash & Kind Rs
			Commodity	Quantity	Value	
1.			1.			
			2.			
			3.			
2.			1.			
			2.			
			3.			
3.			1.			
			2.			
			3.			
4.			1.			
			2.			
			3.			
Total						

*Includes the value of meals given.

Q. 3.23 RENT PAID ON LEASED IN LAND

Cash Payment Rs..

Details of kind Payments:

Sl. No.	Name of the Commodity	Unit	Quantity	Price per Unit Rs	Value Rs
1.					
2.					
3.					
4.					
5.					

Total payment (Cash + Kind) Rs...

Q. 3.24 CROP-WISE HIRING CHARGES IN Rs.

Sl. No.	Name of the Crop	Tractor Rs	Thresher Rs	Pumpset Diesel Rs	Pumpset Electric Rs	Canal Water Rs	Hiring Animals Rs	Total Cost (2-8) Rs
1	2	3	4	5	6	7	8	9
1.								
2.								
3.								
4.								
5.								
6.								
	Total							

Note :Hiring charges should include kind payments.

Q. 3.25 EXPENDITURE ON OWNED ANIMALS DURING THE REFERENCE PERIOD

Sl. No.	Type of Animal	Purchased Feed Rs	Imputed value of home produce Rs	Veterinary expenses Rs	Expenses on man-power to look after livestock Rs	Approx. No of hours spent by family members (weekly)	Total Expe-nses Rs
1.	Draught animals						
2.	Milch animals						
3.	Poultry						
4.	Piggery						
5.	Total:Milch poultry and Piggery (2-4)						
6.	Grand Total (1 + 5)						

Q. 3.26 Gross receipts from livestock Rs.......................................

Q. 3.27 Operating expenses on milch, poultry and piggery Q. 3.25 (5) Rs.......................................

Q. 3.28 Net income from livestock Rs.......................................

Q. 3.29 OPERATING EXPENSES

Sl. No.	Type of Expanses	Amount spent in Rs during the Reference Period
1.	Repair and Maintainance charges of: (a) Tractor (b) Thresher (c) Power Tiller (d) Harvester Combine (e) Pumpset Diesel (f) Pumpset electric (g) Masorny Well (h) Hand Tools	
2.	Irrigation charges for all crops(water charges Q. 3.24)	
3.	Hiring Charges for tractor, thresher and other farm assets.(for all crops Q. 3.24)	
4.	Hiring charges for animal power (Q. 3.24)	
5.	Fuel charges,petrol and diesel	
6.	Electricity charges	
7.	Land Rent(For leased in land) Cash as well as kind Q. 3.23)	
8.	Expenses on storage and Marketing	
9.	Land revenue	
10.	Betterment levy	
11.	Agriculture income tax	
12.	Cost of material inputs(Q. 3.21)	
13	Casual labour cost (Q.3.21)	
14.	Permanent labour cost(Q. 3.22)	
15	Expenditure on owned animals (Q. 3.25)	
16	Interest paid	
17	Others	
	Total operating expenses (1-17)	

Q. 3.30 (a) Gross Receipts from Crops Rs...
(b) Gross receipts from Vegetables Rs...
(c) Gross Receipts from Agriculture By- products Rs...
(d) Total Receipts from crops Rs...
(a+b+c)
(e) Total Operating Expenses (Q. 3.29) Rs...
(f) Net Income from Crops (d-e) Rs...

B. INCOME FROM NON-AGRICULTURAL ACTIVITIES

Q. 3.31 Business / Trade /Commerce / Small and Cottage Industry

(a) Is any member of your household engaged in Trade/Business/Shop/Industry Yes No
If yes, give the following details.

(b) Name of the Business/Trade/Commerce/Industry...
(1) Is the industry seasonal? Yes No
(2) If seasonal, months o f operation ....

....

(c) Products dealt in...

(d) Ownership: (1) Partnership (2) Propietorship
If partnership
Percentage share of said household in the income...

(e) Employment:Household members working in the business/trade/industry

Sl. No as in Q.2	Full Time		Part Time	
	Type of work	*Days worked	Type of work	*Days worked
1.				
2.				
3.				
4.				
5.				

*Days worked should be calculated on the basis of 8 hrs per day

(f) Number of worker employed on wages/salary.

Sl. No.	Name of the Employee	Type of work	Wages/salary per month Rs	Total amount paid during the reference period Rs
1.				
2.				
3.				

(g) Inventories

Sl. No.	Items	Value at the beginning of R.P Rs	Value at the end of R.P Rs	Change (+ or -) Rs
1.	Raw material/goods			
2.	Spares,components			
3.	Finished goods			
4.	Unfinished goods in process			
5.	Others			
	Total			

(h) Investment during Reference Period

Sl. No.	Type of investment (business)	Value at the beginning of R.P Rs	Purchased/ constructed during R.P Amount paid /spent Rs	Sale during R.P amount received Rs	Amount invested during R.P Rs	Change (+ or -) Rs
1.	Premises (a) Land					
	(b) Building					
	(c) Construction					
	(d) Addition etc.					
	(e) Others					
2.	Machinery and equipment					
3.	Other fixed assets					
	Total					

Amount paid during the reference period for part investments already made in previous year or to be completed next year has to be recorded in this column;clearly indicate advance/balance or full payment/investments.

Amount received during the reference period as balance or advance for the assets already sold in the next year has to be recorded in column sales during reference period.

(i) Loan

Rs value of total loan at the beginning of the R.P Rs................................

Rs value of loan taken during the R.P Rs................................

Rs value of loan paid back during the R.P including interest Rs................................

Rs value of loan outstanding at the end of R.P Rs................................

(j) Type of Raw Material Used

Sl. No.	Name of raw material	Average monthly raw material purchased				Annual raw material purchased	
		Unit	Quantity	Value Rs	Purchased From (location)	Quantity	Value Rs
1.							
2.							
3.							
4.							
5.							

(k) List of Machines/Equipment Used

1..
2..
3..
4..
5..

(l) Operating Expenditure

Sl. No.	Type of expenditure	Monthly	Annual
1.	Rent		
2.	Salaries		
3.	Wages		
4.	Fuel/Electricity		
5.	Transportation		
6.	Other running expenses		
	Total		

(m) Receipts from Business

(i) Sales of products and by-products (based on monthly averages) Rs..........................

(ii) Value of products and by-products consumed at home (based on monthly average) Rs..........................

(iii) Other receipts Rs..........................

(iv) Change in inventories Rs..........................

(v) Total receipts Rs..........................

(n) Operating Expenses

(i) Cost of raw material / purchases (based on monthly averages) Rs..........................

(ii) Salaries / wages (paid) Rs..........................

(iii) Interest Rs..........................

(iv) Depreciation Rs..........................

(v) Other running costs,rent,taxes,wages,fuel etc. (Annual) Rs..........................

(vi) Total operating expenses Rs..........................

(o) Net Income of Business / Trade/Commerce/Industry

Total receipts (Annual) Rs..........................

Less:Total operating expenses (Annual) Rs..........................

Net Income (Annual) Rs..........................

Q. 3.32 INCOME OF ARTISANS LIKE BLACKSMITHS,POTTERS,CARPENTERS, TAILORS ETC.

Sl. No. as in Q.2	Type of artisan/ work	Average No. of days worked during R.P				Average wage/income per day			Total income in Rs	Basic of work*
		Kharif	Rabi	Zaid	Total	Cash	Kind	Total		
1.										
2.										
3.										
4.										
5.										
6.										
7.										

*(1) Wage, (2) Contract basis, (3) Independent worker.
In case of independent worker, give the following details:

(a) Wherefrom you get Raw materials...
(b) Type of Raw material used...
(c) Cost of Raw material purchased
(i) Locally Rs ....
(ii) Outside the Block Rs..
Total Rs...
(d) Other running costs like rent, taxes, wages, fuel, etc. per annum
Rs..
(e) Total operating expenditure (c + d) Rs..
(f) Value of total sales during the R.P Rs..
(g) Annual income during R.P (f - e) Rs..
(h) Are you satisfied with your occupattion,
if not what are the main problems ....
....

Q. 3.33 Income from Rent (property)

(i) Gross receipts Rs....................................

(ii) Less maintenance / repairs Rs....................................

(iii) Net income (i - ii) Rs....................................

Q. 3.34 Annual income from interest Rs....................................

Q. 3.35 Remittances
Total remittances received during
the Reference Period Rs....................................

Q. 3.36 Pension
Did any member of your family receive
pension during the Reference Period Yes No
If yes, what was the amount? Rs....................................

Q. 3.37 Income from other sources (Rs.)

1...

2...

3...

4...

5...

6...

7...

BLOCK - IV

Q. 4.00 CONSUMPTION EXPENDITURE

Q. 4.1 FOOD ITEMS

Sl. No	Items of expenditure	Unit	Purchased				Home Produce or received as wage wage/rent (annua		Total annual consumption expenditure	
			Monthly average		Annual					
			Qty	Value Rs	Qty	Value Rs	Qty	Value Rs	Qty	Value Rs
1	2	3	4	5	6	7	8	9	10	11
	(a) Cereals									
1	Rice									
2	Wheat									
3	Maize									
4	Bajra									
5	Jowar									
6	Ragi									
7	Other cereals									
	(b) Pulse									
8	Tur									
9	Gram									
10	Urad									
11	Moong									
12	Other Pulses									
	(c) Other Food Items									
13	Sugar									
14	Gur and Khandsari									
15	Edible oils									
16	Spices									
17	Milk									
18	Milk Products									
19	Eggs									
20	Meat									
21	Fish									
22	Fruits									
23	Vegetables									
24	Bread									
25	Biscuits									
26	Beverage/ Tea / Coffee									

Sl. No	Items of expenditure	Unit	Purchased				Home Produce or received as wage wage/rent (annua		Total annual consumption expenditure	
			Monthly average		Annual					
			Qty	Value Rs	Qty	Value Rs	Qty	Value Rs	Qty	Value Rs
1	2	3	4	5	6	7	8	9	10	11
27	Coocked Meals Received									
28	Intoxicants									
29	Pan- Cigarettes									
30	Medicines									
31	Hotels									
32	Others									
33	Total for food items									

Q. 4.2 NON - FOOD ITEMS
(Cunsumption expenditure contd.)

Sl. No	Item of expenditure	Monthly average Rs	Annual expenditure Rs
34	Kerosene		
35	Firewood (purchased + collected)		
36	Electricity		
37	Coal		
38	Gas		
39	Ready made garments		
40	Dhotis		
41	Sarees		
42	Cloth for garments		
43	Towels, fur, linen		
44	Tailoring charges		
45	Footwear		
46	Toilet goods		
47	Books and stationary		
48	School fees		
49	Entertainment		
50	Conveyance		
51	House rent		
52	House tax		
53	Repair of house		

Sl. No	Item of expenditure	Monthly average Rs	Annual expenditure Rs
54	Domestic services		
55	Services of barber/sweeper		
56	Others		
57	Total (34 - 56 Non food items)		
58	Total of food + Non Food items (33 + 57)		

Q. 4.3 OTHER EXPENDITURE

59	Marriages		
60	Religious function		
61	Festivals		
62	Unexpected travels		
63	Funerals		
64	Others		
65	Total of other expenditure		

Q.4.4 EXPENDITURE ON DURABLE AND SEMI DURABLE GOODS

Sl. No	Type of durable and semi durable goods	Owned at the beginning of R.P (value in Rs)	Sold or given as gift during R.P (value in Rs)	Received as gift during R.P (value in Rs)	Purchased during R.P (value in Rs)	Investments during R.P (value in Rs)	Owned at the end of R.P (value in Rs)
1	2	3	4	5	6	7	8
66	Furniture						
67	Domestic utensils						
68	Electric fan						
69	Sewing machine						
70	Bicycle						
71	Scooter / moter cycle						
72	Watches						
73	Jewellery						
74	Radio etc.						
75	Bullock cart / Horse drawn / vehicle						
76	Others						
77	Total for durable and semi durable goods (66-76)						
78	Total Expenses (58 + 65 + 77)						

Q. 4.5 Did you or any member of your household send any regular remittances in cash or kind to relatives / friends ? ☐ Yes ☐ No

If yes, what was the total amount remitted during R.P Rs..

BLOCK - V

PHYSICAL ASSETS - LIABILITIEA - TRANSFERS

Q. 5 Did you or any member of your household own / purchase / or sell any land ? ☐ Yes ☐ No

If yes, give the following details:

Q. 5.· **INVESTMENT IN AGRICULTURAL LAND**

Sl. No	Type of land	Land owned at the beginning of the R.P		Land Purchased during the R.P		Land inherited or received as gift during R.P (Area acres)	Land sold during R.P		Land given away as gift during R.P		Land owned at the end of the R.P		Total invesment during R.P Rs
		Area in acres	Value in Rs	Area in acres	Amount spent (Rs)		Area in acres	Amount received Rs	Area in acres	Value in Rs	Area in acres	Value in Rs	
1	2	3	4	5	6	7	8	9	10	11	12	13	14
1	Bunding												
2	Fencing												
3	Levelling												
4	Terracing												
5	Reclamation, etc												
6	Others (specify)												
	Total Cost												

Note

Amount spent during the Reference Period as balance or advance for the land already purchased in the previous year or to be purchased in the next year.has also to be recorded in the 'amount spent' column.

Amount received during the reference period as balance or advance for the land already.sold in the previous year or to be sold in the next year has also to be recorded in the 'amount received ' column.

Q. 5.2 LAND DEVELOPMENT

Sl. No	Type of Development	Material cost Rs	Hired labour charges			Permanent labour			Family labour		Total cost of Development of land Rs (2+5+8)
			No. of days worked	Average wage payment (cash + kind) Rs	Total wages paid Rs	No of persons	Days worked	Inputed value of wages Rs	No . of persons	Days worked	
1	2	3	4	5	6	7	8	9	10	11	12
1	Bunding										
2	Fencing										
3	Leveling										
4	Terracing										
5	Reclamation, etc.										
6	Others										
	Total cost										

Note: Record all the expenses incurred during the reference period only.

Q. 5.3 FARM ASSETS

Sl. No	Type of Assets	Owned at the beginning of reference period		Purchased / constructed during R.P		Sold during reference period		Net investment during R.P		Value at the end of R.P		Sources of funds
		No	Value Rs	No	Value Rs	No	Value Rs	No	Value Rs	No	Value Rs	
1	2	3	4	5	6	7	8	9	10	11	12	13
	A. Irrigation											
1	Well											
2	Tubewell/ electric pumpset											
3	Persian wheel											
4	Diesel pump set											
5	Irrigation channel											
6	Others											
	B. Equipment											
7	Tractor											
8	Harrow											
9	Cultivator											
10	Harvester combine											
11	Power tiller											
12	Leveller											
13	Seed drill											
14	Weeder											
15	Thresher											
16	Sprayer											
17	Winnower											
18	Chaff cutter											
19	Rice pounder											
20	Cane crusher											

Q. 5.3 Contd...

Sl. No	Type of Assets	Owned at the beginning of reference period		Purchased / constructed during R.P		Sold during reference period		Net investment during R.P		Value at the end of R.P		Sources of funds
		No	Value Rs	No	Value Rs	No	Value Rs	No	Value Rs	No	Value Rs	
1	2	3	4	5	6	7	8	9	10	11	12	13
21	Improved plough											
22	Yoke											
23	Others											
24	Farm house											
25	Godown / warehouse											
26	Bullock cart											
27	Others:											
	(a) Additions and improvements (b) (c)											
28	Total											

Q. 5.4 LIVE STOCK WEALTH

Sl. No	Animals	Owned at the beginning of Reference Period		Purchased during Reference Period		Sales made during Reference Period		Change due to birth and death during Reference Period		Owned at the end of Reference Period		Total Investment during Reference Period Rs	Source of funds
		No	Val-ue Rs	No	*Amount spent Rs	No	**Amount Received Rs	No	Val-ue Rs	No	Val-ue Rs		
	Type of animals												
1	Cows in Milk(Imp)												
2	Cows in Milk(local)												
3	Cows Dry (imp)												
4	Buffaloes in Milk												
5	Buffaloes in Milk(Local)												
6	Buffaloes Dry												
7	Bullocks												
8	Goats												
9	Sheep												
10	Poultry Birds												
11	Pigs												
12	Camels												
13	Mules												
14	Total												

Note: *Amount paid during the Reference Period as balance or advance for the animal already purchased in the previous year or to be purchased in the next year has also to be recorded in the 'Amount spent' column.

**Amount received during the Reference period as balance or advance for the animal already sold in the previous year or to be sold in the next year has also to be recorded in the 'Amount received' column.

IMPROVEMENT TO HOUSE

Sl. No	Type of Investment	Owned at beginning of R.P		Purchased/ Constructed during R.P		Sold during R.P		Value at end of R.P		Invest-ments during R.P
		No	Value Rs	No	Amount Spent Rs	No.	Amount received Rs	No	Value Rs	Rs
1	Residential Plot									
2	Residential building									
3	Construction of buildings									
4	Additions and improvements									
5	Total									

Q. 5.6 Did you rent out any portion of your house during the reference period? Yes
If yes, how much rent did you receive during R.P. ? Rs...

Q. 5.7 Did you incur any expenditure on repairs and maintenance of house(s) owned by yc during the Reference period Yes No

Q. 5.8 If Yes, what was the Amount you spent? Rs..................................
House tax (if any) Paid during R.P Rs..................................

Q. 5.9 Net income from property (rent) Rs..................................
(Q. 5.6 - Q. 5.7 + Q 5.8)

Q. 5.10 FINANCIAL ASSETS

Did you or any member of your household have any deposits in the form of Saving Accounts, Current Account, Fixed, Recurring, Shares etc. at any time during R.P? Yes No

If yes, give the following details

Sl. No	Details	Value of deposit a the beginning of R.P Rs	Amount deposite during R.P Rs	Interest / dividend received during R.P Rs	Value at th end of R.P Rs	Net change Rs
1	Commercial Banks (a) Saving					
	(b) Fixed					
	(c) Recurring / cumulative					
2	Cooperative Bank					
3	Cooperative Societies					
4	Unit Trust					
5	Chit Fund					
6	Shares etc.					
7	Post office Savings					

Q. 5.11 Did you or any member of your household have any life insurance policy at any t during reference period ? Yes No

If yes, what was the total premium paid on all policies during Reference period?
Yes No

Q. 5.12 SHARES / SECURITIES/ SAVING CERTIFICATES

Sl. No	Details	Purchased during R.P Rs	Sold during R.P Rs	Net Change Rs
1	Companies / Cooperatives / Government / Units			
2	N.S.C			
3	C.T.C			
4	Seven Years NSC			
5	Plan Certificates			
6	P.O. Deposits			

Q. 5.13 LENDING

(a) Amount outstanding at the beginning of R.P Rs..............................
(b) Amount lent out during R.P Rs..............................
(c) Interest accured during R.P Rs..............................
(d) Repayment received during R.P Rs..............................
    (i) Principal.............................. Rs..............................
    (ii) Interest.............................. Rs..............................
    (iii) Total (i + ii).............................. Rs..............................
(e) Amount outstanding at the end of R.P Rs..............................

Q. 5.14 CHANGE

(a) Net borrowing during R.P Rs..............................
(b) Net lending during R.P Rs..............................
(c) Chance in liabilities (a - b) Rs..............................

Q. 5.15 TRANSFERS

Receipts during R.P from

(i) Matured Insurance Policy Rs..............................
(ii) Provident Fund Rs..............................
(iii) Chit Fund Rs..............................
(iv) Lotteries Rs..............................
(v) Gifts Rs..............................
(vi) Inheritance Rs..............................
(vii) Others (specify) Rs..............................
(viii) Total Receipts, Capital Gains Rs..............................

Q. 5.16 PAYMENTS DURING R.P

(i) Gifts given during R.P Rs..............................
(ii) Regular remmittances to friends and relations Rs..............................
(iii) Total payment Rs..............................

Q. 5.17 CHANGE IN TRANSFER Rs..............................

Q 5. 18 LIABILITIES / BORROWINGS

Did any member of your household borrow any money (cash kind) during the reference period Yes No

If yes, give the following details

Sl. No	Purpose of Borrowing	Source	Amount outstanding at the beginning of R.P Rs	Amount borrowed during the R.P Rs	Amount re-paid during R.P Rs	Amount outstanding at the the end of R.P Rs	Rate of Interest at which borrowed	Duration for which borrowed	Remarks
				Cash + Kind	Principal + Interest			Year Month	
1	For buying agricultural inputs, seeds, fertilizers, etc.								
2	For buying consumption goods								
3	For performing religious or social rites								
4	For repayment of loan								
5	Land improvement								
6	Pumping sets, Tractors, etc.								
7	Business/Trade/Commerce								
8									
9									
	Total								

Hereditary loan if any. Rs. ____________

1+Money lender, 2+Co-operative society, 3+Commercial bank, 4+Government, 5+Chit fund, 6+Provident fund, 7+LIC, 8+Others (Specify)

BLOCK - VI
HOUSE CONDITIONS

Type of House Construction
(Obtain this information through observation.)

A. Construction

(1) Tin roof with brick walls
(2) Tin roof with mud walls
(3) Tin roof with banboo walls
(4) Tiled roof with brick walls
(5) Tiled roof with mud walls
(6) Tiled roof with bamboo walls
(7) Thatched roof with mud walls
(8) Thatched roof with bamboo walls
(9) Pucca house (Brick walls and concrete roof)
(10) Other (specify)

B. Type of floor (observe)

1. Mud and dung
2. Bricks (pucca)
3. Cement Plaster
4. Others (specify)

C. Accommodation

How many rooms are there in the house?
Describe use of each by ticking off appropriately.

Used for — Number of room

1. Kitchen
2. Sleeping
3. Sleeping and sitting
4. Sitting only.
5. Sleeping/sitting/kitchen and animal rearing
6. Animal rearing only (specify)
7. Total number of rooms

D. Open space

Is there open space:
(a) In front of house
(b) Back side of house
(c) Both
(d) Middle of house
(e) No open space

E. Environmental Sanitation and Hygiene (Observe)

Sl. No.		V. Bad 1	Bad 2	Fair 3	Good 4	V. good 5
1.	Ventilation					
2.	Sunlight					
3.	Cleanliness					

F. Pests

Sl. No.	Type of Pests	Always present 1	Mostly presents 2	Generally absent 3	Totally absent 4
1.	Rats				
2.	Sparrows				
3.	Mosquitoes				
4.	Flies				
5.	Bed bugs				

G. Source of Drinking Water and its Distance from house.

Sl.	Source	Distance
1.	Tap	
2.	Hand Pump	
3.	Open well	
4.	Stream/river	
5.	Pond	
6.	Others (specify)	

H. Are steps taken to made it safe? ☐ Yes ☐ No

If yes, (a) At home ☐

(b) By community ☐

I. Where do the animals

(a) Drink water

(b) Bathe

J. Where do the people

(a) Bathe

(b) wash clothes

K. Water disposal

1. Soak pit. ☐
2. Open drains ☐
3. Covered drains ☐
4. Let out in open space. ☐
5. Others. ☐

L. Refuse disposal

1. Dumping outside the house. ☐
2. Dumping in pits ☐
3. Composting ☐
4. Burning ☐
5. Others (specify) ☐

M. Defecation facilities

(a) Space in the house ☐

1. Septic tank ☐
2. Bore hole. ☐
3. Others (specify) ☐

(b) Separate space outside thehouse

1. Septic tank

2. Bore hole ☐
3. Others (specify) ☐

(c) Open fields:
Distance from residence

(d) Do people defecate far from source of drinking water? ☐ Yes No ☐

N. Is the street around the house clean? Yes No

(a) Is water collected in the street during the rains? ☐ Yes ☐ No
(b) Proximity to any stagnant water (distance)...
(c) Proximity to garbage/ cow dung heap...

☐ ☐ ☐
House hold No.

SUMMARY STATISTICS OF HOUSEHOLD

A. Identification

1. Family size Male...............Female.............Total..........
2. Workers Male...............Female.............Total..........
3. Household workers Male...............Female.............Total..........
4. Infants (up to 5 years) Male...............Female.............Total..........
5. Students Male...............Female.............Total..........
6. Non- Student Male...............Female.............Total..........
7. Unemployed persons Male...............Female.............Total..........
8. Retired Male...............Female.............Total..........
9. Disable Male...............Female.............Total..........
10. Family size (16-60) years of age Male...............Female.............Total..........
11. Workers (16-60) years of age Male...............Female.............Total..........
12. Unemployed household members (16-60) years of age Male...............Female.............Total..........
13. Household members working less than 100 days (16-60) years of age Male...............Female.............Total..........
14 Female reporting household work as primary Occupation (16-60) years of age Male...............Female.............Total..........
15. Land owned by the household (area in acres) Total..........
16. Number of pieces of land (No.)
17. Area irrigated in acres ....

B. Receipts

18. Income from agricultural wages (q. 2.4) Rs...................................
19. Income from non agricultural wages (Q. 2.4) Rs...................................
20. Income from salaries (Q. 2.5) Rs...................................
21. Net income from orchards Rs...................................
22. Net income from allied agricutural activities (Q. 3.17) Rs...................................
23. Income from land leased out (Q. 3.18) Rs...................................
24 Income from hiring out farm assets (Q. 3.19) Rs...................................
25. Net income of professionals (Q. 3.20) Rs...................................

26. Net income from Livestock (Q. 3.28) Rs...................................
27. Net income from crops (Q. 3.30) Rs...................................
28. Income from business / trade / commerce (Q.3.31) Rs...................................
29. Income from small and cottage industries (Q. 3.31) Rs...................................
30. Income of artisans (Q. 3.32) Rs...................................
31. Income from property (Q. 3.33) Rs...................................
32. Income from interest (Q. 3.34) Rs...................................
33. Remitttances received (Q. 3.35) Rs...................................
34. Pension (Q. 3.36) Rs...................................
35. Income from other sources (Q. 3.7) Rs...................................
36. Total income (18-34) Rs...................................
37. Amount borrowed during R.P (Q. 5.18) Rs...................................
38. Miscellaneous receipts like insurance policy, provident fund chit fund, gifts, inheritances, lotteries, etc. (Capital gains) (Q. 5.15) Rs...................................
39 Total Receipts (from all sources) (Q. 36 - 38) Rs...................................

C. Disposition - Expenditure / Investment

40. Consumption expenditure non-food items Rs...................................
41 Consumption expenditure non-food items Rs...................................
42 Other expenditure (Q. 4.3 - 6.5) Rs...................................
43. Expenditure on durable, semi durable goods Rs...................................
44. Total expenditure (58 +65+ 77) Rs...................................
45. Agricultural land (Q. 5.1) Rs...................................
46. Land development (Q. 5.1) Rs...................................
47. Farm assts (Q. 5.3) Rs...................................
48. Livestock (Q. 5.4) Rs...................................
49. Investment in house construction / addition (Q. 5.5) Rs...................................
50. Saving (Q. 5.10) Rs...................................
51. Insurance premium (Q. 5.11) Rs...................................
52. Shares / securities / saving certificates (Q. 5.12) Rs...................................
53. Lendings (Q. 5.13) Rs...................................
54. Amount of loan repaid Rs...................................
55. Miscellaneous payments, gifts, remittances (Q. 5.16) Rs...................................
56. Total expenditure / investment / disposition (Q. 44 - 56) Rs...................................
57. Change (38 - 55) = (+ -) Rs...................................

(i) Name of the interviewer ....
(ii) Number of calls made ....
(iii) Date of interview ....
(iv) Duration of interview ....
(v) Supervisor ....
(vi) Edited by ....
(vii) Coded by ....
(viii) Remarks, if any ....

Appendix III

SCHEDULE FOR HEALTH STATUS OF POPULATION

VILLAGE	NUMBER

INTERVIEW	NUMBER	

Name of the village...

Name of the project...

Reference Period ....

HEALTH STATUS OF POPUPLATION

Interview No. [ ] [ ] [ ]

Q.1 IDENTIFICATION

1.1 Name of respondent : ______________________

1.2 Is respondent economic or social head or both or none of the family?

Economic Head	Social Head	Both	None

1.3 Respondent's sex Male( ) Female( )

1.4 Occupation of the head of the household

Main Occupation ______________________ Subsidiary occupation ______________

1.5 Caste ______________________

1.6 Religion ______________________

Q.2 TYPE OF HOUSE CONSTRUCTION (Obtain this information through observation)

2.1 CONSTRUCTION

(a) Tin roof with brick walls 1 [ ]
(b) Tin roof with mud walls 2 [ ]
(c) Tin roof with bamboo walls 3 [ ]
(d) Tile roof with brick walls 4 [ ]
(e) Tile roof with mud walls 5 [ ]
(f) Tile roof with bamboo walls 6 [ ]
(g) Thatched roof with mud walls 7 [ ]
(h) Thatched roof with bamboo walls 8 [ ]
(i) Pucca house (brick walls and concrete roof) 9 [ ]
(j) Other (specify) ______________________ 10 [ ]

2.2 **TYPE OF FLOOR** (Observe)

(a) Mud and dung 1 [ ]
(b) Bricks (pucca) 2 [ ]
(c) Cement plaster 3 [ ]
(d) Other (specify) ______________________ 4 [ ]

2.3 ACCOMMODATION

How many rooms are there in the house? Describe use of each by ticking off appropriately.

Used for — Number of rooms

1. Kitchen 1. [ ]
2. Sleeping 2. [ ]
3. Sleeping & sitting 3. [ ]
4. Sitting only 4. [ ]
5. Sleeping / sitting / kitchen and animal reating 5. [ ]
6. Animal rearing only (specify) 6. [ ]
7. Total number of rooms 7. [ ]

2.4 OPEN SPACE

Is there open space?

(a) In front of house

(b) Back side of the house

(c) Both

(d) Middle of the house

(e) No space

Q.3 ENVIRONMENTAL SANITATION AND HYGINE (Observe)

	V.Bad	Bad	Fair	Good	V.Good
1. Ventilation	1	2	3	4	5
2. Sunlight	1	2	3	4	5
3. Cleanliness	1	2	3	4	5

Q. 3.1PESTS

	Always present	Mostly present	Generally absent	Totally absent
1. Rates	1.	2.	3.	4.
2. Sparrows	1.	2.	3.	4.
3. Flies	1.	2.	3.	4.
4. Mosquitoes	1.	2.	3.	4.

Q.4 (a) SOURCE OF DRINKING WATER AND ITS DISTANCE FROM HOUSE

Source	Distance
1. Tap	
2. Hand pump	
3. Open well	
4. Stream / river	
5. Pond	
6. Other / (specify)	

4.1 Are steps taken to make it safe ? ☐ Yes ☐ No

If yes, (a) At home

(b) By Community

4.2 Where do the animals

(a) drink the water ______________

(b) bathe ______________

4.3 Where do the people

(a) Bathe ______________

(b) Wash clothes ______________

4.3 Number of family members suffering from water-born diseases during the Reference Period

Sl. No	Age	Sex	Average number of times each such members suffered during R.P
1.			
2.			
3.			

Q. 5 **Water disposal**

1. Soak pit 1 ☐
2. Open drains 2 ☐
3. Covered drains 3 ☐
4. Let out in open space 4 ☐
5. Other (specify) 5 ☐

Q.6 **REFUSE DISPOSAL**

1. Dumping outside the house ☐
2. Dumping in pits ☐
3. Composting ☐
4. Burning ☐
5. Others (specify) ☐

Q. 7 **DEFECATION FACILITIES**

(a) **Space in the house**
   1. Septic tank ☐
   2. Bore hole ☐
   3. Other (specify) ☐

(b) Separate space outside the house
   1. Septic Tank ☐
   2. Bore hole ☐
   3. Others (specify) ☐

(c) Open Fields : Distance from residence

(d) Do people defecate far from source of drinking water? Yes ☐ No ☐

Q. 8 Is there space for kitchen garden? ☐ Yes ☐ No

If yes, please give season-wise vegetables grown

Name of the vegetable Production during R.P

1
2
3
4
5
6

Q. 9 Is the street around house clean? Yes ☐ No ☐

(a) Is water collected in the street during the rains Yes ☐ No ☐
(b) Proximate to any stagenant water (distance) ____________
(c) Proximity to garbage / cow dung heap ____________

Q. 10 HOUSEHOLD PARTICULARS

Total no. of the family members (   ) No. of males (   ) No. of females (   )

No. of earners - Males (   ) Females (   ) No. of married couples (   )

Sl. no.	Name	Relation to the head of the household	Sex	Age (Completed years)	Marital status	Education	OCCUPATION			Remarks Preg./Lac.
							Main	Subsi-diary	Activity status	
1	2	3	4	5	6	7	8	9	10	11
1										
2										
3										
4										
5										
6										
7										
8										
9										
10										
11										
12										
13										
14										
15										
16										
17										
18										
19										
20										
21										
22										
23										
24										

Q. 10 HOUSEHOLD PARTICULARS

Total no. of the family members ( ) No. of males ( ) No. of females ( )
No. of earners - Males ( ) Females ( ) No. of married couples ( )

Sl. no.	Name	Relation to the head of the household	Sex	Age (Completed years)	Marital status	Education	OCCUPATION			Remarks Preg./Lac.
							Main	Subsi-diary	Activity status	
1	2	3	4	5	6	7	8	9	10	11
25										
26										
27										
28										
29										
30										
31										
32										
33										
34										
35										
36										
37										
38										
39										
40										

Note: Illiterate, literate if educated, Class completed; if student, class studying
Earner-E, Dependant-D
Against married females mark L for lactating and P for pregnant

Q. 11 INCIDENCE OF ILLNESS AND TREATMENT DURING REFERENCE PERIOD

Sl.no as in Q.10	Age in completed years	Name of the disease or description	Duration of disease in days	By whom treated		Satisfied with treatment Yes/No	Satisfied with cost Yes/No	Period unfit for work in each case (days)	Possible known cause of the disease
				Within village	Outside village				

Q. 12 BIRTHS IN THE FAMILY

(In three preceding year)

Sl. No	Details	Year		Year		Year	
		I Birth	II Birth	I Birth	II Birth	I Birth	II Birth
1	Name of the Mother (Sl. No. Q. 10)						
2	Relationship to H.O.H						
3	Age of Mother						
4	Number children born Alive						
5	Number of Children alive at present						
6	Result of delivery: Live Birth/ Still Birth						
7	Type of Birth Simple/Multiple						
8	Sex of New Born : Male / Female						
9	Name of Child						
10	Date of Birth						
11	Place of Birth : Home/ PHC/ Govt. Hospital/Pvt. Hospital/ Other						
12	Who conducted the delivery : Doctor/ Lhv/ ANM / Trained Dai / Untrained Dai						
13	Is the child alive at present : Yes / No						
14	If yes, present age of child (month)						
15	If dead, age at death (Days)						
16	Type of feeding: Breast fed/ Breast fed & top fed only						
17	Whether the child was taken to well baby clinic for check up						
18	If yes, Number of Visit						

Q. 12 BIRTHS IN THE FAMILY (Contd)
(In three preceding year)

Sl. No	Details	Year		Year		.Year	
		I Birth	II Birth	I Birth	II Birth	I Birth	II Birth
19	Normal Delivery / Abnormal						
20	If assisted delivery, satisfication with assistance, satisfication with cost						
21	Condition of the new-born (a) O.K (b) Under weight / Any. abnormality						
22	IMMUNISATION (a) Small Pox (b) Tetanus (c) Polio (d) B.C.G (e) Diphtheria (f) Whooping Cough						

Q. 13 DETAILS IN THE FAMILY DURING THE LAST THREE YEARS

Sl. No	Details		Year		Year		Year
		I	II	I	II	I	II
1	Name of the deceased (Sl. No. Q. 10)						
2	Relation to H.O.H						
3	Sex of Deceased Male / Female						
4	Age at Death (Completed years)						
5	Cause of Death / Type of Disease / complaints						
6	Place of Death - Inside / Outside village						
7	Medical Attention before Death codes						
	1. No/						
	2. Qualified Pvt. Allopathic						
	3. Qualified Pvt. Homeopathic 4. Qualified Pvt. Unani						
	5. Quack						
	6. Folk Medicine						
	7. PHC						
	8. Hospital						
	9. Govt. Dispensary						
	10. Ayurvedic						
	11. Others						
8	Duration of sickness in days						
9	Cost of treatment						
10	Satisfication with Treatment Yes / No						

Q. 14 INCIDENCE OF ABORTIONS IN THE FAMILY DURING THE R.P

Family Member Sl. No as in Q. 10 (Name of the Mother)	Age	Gestation period No. of months Full time Premature	If natural Cause (accident etc.)	IF INDUCED, METHOD			Particular	Mother's condi tion codes
				Surgically terminated (F.P)	Use of Oral Medi-	Helped Mid wife(F.P)	Reasons (Code)	

Code for Reasons:

(1) Pregnancy seriously endangering the health.
(2) Couple could not afford another child.
(3) Couple did not want any more chidren.
(4) Using birth control and got pregnant.
(5) Believes something might be wrong with the baby (like hereditary diseases, deformity & others)
(6) Combination of health and economic reasons.
(7) Health and accidental reasons.
(8) Daughter or daughter-in-law started to have her own children.
(9) Combination of all factors.
(10) Others (specify)

Mother's condition code:

(1) Died because of abortion.
(2) Healthy.
(3) Diseases - Type

Q. 15 PARTICULARS OF PREGNANT WOMEN AT THE TIME OF SURVEY.

	Details	I	II
1.	Name of woman		
2.	Relation to the H.O.H		
3.	Age in completed years		
4.	Month of Gestation(weeks)		
5.	**Complaints**		
	1. None	1 ☐	1 ☐
	2. Tired	2 ☐	2 ☐
	3. Pain	3 ☐	3 ☐
	4. Fever	4 ☐	4 ☐
	5. Sleeplessness	5 ☐	5 ☐
	6. Headache	6 ☐	6 ☐
	7. Others (specify)	7 ☐	7 ☐

	Details	I	II
6.	General Appearences		
	1. Healthy	1 ☐	1 ☐
	2. Pale	2 ☐	2 ☐
	3 Oedematous	3 ☐	3 ☐
7.	Antenatal Care Agency / Personnel Rendering the cares		
	1. Not receiving	1 ☐	1 ☐
	2. P.H.C	2 ☐	2 ☐
	3. L.H.W	3 ☐	3 ☐
	4. A.N.M	4 ☐	4 ☐
	5. Trained Dai	5 ☐	5 ☐
	6. Untrained Dai	6 ☐	6 ☐
	7. Relatives	7 ☐	7 ☐
	8. T.B.A	8 ☐	8 ☐
	9. Others	9 ☐	9 ☐
8.	Investigations		
	Haemoglobin		
	1. Not Attending	1 ☐	1 ☐
	2. Not done	2 ☐	2 ☐
	3. Done	3 ☐	3 ☐
9.	Urin		
	1. Not Attending ANC	1 ☐	1 ☐
	2. Not done	2 ☐	2 ☐
	3. Done	3 ☐	3 ☐
10.	B.P		
	1. Not Attending ANC	1 ☐	1 ☐
	2. Not taken	2 ☐	2 ☐
	3. Taken	3 ☐	3 ☐
11.	Tetanus Toxoid		
	1. Not Attending	1 ☐	1 ☐
	2. Not taken	2 ☐	2 ☐
	3. Taken	3 ☐	3 ☐
12.	Physical Examination		
	1. Not attending ANC	1 ☐	1 ☐
	2. Not Examined	2 ☐	2 ☐
	3. Examined	3 ☐	3 ☐
13.	Weight		
	1. Not Attending ANC	1 ☐	1 ☐
	2. Not recorded	2 ☐	2 ☐
	3. Recorded	3 ☐	3 ☐
14.	Iron and Folic Acid		
	1. Not Attending ANC	1 ☐	1 ☐
	2 Not taking	2 ☐	2 ☐
	3. Taking	3 ☐	3 ☐

Q. 16 Family Planning:What Family Planning method you have heard about?

Sl. No.	The Method	Age		Awareness	Knowledge	Source of Knowledge	No. of Users in the Family	Non-Users. Reasons for not using
		Male	Female	(1) No (2) Yes				
Ist Couple								
1.	Sterlization of Husband							
2.	Sterlization of wife							
3.	I.U.D							
4.	Condom							
5.	Other/specify/abortion							
2nd Couple								
1								
2								
3								
4								
5								
3rd Couple								
1								
2								
3								
4								
5								

Q.17 PROTECTIVE DIET

1. Average Number of meals in a day (Average for family)
2. Number of family Members using milk
3. Average quantity of Milk consumed — Kg — Gram

    PER DAY
    PER WEEK
    PER MONTH

4. Is horsegram/ whole gram / soya bean/ gram used in the home? — Yes — No
    If yes, average quantity consumed ? — Kg — Gram

    PER DAY
    PER WEEK
    PER MONTH

5. No ofFamily members using Non-Vegetarian foos
    Average quantity of meat consumed

    Kg — Gram

    PER WEEK
    PER MONTH

6. Are eggs consumed in the Home? — Yes — No

    If yes, average quantity consumed.

    Number of Eggs

    PER WEEK
    PER MONTH

Q. 7 Which of the following are consumed and how often

Sl. No	Type	Daily	Twice a week	Thrice a week	Weekly	Bi- Monthly	Monthly
1	Milk						
2	Meat						
3	Dal						
4	Fish						
5	Eggs						
6	Grains						
7	Nuts						
8	Green leaf						
9	Vegetables						

Q. 18 GRANDMA TYPE CURES

1. Do you grow any medicinal plant including Tulsi? Yes No
2. If Yes, please name plants / herbs you know and their use for different ailments

	Name of the Plants	Uses
1		
2		
3		
4		
5		
6		
7		
8		

3. Please name known allopathic medicines and their uses for different ailments

	Name of the Medicine	Ailment for which used
1		
2		
3		
4		
5		
6		
7		
8		

3. Who gives first advance on children's diseases?

Q. 19 EPIDEMICS

1. In your memory has there been a case of epidemics, if so how many years past? Name the scourge.
2. How was it combated?
3. Who do you think will inform/ or should inform relevent authorities on the visitation of such difficulties?

Q. 20 MEDICAL FACILITIES

Q. 20(a) **Satisfacation with Existing Medical Facilities**

	Type of Facility	How far this facility is located from your home Distance	Number of times used	Are you satisfied with location	Are you satisfied with treatment	Are you satisfied with cost
1.	Hospital					
2.	Primary Health Centre					
3.	Sub-Centre/ANM					
4.	Family Planning Centre					
5.	Chemist/Druggist					
6.	Pvt Practitioner					
	(a) Registered					
	(b) Non-registered					
7.	Ayurvedic					
8.	Unani					
9.	Siddha					
10.	Homoeopath					
11.	Hospital Mobile Van					
12.	Village Health Worker If any					
13.	Which is the nearest good Hospital (Where serious cases can be taken)					

Q. 20(b) Does any mobile medical van visit your visit? [Yes] [No]

If yes, Periodicity of mobile medical van visit.

1. Weekly
2. Bi-weekly
3. Bi-Monthly
4. Monthly
5. No Visit

1. Is there a medical store mearby? [Yes] [No]

   If yes, state distance ____________________

2. Does some local shop keeped sell simple medicines? [Yes] [No]

3. Immunisation Facilities — Distance

   1. Smallpox
   2. Cholera
   3. Typhoid
   4. Polio
   5. B.C.G
   6. Triple
   7. Others specify

4. Do you think diseases are preventable? [Yes] [No]

5. Do you think poor food has to do with people being ill? [Yes] [No]

6. If we form a health committee, will you be willing to serve or recommand any one else? [Yes] [No]

7. What exacty are you willing to contribute?

Work	Time	Organisation	Help	Money

8. Are you willing to pay a small monthly fee(how much) to support a Village Health WorkerService for total health care? Yes No

   If yes, Say Rs/Paise P.M

   Say Rs/Paise P.M

   Say Rs/Paise P.M

Q. 21 Personal Hygiene

21.1 Do you brush your teeth daily? [Yes] [No]

21.2 Do you take bath daily? [Yes] [No]

21.3 Do you wash your hands before taking meal? [Yes] [No]

21.4 Do you use washing soap for cleaning cloths? [Yes] [No]

21.5 Do you have metallic utensils for cooking food? [Yes] [No]

21.6 Do you cover cooked preparations? [Yes] [No]

21.7 Where do you wash your cloths?

21.8 Where do you wash your utensils?

21.9 What steps you take to keep off flies?

(1) ____________________

(2) ____________________

(3) ____________________

21.10 What steps you take to escape from mosquitoes? (1) ________
(2) ________
(3) ________

21.11 What according to you promote family health? (1) ________
(2) ________
(3) ________

21.12 How many times you have received audio-visual lessons on health during the last one month / one year? ________

APPENDIX IV

WORKING SHEETS FOR IRRIGATION PLANNING

PROFORMA I

Month	Year-wise distribution of rainfall in the area for the last ten years (in mm)										Average rainfall (in mm)
	1	2	3	4	5	6	7	8	9	10	
January-December											

PROFORMA II

VILLAGE-WISE AND VLW CIRCLE-WISE EXISTING MEANS OF IRRIGATION

Year.................

Sl. No.	Village	VLW Circle	State Tube Wells		Private Tube Wells		Masonry Wells	Persian Wheels	Pumping Sets	Canals (Length in kms)			Bundhies/Ahars	Channels/Pynes (Length in kms)	Others if any
			Diesel	Electric	Diesel	Electric				Main	Distributories	Minors			

PROFORMA III

VILLAGE-WISE, VLW CIRCLE-WISE AND MEANS-WISE PRESENT IRRIGATED AREA

Year ....

Sl. No.	Village	VLW Circle	AREA IRRIGATED BY (IN ACRES) State Tube Wells		Private Tube Wells		Masonry Wells	Persian Wheels	Pumping Sets	Canals (Length in kms)			Bundhies/Ahars	Channels/Pynes (Lenth in kms)	Others if any
			Diesel	Electric	Diesel	Electric				Main	Distributories	Minors			

PROFORMA IV
LAND USE : 19

(Area in acres) ....

Sl. No.	Village	VLW Circle	Net Cultivated Area Irrigated				Cultivable waste	Net area to be brought under irrigation (total of unirrigated cultivated area including current fallow and old fallow and cultivable waste)	Seasonally irrigated area to be brought under perennial irrigation	Area which may have to be left uncovered
			Seasonal	Perennial	Unirrigated	Total				

PROFORMA V
PLAN PROPOSALS

Sl. No.	Scheme	Number Suggested	Net area to be irrigated (in acres)	Estimated cost (Rs.)	Materials required		Others
					Brick	Cement	

Notes and References

1. Basic Source: AVARD: *Block Level Planning* (New Delhi: Vikas Publishing House) 1980.
2. Organising the rural poor is still a far cry. This will be discussed in the methodology again at a later stage.
3. This has been explicitly recognised now in the decentralized planning set up of WestBengal. See District Planning Committee: *Village Based District Planning Process* (Midnapore: Government of West Bengal) 1984.
4. R.P. Misra has of late been a leading proponent of this view. See Misra R.P.: "On the Task of District Planning", in Yugandhar, B.N. and Mukherjee, Amitava (eds.): *Readings in Decentralized Planning* Vol. I (NewDelhi: Concept Publishing Company) forthcoming, pp. 1-12. See also Misra, R.P. (ed.): *Gandhian Model of Development & World Peace* (New Delhi: Concept Publishing Company) 1988.
5. This is a real problem in agriculture now on account of commmercialisation of agriculture. See Nadkarni, M.V.: Agricultural Development and Ecology—An Economist's View", in Ramachandran, H. : *Environmental Issue in Agricultural Development* (New Delhi: Concept Publishing Co.) 1990.
6. There is considerable debate about the actual quantum of area under forest, but it is there is a virtual unanimity that the acceptable economically stable forest cover of 33.3 per cent of land mass, is nowhere near sight in this country. See Dewan, M.L.: *Himalayan Eco-system* (NewDelhi: Concept Publishing Company) 1990.
7. The local terminology for this can vary. For instance, in the case Jaunsar Babbr area of Dehradun District, the term used is "Maafi", whose transliteration is "condone". See Srivastava, P.C. and Srivastava, S.S.: *Working Plan for Chakrata Forest Division* (Nainital: Government of Uttar Pradesh, Forest Department, Tehri Circle) 1977 p. 558 for such rights. See also Notification No. 104/XIV-27 dated 24th January 1921, G.O. No. 1222/XIV-217 dated 17th July 1926 and G.O. No. 1021 (2)/XIV-216 dated 12th December 1936.
8. TRYSEM under IRDP of Government of India is one later version of this activity. See Government of India: *Integrated Rural Development Programme and Allied Programmes of Training of Rural Youth for Self-Employment (TRYSEM)* and *Development of Women and Children in Rural Areas (DWCRA): A Manual* (New Delhi: Department of Rural Development, Ministry of Agriculture, Government of India) November, 1988, pp. 20-23.
9. This has been the tenor of the Minimum Needs Programme of the Government of India which was anticipated in the Rayalaseema Plan. See Venugopal Reddy, V: "Regional Development Plan for Rayalaseema: A Case Study" in Misra, R.P. et. al. (eds.): *Regional Planning and National Development* (New Delhi: Vikas Publishing House)1978.
10. As a first guide, the norms set forth in the *Report of the Working Group on District Planning* (New Delhi: Planning Commission) 1984, may be followed though Revised Minimum Needs Programme of the Planning Commission, Government of India, NewDelhi as given in the Sixth Plan document is the one suggested by both the *Report of the Working Group on Block Level Planning* (New Delhi: Planning Commission) 1978 and AVARD: loc. cit. 1980.
11. See Minhas, B.S. : *Inaugural Lecture* in Yugandhar, B.N. and Mukherjee, Amitava: *Readings in Decentralised Planning*, Vol. I (New Delhi: Concept Publishing Co.) 1990.
12. An early evaluation of the Antyodaya programme of Rajasthan is Mukherjee, Amitava and Neela Mukherjee: "Rajasthan's Antyodaya Programme : An Analytical Study", *Yojana*, April 16, 1979, Vol. XXIII, No.7.

13. Association for Voluntary Agencies for Rural Development: *Block-Level Planning* (New-Delhi: Vikas Publishing House Pvt. Ltd.) 1980.
14. Misra & Sundaram has called these plans "Block Level Plans prepared by Voluntary Agencies". See Misra, R.P. and Sundaram, K.V.: *Multi-Level Planning for Integrated Rural Development in India* (New Delhi : Heritage Publishers) 1980, pp. 113-115. See also Mukherjee, Amitava: *Researches in Decentralisation* (New Delhi: Heritage Publishers) 1990, being Volume 1, of this series, chapter II for a list of plans prepared by AVARD.
15. Roy, Prodipto and Patil, B.R.: *Manual for Block Level Planning* (New Delhi: MacMillan) 1977.
16. This was one of the recommendations of the International Expert Group Meeting on Decentralized Planning, held at the L.B.S. National Academy of Administration, Mussoorie, from 11th to 13th June 1990. See *Recommendations* (Mussoorie: L.B.S. National Academy of Administration, Government of India) June 1990, which was circulated at the 42nd meeting of the National Development Council, Planning Commission, Government of India, held on 11th October 1990, at New Delhi.
17. See Mukherjee, Amitâva: *Foundations of Decentralisation* (New Delhi: Heritage Publishers) 1990, p. 286, for a summary of the principle.
18. The pro-poor stance in other methodologies like the ones adopted in the case of West Bengal is a much later phenomenon.
19. See for an early evaluation of Antyodaya programme in Rajasthan. Mukherjee, Amitava et al.: "Rajasthan's Antyodaya Programme: An Analytical Study", *Yojana*, New Delhi; Vol. XXIII, No. 7, April, 16th 1979.

CHAPTER VIII

BLOCK AS A PLANNING UNIT, PROGRAMME CONTENT AND CRITERIA FOR THE SELECTION OF THE BLOCK[1]

(DANTWALA COMMITTEE METHODOLOGY)

I. INTRODUCTION

Systematic planning at the national level and to some extent at the State level has been established, and in both the national level and the state level plans, allocations of outlays are made to major sectors of the economy in the light of accepted priorities and desired targets of growth. Nevertheless, the remoteness of the locus of planning, of decision making and of the planning agencies from areas of implementation, and the wide geographical coverage of each set of plan, imposes a severe limitation upon the efficiency of the plans in the matching of sectoral financial allocations with location-specific needs, as well as potential to regulate the distribution of the gains of development. Additionally, the sectoral allocations fail to get integrated such that returns in terms of production, employment and the incomes of the community in general and of the people below the poverty line in particular, are optimized.

Certain developmental schemes like power and major irrigation have to be planned necessarily at supra-district level, namely, the state level or even at the national level, and for certain types of regions (hilly regions or arid zones) and socio-cultural situations (tribal areas), the planning techniques, processes and machinery will have to be different from those suggested in this methodology, though underlying concepts and ideas contained in the *Report* can be adopted even in these special situations after making allowances for variations in conditions in such special class of regions.

At the sub-state or divisional level, the issue whether a district or a block is more appropriate for the purpose of planning need not be viewed with rigidity, and therefore, it is not an 'either-or' type of choice. The main purpose of block-level planning is to accelerate the process of decentralisation, because a more systematic planning effort with a smaller coverage is expected to help speed up the development process and, at once, improve planning efforts qualitatively in the sense of making planning more responsive to the needs of the people, particularly the weaker sections of the community.

Block level planning is to be viewed as a link in a hierarchy of several levels of planning, from a cluster of villages below the block level to the district, regional and state levels. Its relevance as a unit of planning will become apparent in course of our discussion.

II. CONTENTS

The block is distinguished by a certain community of interests, which is sufficiently small both in terms of area and population to enable intimate contact and understanding between all "parties" to the planning process, namely, the planners, the departments or development agencies responsible for implementation of the plan and the people. It provides an observation platform in close proximity of the target group and thus helps to:

(a) appreciate more clearly the felt needs of the people and factors which inhibit the upliftment of the weaker sections of society;
(b) ascertain area specific (in this case block-specific) physical and human resource potential;
(c) identify constraints which inhibit socio-economic and technological growth; and
(d) expand the scope of people's participation in the preparation and implementation of plans for development of their respective areas.

A primary task of block-level planning is, therefore, to demarcate the functional subjects to be covered in block-level planning from that of the district and state levels. The block plan has, therefore, to be related on the one hand to the district plan and the state plan and, on the other, to the plans for the sub-block level which may consist of clusters of villages within the block, like a Gram Panchayat or Mandal Panchayat.

The sectors or sub-sectors which should fall under the purview of block-level planning may be broadly indicated as under:

(a) Agriculture and allied activities.
(b) Minor irrigation.
(c) Soil conservation and water management.
(d) Animal husbandry.
(e) Fisheries.
(f) Forestry.
(g) Processing of agricultural produce.
(h) Organizing input supply, credit and marketing.
(i) Cottage and small industries.
(j) Local infrastructure.
(k) Social Services:
    i) Drinking water supply,
    ii) Health and nutrition,
    iii) Education,

iv) Housing,

v) Sanitation,

vi) Local transport and

vii) Welfare programmes.

(l) Training of local youth and unskilled population.

There are several other linked activities which have to be undertaken as a part of a larger resource development programme cutting across block boundaries, in which cases the role of each of the concerned blocks would be to develop a preparatory plan to speed up the absorption (or utilization) of the benefits emanating from these projects. For example, the methodology envisages that in a command area covering several blocks, the utilization of the newly available irrigation facilities for increasing productivity and employment can be accelerated through the block level plan, under which complementary programmes of land shaping, distributory channels, crop planning, agricultural extension, supply of inputs and credit, will have to be undertaken. Planning for these complementary programmes clearly requires both the identification of the needs for various inputs and an appropriate sequencing of activities. Without such complementary planning, delays in availing of the benefits of such area programmes would ensue and it may generate dualistic economies (or entrench deeper, the existing ones) as in cases of investments in large industrial projects in the tribal areas of East Central India where the local population experienced, not the growth effects, but the backwash effects of development.

If the linkages with the programmes of larger area level are not visualized, bottlenecks may be caused, because local development schemes have to be coordinated with the larger projects that lie beyond the bounds of the block as regards their respective requirements of raw materials and manpower, which is essential to avoid emergence of shortages, whereby avoid delay in the execution of projects at both block and supra-block levels and avoid adding to the cost over-runs.

Granted the foregoing, the block-level plan would encompass programmes for intensive development of agriculture and allied activities mentioned earlier, and the provision of the related economic and institutional infrastructure through a large number of programmes directed at serving the needs of targeted groups comprising landless labourers, marginal and small farmers, artisans, women, children, and other weaker sections of society would be abundantly made.

III. OBJECTIVES

While the development programmes should aim at the creation of productive assets, they will have to be so designed as to generate the maximum possible employment. Production or employment programmes and the provision of economic infrastructure will not, by themselves, be adequate for accelerating the tempo of economic development, unless a programme for meeting the basic minimum needs like health care, drinking water, child nutrition, education, house-sites, rural roads and electricity is concurrently undertaken. Comprehensive block planning would, thus, have a distinct component of location-specific plan for the provision of basic minimum needs, which will reach those below the poverty line, generate employment and in the process improve the quality of the labour force.[2]

Another component of the block level plan is the provision of adequate institutional support for the removal of the socio-economic constraints that hinder the implementation of the plan. The form of such institutional support and the manner in which these have to be organized are discussed later.

The major components of a block level plan thus are:

(a) Production programmes for the target groups in the area in the light of the resource potential.
(b) Manpower planning and skill development in relation to the production programmes.
(c) A programme for the provision of basic minimum needs.
(d) Programme for institutional support.

IV. THE FOCUS OF THE PLANNING PROCESS AT BLOCK LEVEL

It would appear on first inspection that planning at block level would be a miniature of planning at higher levels,[3] and the financial resources available for the block plan would be a fraction of those available at the State and the District levels and the range of projects or programmes would be restricted accordingly, impressions that may not always be true. The smallness of the size and scale will indeed provide an opportunity for a more intensive plan formulation[4] (see Figure 8.1) and plan implementation and make the plan formulation more realistic and plan implementation more effective. And then, what may be missed in a global view, whatever it may be, from a latent resource or an incipient constraint, can be discerned in a block planning exercise through closer observations with a sharper focus. A closer contact with people would sharpen the awareness of the planners regarding people's problems which need to be solved, their priorities and the obstacles to finding their solutions. The proximity of approach may encourage the people to reflect on collective wisdom of the planners with regard to the programmes which have succeeded and which have failed, and causes thereof. It should be borne in mind, however, that the same proximity may raise people's expectations to higher levels and non-performance would be more severely exposed than is otherwise the case.

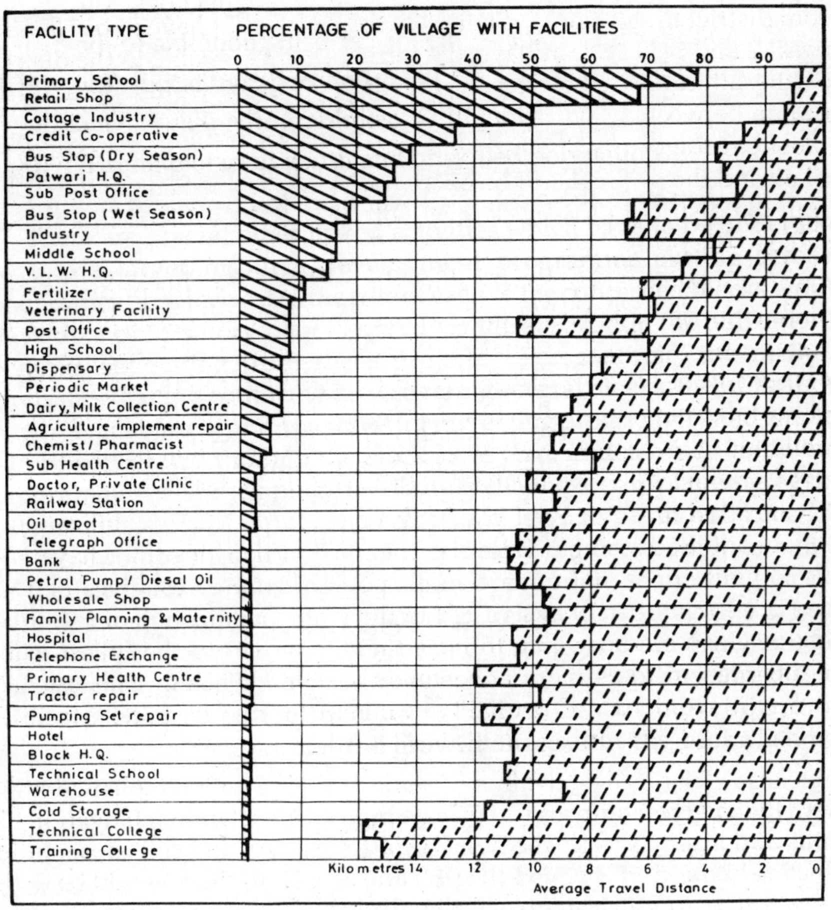

Figure 8.1 Presence of facilities and average travel distance across twenty

Therefore, any inference that a smaller area and a smaller plan implies less scope or requires a lower level of planning competence is clearly misplaced.

V. FINANCIAL RESOURCES

The planning team will need an initial 'briefing' with the State level planning body for obtaining a broad idea about the (a) financial parameters within which to plan and (b) the continuing schemes or on-going for which a part of the expenditure is committed.[5]

Before the financial base of the blocks and the district comes to be built up through area development, the financing of the block level planning will depend on the devolution of financial resources from the State to the districts and from district to the blocks. State Plan outlays would have to be classified into *divisible* and *indivisible* outlays, the former being allocable to the districts. Out of the allocations received by the district, there would be a further distribution between schemes identified as those of the district level (having inter-block coverage or linkage) and those for schemes forming part of the block level plan; and the principles of resource transfer from the State to the district and from the district to the block level will have to be evolved in a manner acceptable to the people.

Even after making allowance for substantial increases in the priority sectors of agriculture, irrigation, power generation, the minimum needs programme, and a step-up in central assistance towards schemes of integrated rural development at the block or district levels, the gap between the needs and the availability of resources at the block level will continue to be significant. Augmentation of the resource availability through provision of institutional credit for bankable schemes or bankable projects will be essential.

Intensification of block level planning would necessitate mobilization of financial resources at the block level. The local authorities (Panchayati Raj Institutions) either did not have enough power to raise resources or were reluctant to exercise the powers vested in them for mobilization of resources, (just as the States are unwilling to raise their resources to the fullest extent possible) because of, possibly, "non-economic" expediencies. This question may be carefully examined and suitable arrangements may be made to facilitate larger mobilization of resources at the local level.

All blocks will have several minor irrigation projects under implementation, and they will have commitments in private investments in minor irrigation like dug wells and lift irrigation schemes. The afforestation and soil conservation works have also been executed in the past and several of them would be under execution, just as in cases of animal husbandry and dairy programmes. Resources committed to such ongoing programmes will have to be provided for and the new programmes will have to be coordinated and dovetailed with the on-going ones as well as with the completed ones. Wherever infrastructure work programmes have been completed or are under implementation, production and employment programmes for the farmers and landless labourers will have to be conceived. For example, if in a block, dairy marketing infrastructure has been built in the shape of a chilling plant, dairy, etc., complementary programmes like artificial insemination facilities, provision of credit etc. will have to be planned and implemented.

VI. RESOURCE INVENTORY

(a) Inventory

This brings us to the problem of resource inventory. Usually the planning exercise begins with the compilation of a resource inventory. Proformae or schedules are prepared for collecting information, mostly statistical, without any precise idea about its utility or relevance for the planning exercises, and more importantly, information (as distinguished from statistics which can be neatly accommodated in a proforma) which may be quite crucial for the planning exercise, may be overlooked. Proformae are prepared by an economist or statistician on the basis of his general understanding of the importance and availability of data without any idea (cannot be expected to have much) of the exact kind of data that a particular subject matter specialist would need. Therefore, the compilation of inventory may be made after the subject matter specialist indicates his requirements, upon receiving his briefing from the State Planning Department and subsequent to a full length discussion with the district planning team.

The type of resource inventory necessary for block level planning should be relevant to planning at the level we are presently concerned, namely, block level. For example, if there are substantial iron ore, and coal deposits in the block, the resource inventory for block level planning need not concern itself with resources of such a nature. Further, the resource inventory should lead to certain specific action programmes which can be built into the block level plan rather than merely cataloguing certain possibilities which may or may not be germane to the block level planning at all. For example, for the purpose of block-level planning it is redundant to state that because of forest resources, a paper mill is a possibility, because planning of such a project like a paper mill should really be the concern of planning at the State level and will indeed be done at the State level if not at the national level. *To be precise, resource inventory should necessarily concentrate on identifying potentialities which can be best exploited at the block level and which will directly contribute towards increasing in the value added component of the largest segment of population* (of the block).

Resource inventory as contemplated is not a once-overall exercise but is a continuous process, with resource inventory initially concentrating on the clearly most dominant activity of the block. To illustrate, it is clear that in Konkan region of Maharashtra, because of the terrain, the economic activity has to be tree based with emphasis on horticulture crops like mangoes and cashews. Identification of such a dominant economic activity would be easy for almost every block and in many cases it will be seen that there is a great deal of scope for further augmentation of this activity and fuller exploitation of its potential for the betterment of the people of the area.

(b) On-Going Programmes

The first task of the planning team for block-level planning would be to acquaint itself thoroughly with the earlier and the on-going projects and programmes and review their performance, particularly so with regard to their successes, failures and the reasons thereof. "New investments should be in the nature of complementary investments, first deployed to maximize the yield potential of past investments and disseminate it as widely as possible." It is not very unlikely that further investment in the project per se (like irrigation) may be found to be unnecessary but investment may be essential in the infrastructure needed for the fuller and better utilization of the potential created (through field channels and prevention of water-logging) by the project. Or, for instance, in the development of animal husbandry the need may be not merely more and better cattle, but streamlining of forward and backward linkages (roads, vehicles, chilling plants, fodder supply, veterinary service) for fully utilizing the potential created by earlier investments in animal husbandry.

(c) Status Paper

Thus, the task of building up a resource inventory should not be confined to watertight compartments, because, the operational task of full utilization of the resources and facts and their analysis should not be a sequential process. For example, the phenomenon of low productivity or low growth-rate in agriculture acquires relevance only if the underlying causes are analyzed, constraints are identified and measures can be suggested for their removal. The gathering of facts, identification of constraints and determination of development potential should all form parts of the same exercise, and therefore, instead of compiling inventory of statistics as an independent exercise, a *Status Paper* should be prepared for each major sector (like agriculture, irrigation, animal husbandry, forestry, health and education) giving a complete picture of the past quantitative and qualitative performance, factors which contributed or inhibited the progress, constraints (physical, financial, technological, administrative) experienced, suggestions for removal of those constraints, realistic assessment of potential (immediate, short-term and long-term) and projects to be undertaken during the Plan period under reference with all the details including cost-benefit calculations and analysis.

Thus while preparing the *Status Paper*, inter-sectoral linkages should be identified through a joint multi-disciplinary discussion, and the attempt should be to evolve an integrated plan from sector *Status Papers*, in which process, information gaps may also be discovered and filled up. This status paper would form the basis for consultation with professionals, scientific institutions and management experts. At the same time there is a whole lot to learn from the people themselves, all those who have benefited and who have not benefited, from past efforts at planning and development.

(d) Identification of Poor

A very important information which the planning team should collect appertains to the number of families living below the poverty line, which need not have academic precision but be an informed judgement about the nature of the problem, the magnitude of the problem and the types of programmes which have to be launched immediately to make a visible impact in obviating the problem. The package of this programme will have to have two elements:

one, a transitory relief element, and

two, a more enduring element which will provide a viable solution to the problem of poverty.

Model proformae and schedules for the collection of resource inventory, can be obtained from the Indian Institute of Management (Ahmedabad) Model,[6] AVARD Model,[7] Manual on Block Level Planning prepared by Prodipto Roy and Dr. B.R. Patil[8] and Comprehensive Area Development Corporation, West Bengal all of which contain various kinds of proformae and schedules as well as elaborate instructions for the collection of information relating to resource inventory. These proformae or schedules are adequate from the point of view of indicating the type of information that needs to be collected, and any one such proforma or schedule would generally serve the purpose of planning at block level.

Each block level planner or sectoral specialist has to adopt these proformae or schedules to the specific requirements of the block which has been chosen for the planning exercise, which imparts sufficient flexibility to the block planner or the sectoral specialist to enable him or her to prepare his own proformae or schedules to suit local needs, resources and priorities. If any assistance is needed it may be obtained from the training institutions.

It is not enough to augment allocations or indicate new priorities: the planning process itself will have to be different from earlier planning efforts. The differences that need be emphasized are mainly in regard to

(a) learning from past experiences and activizing previous investment;

(b) vigilance on distribution of gains from development;

(c) rectifying infrastructure (not ignoring the agrarian structure, e.g. land ownership) and institutions which restrict growth and distort gains; and

(d) learning from the people themselves.

It would have been a whole lot better if restructuring of the administrative apparatus aiming at strengthening of horizontal linkages and loosening of the vertical (departmental) command line were possible, as this would facilitate a better appreciation of inter-sectoral linkages and furtherance the process of decentralisation. These, however, are beyond the scope of planning at the level referred to here and is therefore, naturally not pursued any further.

Several development activities that are considered suitable to the requirements of the State have been entrusted to the Boards and Corporations such as Electricity Boards and State Road Transport Undertakings as also multi-functional Regional Development Corporation. Gujarat for instance had set up a Rural Development Corporation for undertaking Rural Development Programmes, including area development programmes like Command Area Development Programme, Drought Prone Area Programme, and Tribal Development Programme. Block level planning will have to take a note of the role of all these Corporations and programmes and as such others, so that their activities within the block converge towards the achievement of the employment and production goals of block-level planning.

The great advantage of block-level planning and, in a way, its justification lies in its ability to observe the functioning of the local economy and the growth process from close proximity and draw appropriate lessons for better planning, both for the purposes of accelerating growth and for better distribution of the gains of growth. The merit of planning is usually judged by the quantum of investment and its sectoral allocations, but an equally important component of planning, particularly so if it is to be oriented to the needs of the weaker sections, is the institutional framework within which the economy functions, which is largely ignored. The methodology suggests that the success of the block plans would critically depend upon their ability to bend the existing institutions and improvise new ones to subserve the objectives of the plan at the block level.

(e) Minimum Needs Programme

The minimum needs programme will have considerable importance in block planning, because this programme cannot be planned meaningfully from above, say at the supra-district level. Block level planning has to play a crucial role to make the minimum needs programme operational. "What is needed is not so much an inventory of age-groups of children or an inventory of sickness or malnutrition but the analysis of the causes which inhibit the poor from availing of these opportunities."[9] The despicable spectacle of a school without a teacher or conspicuous absence of SC/ST boys from school, or health centres without even a nurse or medicines, is the one with which the block level planners will have to contend with. In brief, a block level plan should not be a slice cut out of the district plan cake, but a self-contained plan in its own right addressing itself to appropriate spheres such as the minimum needs programme, and where the nature of the projects or programmes necessitates a bigger area or a larger scale of planning, it will seek to establish structural and operational linkages with the plans at the higher levels in the planning hierarchy. The planners at the block level should be able to set into motion a process of change in working of the economic system at the sub-district level, which would tilt the distribution of gains of development in favour of the weaker sections of society, but obviously their success in this regard would critically depend on the backing provided by political will at the local and the State level.

VII. SPATIAL PLANNING FOR SOCIOECONOMIC INFRASTRUCTURES: CONCEPT OF SPATIAL PLANNING

Spatial planning implies a systematic effort to locate facilities (such as roads, schools, factories and houses) in relation to human settlements where all people can use them to maximum advantage. Unless this is deliberately done, infrastructural investments of sectoral programmes would be made in locations randomly determined, which may not *converge* in desirable combinations at the most optimal locations, which can effect economies of scale in movement of men and materials and better utilization of facilities. Unplanned development may result in location of an agricultural market and an agricultural processing function in different places; or that of middle school and health sub-centre in different villages. The point cannot be over-emphasized that there will be great advantage in planning to build facilities in a single location in that the farmer who comes to sell his produce in the market-place can be is provided with the facilities of having his goods processed at the same place and facilities to pick up some essential requirements, like drugs and medicines. Granted this, when locational planning is not inter-sectorally integrated, or when locational planning is guided by political "distributive justice", villages will continue to compete with each other and ultimately neither of them will succeed in achieving viability, nor will all sections of the people be able to obtain adequate service. Thus, for optimum growth of infrastructure with social justice in spatial planning, it is necessary to rationalize the locations of the various sectoral infrastructure investment programmes.

A block plan is a continuum of neighbouring block plans, the district plan or in the broader context of a geographic region, of the State plans. Each of the social and economic infrastructures has a hierarchy of functions and has evolved its own threshold populations and distance norms or standards.

At the block level, there are three types of activities which require locational decisions:

(a) The key projects and supporting subsidiary projects that are identified in the area in the productive sectors of the economy.

(b) The provision of basic infrastructure which will include electricity, buildings, roads, marketing yards, warehousing, processing facilities, and agricultural services of various kinds, and social infrastructure for the provision of the basic minimum needs to people like schools and dispensaries.

(c) The setting up of organizations such as cooperatives, service societies or agencies at the grassroots level which cater to the poorer sections.

The first of the three activities, namely those at (a) above, has a generative role and will be concentrated at a few specific locations which may be called "rural growth centres". The activities mentioned in (b) and (c) will have a servicing role and will be dispersed in as many locations as necessary, to make them accessible to the local population within a reasonabling specified minimum distance. Those will be "rural service centres". *"Thus, the convergence of rural growth centres and service centres will constitute an essential part of area planning."*

VIII. PLANNING FOR INFRASTRUCTURE

The task of planning for infrastructures is not easy. The selection of locations for infrastructures in the rural areas will have three basic constraints: *one,* Service population, *two,* maximum travel distance and *three,* finance. Systematic planning would involve firstly, determining the existing norms for population and distance on the basis of the availability of the existing facilities and then setting of appropriate distance and population standards, taking into account the various constraints, including constraints of topography and the settlement pattern. The "National Minimum Needs Programme" implemented during the Fifth Plan spelt out some population and distance standards for some services as given in Figure 8.1, which has been recommended by the Government of India in "National Minimum Needs Programme", *Fifth Five Year Plan* (New Delhi: Planning Commission) 1974. The Pilot Research Project on Growth Centres which was conducted during the Fourth Plan in 20 blocks gathered data on a wide range of facilities as in Figure 8.2. The lessons learned and methods of planning evolved in these pilot projects will be useful in this context.

Facilities/Activities	Max. Travel Distance (Km)	Other Standards
Regulated Market	16	Quantity of produce
Godown Cold Storage		to be marked
Technical College		1 per 40,000 to
Hospital Hardware		50,000 pop.[10]
Tractor & Pump Repair		
P.H.C. Bank		
Technical School	12	Minimum population
Collection Yard	to	or money flow
Doctor	16	
High School S.H.C.	4	8 km[10]
Veterinary Dispensary	to	1 per 40,000 to
Fertilizer & Seeds	8	50,000 pop.[10]
Middle School		5 km[10]
Post Office	2	
Daily Shopping	to	
Cycle Repair	4	
Primary School	Under 2	1.5 km[10]

Figure 8.2: Typical Standards for Spatial Distribution of facilities

The Figures referred to above are meant only as illustrations and the standards mentioned need not be applied mechanically to any specific area. The standards should be locally established in the light of the local conditions so that they would be realistic, which is essential in the local planning process. The block plans will, therefore, have to begin by ascertaining the existing situations and the setting of appropriate distance and population standards, which indicates that collection of adequate data and some cartographic analysis are necessary for this purpose.

While making the inventory of resources, the inventory of all infrastructural facilities, institutions and services should also be made. Further data on both the quantum and the qualities of such services available should be collected to the extent possible, and the information available on these aspects should then be mapped and their spatial reach (catchment areas) to the village communities should be identified. On the basis of realistic norms, the spatial and functional gaps must be identified and a suitable programme should be drawn up on the basis of such analysis. This, *in short, is the methodology for service centre planning.* For identifying the spatial and functional gaps and for working out a hierarchy of service centres, simple methods have been devised, and the experiments made on the basis of the pilot project exercises on rural growth centres. The *Report* advocated the use of such simple methods for this purpose.[11] The pilot project exercise and other projects have also worked out computer programmes for locational planning seeking to optimize spatial reach and service population along with the most rational sequencing of locations.[12]

Before working out service centre planning discussed above, it is necessary to decide upon, *one,* the package of basic services or minimum needs which makes a rural area or cluster of villages socially and economically viable, and *two,* the minimum population threshold and distance standard at which these services should be made available. The minimum social and economic services, the methodology envisages, should be provided within say a half hour to one hour travel distance which would be equivalent to a geographical distance of about 3 to 5 km from any village. The basic infrastructures should include an agricultural seed-store, fertilizer or storage godown, elementary education, a sub-health centre or dispensary, a pucca road and electricity. As regards establishing the minimum threshold population and distance standard, it should be a collective decision taken by the concerned departments (agriculture, education, health, roads, and electricity) taking the terrain conditions and the settlement pattern of the area being planned for into account, and obviously enough, only when these standards are mutually agreed upon by the operational agencies or departments concerned with making available certain services at the local level, that their physical convergence as envisaged at appropriate locations could be achieved. The Planning team should, therefore, strive to bring about mutual consensus between different operational agencies or departments, and work out a realistic compromise of standards.

To recapitulate, the problem of locational planning for social and economic infrastructures must address itself to something like the following:

i) Examine the existing hierarchies of facilities available in the block, in the broader context of the district as geographic region.

ii) Attempt at the convergence or integration of the various public and private infrastructures at various levels in the hierarchy at one location. Because the district and block levels have already had some established integration, the main focus of attention in block planning, will be the primary service centres, or growth centres, between the block headquarters and the revenue village which can be integrated into a viable sub-block micro-region. The decision on which village should be selected as the service centre and the delineation of the viable micro-regions within the block is the second important step.

iii) Contingent in the second step, is the establishment of resource, population and distance standards and deciding upon the actual services to be provided, and the capacity and quality of services.[13]

It should be emphasized that infrastructural investment is both for filling existing gaps and the gaps that may emerge within the "expectational horizon", and it must be viewed dynamically as the prime mover for generating fuller employment and greater equity. A special public works programme of roads, canals, minor irrigation, soil conservation, afforestry, inland fisheries can be used as an employment scheme and cause a massive transfer of resources to the labouring classes. For this purpose, *first*, sensitively designed integrated multi-sectoral approach, with multi-level spatial planning should be used together with various labour-intensive intermediate technologies; *second*, the scale should be large enough to create a psychological, political and economic impact and *third*, better technical planning, maintenance and more decentralisation should be used resulting in better management and mobilization of local talents and skills. These public works investments will then stimulate better agriculture, provide better health and nutrition, provide better schools (and introduce more relevant, non-formal adult education), provide better roads and buses, make available more electricity and perhaps bring to the countryside some of the good things of life—radios, bicycles, cinemas, better clothes and better housing. These basic or minimum needs when actually provided will become a massive consumption and employment generator for 60-80 per cent of the rural population. Evaluation of the achievements of any block plan, should be calibrated towards sensitive measurements of the availability of these basic needs to the target groups of each micro-region of the block.

IX. INSTITUTIONAL CHANGE AND ORGANIZATION OF THE POOR

For the allocation of resources to agriculture and rural development to make real impact on reduction of poverty and unemployment, serious attention will have to be given to the removal of structural, institutional and organizational constraints on growth and its benefits accruing to the weaker sections of society.

Absence of basic records of rights in land in many districts has proved a major obstacle in the implementation of land reforms including those relating to granting of protection to tenants and ceilings on land holdings, extension of irrigation facilities, supply of inputs and deployment of credit. The condition obtaining today has not changed much. In those blocks where such records of rights in land do not exist, their preparation should receive a high priority in the block-level plan.

Poverty and unemployment are consequences of a social and economic process, which has resulted in the "inegalitarian structure of ownership of income-earning assets and skills", and which has the characteristic that it utilizes certain institutional mechanisms to perpetuate if not aggravate the inegalitarian character of the economy and the polity. Thus, in addition to the imperativeness of structural change, obliterating the deleterious effects of the existing institutions and establishment of new ones and for the weaker sections of society become absolutely necessary in the block planning exercise.

The first step in organizing the poor is the *conscientisation process*, that is, the weaker sections of society should be made aware of their rights under the existing laws, covering areas such as tenancy, minimum wages, bonded labour, various concessions and subsidies available to them (for example under SFDA, MFAL, house sites), right to make use of community wells for drawing drinking water, credit from banks at concessional rates of interests for productive activity and for consumption loans. Field surveys have revealed that the beneficiaries are not always even aware of their legitimate rights, which makes them vulnerable to exploitation by vested interests. The functioning of the official agencies entrusted with the responsibility of planning and implementation of the so-called special programmes for the poor does not reveal that they have in full measure the will or capability to undertake the task of the conscientisation. The role of the voluntary agencies, provided they are immune to political pressures, can be significant in this regard.

The methods of 'conscientization' and functional adult education are being effectively developed by various bodies which follow the Paulo Freire or Ivan Illich Schools, and the Government's National Adult Education Programme (NAEP) has included these procedures in their purview and has also provided substantial financial resources. The methodology envisages that the organizations of the poor can be given direction and skills with such assistance. Such motivation and training of the poor is a necessary condition for organizations of the poor to become self-reliant and be able to withstand the exploitative forces in the political-economic real world. The procedures for motivating and training the poor should be linked specifically to the projects or programmes mentioned above which are taken up for implementation in the block level plans.

Conscientisation and awareness are not enough, because the weaker sections of society are unable—and sometimes even unwilling—to assert their rights, because of two major constraints: *One*, "despondency constraint" inhibits the poor from taking any positive action because of the despair they have inherited through generations, which may not be irrational (as it may seem to us) for experience has taught them that the consequences of assertive behaviour, more often than not, evinces trouble, if not setback and accentuates suppression; and *two*, the total dependence on the landlord of the poorer sections of society or on the money-lender-trader nexus for their day to day needs and more so in times of calamity. The fate of the 'freed' bonded labour, revealed both through public media and serious studies amply illustrate the point.

Granted these circumstances, it is worth pondering over the options open to the planner, which are necessarily limited, and the strategy of the plan should be to buttress the resistance capacity of the poor and reduce his vulnerability to exploitation, which would need identification of all vulnerable situations and devise institutions which would close the private exploitation trap with a public support system. No elaborate study of the causes of poverty or the process which perpetuates it is necessary to identify the exploitation traps, for some of them are quite obvious, and to begin with it should suffice if concrete steps are immediately taken to close them.

Some of the social and economic constraints which afflict the weaker sections of society and which the block level planner should strive to remove within the ambit of his authority, are:

(a) Lack of income-yielding assets and skills with the poorer sections leading to:
   i) total unemployment or severe under-employment;
   ii) low income resulting from low wages and low productivity; and
   iii) total dependence on money-lender and trader for credit and marketing.

(b) Crop failures and cattle mortality.

(c) Subsistence constraint particularly during the lean seasons.

(d) Lack of medical aid for treating serious illness in the family.

(e) Ignorance and illiteracy.

(f) Social customs exercising pressure to incur expenditure beyond their means on social occasions like births, marriages and funerals.

A complete blue-print of institutions and organizations which would be able to remove all the above constraints cannot be enumerated, apart from the fact that some of the constraints such as lack of assets, crop and cattle insurance would need action at a much higher level than that of block-level planning.

However, other constraints, like illiteracy and lack of medical facilities are certainly within the ambit of block planning, and have attracted considerable attention in the Ministries in the Government concerned and by expert bodies, and the solutions evolved are seemingly satisfactory enough. However, some concrete suggestions in regard to two ingredients of this programme: *one*, removal of subsistence constraints and *two*, institutional support for rural crafts and artisans, seems to be in order. The questions of employment planning and institutional credit need also be looked into.

(i) Subsistence Constraint

During lean seasons, particularly so in a mono-crop areas, poor families have no employment and often run out of stocks of food. It is during this period that the dependence of the poor families on the landlord-moneylender -trader nexus becomes absolute, forcing them to borrow in cash or kind at exorbitant rates of interests and as a consequence sink into chronic indebtedness. If some arrangements could be made to provide the rural poor with minimum subsistence support during lean seasons, their dependence on the vested interests can be considerably reduced, though not totally eliminated and thus be saved from getting enmeshed in chronic indebtedness. One such mechanism could be the development of a "Community Grain Gola" for the landless and the marginal farmers, many of whom work in others' fields, at times on a wage which is just subsistence wage below the prescribed minimum wage, trapping them into this subsistence constraint. The Community Grain Gola can develop the self-reliance of the poor, if it can be operated on the basis of the savings of the rural poor themselves, coupled with the programme of additional employment and income during the succeeding years. Thus, if the landless and the marginal farmers can be induced to save about 5 to 10 percent of their meagre earnings during their working period of about 150 to 200 days in a year, it may work out to be about Rs. 50 to Rs.100 per worker per year. If the irrigation and other allied programmes are taken up simultaneously in the area employing credit from Banks or some such similar organizations, the prospects of better incomes and employment during the next year would considerably improve. The resources so gathered may be used to store grain, to be supplied to the rural poor during the lean season. Hopefully, the additional income which will accrue to them during the next season and in the next year will enable them to repay the grain loan obtained during the earlier period of the working season. The Community Grain Gola is, therefore, a purely interim measure bridging the time gap between the achievement of full employment and the situation obtaining now, when most of the poor families are unemployed and experience severe food shortage often for as many as six months in a year. Once it can be demonstrated that there is a self-reliant source *now* through which the poor can overcome their subsistence constraint, they may move substantively towards breaking their dependence on the vested interests and in the process will be inclined to develop their own self-reliant agencies or departments or organization. Initially, however, the planning and implementing organization will have to take the initiative and work out the organizational details and provide financial support.

The scope of the Community Grain Gola can be enlarged by including in it provisions for other important consumption goods like cloth, salt, fuel and urgently required-hand tools like sickle, and axe. It may be necessary in the initial period for the public authority to bear the cost of storage and management.

Ostentatious expenditure (in terms of their income and saving capacity) on ceremonial occasions, often dictated by local or caste customs is a major potent source of chronic indebtedness, and evidence suggests that this is one of the causes of bonded labour conditions. The experiments aimed at the introduction of institutional line of credit for meeting such consumption credit requirements of the weaker sections has not succeeded. Probably, the only solution could be some sort of social sanction. If the Panchayats of the low income families could be persuaded to impose ceiling on such expenditure and chit-fund type of institutions could be initiated to provide loans for the purpose, the problem may become manageable. Though this is not a part of block-level planning, but it certainly is a problem which cannot be isolated from the task of fulfilling the plan objectives of eradication of poverty and destitution.

If rural development—in the sense of more income to more people—is to be accelerated, it would be necessary to pay greater attention to the non-farm sector of the rural economy. A further increase in labour intensity in Indian agriculture will need a substantial step-up in fixed and current capital per unit of land used as well as radical structural change in ownership and use of land which may not be possible immediately. In any case, because of the prevailing severe under-employment and because of the expected large additions to the labour force, reduction of the excessive dependence of the poor on farm land through diversification of the rural economy would be necessary, which will be put to test the ingenuity and dynamism of the planner. Ways and means to revive and strengthen the non-farm economy, which includes animal husbandry, forestry, horticulture, fisheries and above all rural crafts and cottage industries are not clearly known, and though these sectors in the recent past have received considerable attention both from the planners and voluntary agencies and even a break-through in some sectors like cattle-breeding and dairying has been achieved, and a shift in emphasis in favour of small-scale and village industries is noticeable, yet the diagnosis of the maladies which afflict the small entrepreneurs and village artisans leaves much to be desired. Once again, the organizational and institutional aspects of the problems have received scant attention vis-a-vis what they deserve. In the following section a few suggestions are made to this effect.

(ii) Institutional Support for Rural Crafts and Artisans

For any programme for crafts and artisans aimed at raising the artisan's incomes, 'self-employment' and 'self-reliance' should be the catchwords together with making the craft capable of self-generating growth. The institutional support for rural crafts and artisans must be geared to help protect the artisans from exploitation by traders-moneylenders nexus or by their own peers, which is tantamount to helping the rural artisans to organize themselves and developing their capabilities to manage their own institutions. Educational and Training Institutions, Khadi Commission, Cooperatives, Voluntary Agencies, Banks, and other financial institutions, could be involved as primary intervenors with Government providing necessary infrastructural and financial support, in this regard.

The kind of institutional support required for each craft will depend on the functions, skills and support levels involved in the development of the crafts. Given the foregoing, broadly, the functions will include:

(a) Development functions which will include development of people, process, technology, management and organization skills, development of appropriate raw materials and of finished products.
(b) Procurement functions, which may be related to procurement of equipment, raw materials or of finished products.
(c) Functions related to the production of finished goods.
(d) Functions relating to finance (loans, costing, pricing, etc.).
(e) Marketing functions (including research, testing, grading, selling, servicing, storage, packing and despatch).

The support could be in relation to four aspects each of which need *distinct skill* and perhaps a different level and form of involvement, as:

(a) Individual artisan learning technological, managerial, social and environmental aspects;
(b) learning for intervenors, field workers, support institutions, etc.;
(c) process work involving action by intervenors to influence values, attitudes and behaviour of participant-artisans with a view to activate them to work together and develop self-reliance by building their own organization; and
(d) commercial participation in logistic flow of resources (banks, market channels, etc.).

There could be three *support levels* and the support resource institutions could operate at one or more of the following levels:

(a) *first order level institutions* (like National Laboratories and IIMs, involved in) training;
(b) second order level institutions (like Universities, departments and other training institutions) which in turn impart training;

(c) third order level institutions (for example, agencies, intervenors and field workers) training; and

(d) artisans, both individual artisans and artisans' organizations.

X. EMPLOYMENT PLANNING

Employment strategy consists of devising ways and means for bridging the gap between supply and demand for work where supply outstrips demand. The prevailing view is that as a first step in the strategy, a man-power budget should be prepared. In other words, we should measure the magnitude of unemployment problem and study its anatomy.

The planning team should be given a direction to the effect that while preparing the individual sectoral plans and the final integrated plan, the major objective of augmenting employment opportunities especially for the weaker sections (small and marginal farmers, landless labourers, village craftsmen, scheduled castes and tribes, and women) should constantly be kept in view, and also policy implications to the adoption of these guidelines such as the desired direction of land reforms, farm mechanization, upgrading of technology, reorientation of credit and marketing institutions, should also be clearly spelt out.

Given the directive in regard to the priority attached to employment generation in block or district planning, the sectoral planner should devise projects or programmes for augmenting the period of employment of various categories of persons (men, women, self-employed, wage labourers) in their *existing occupations.* For example, if irrigation potential exists in the agricultural sector, the period of employment of all persons engaged in cultivation can be extended by increasing the intensity of cropping. Consistent with the accent on employment generation, the planners should attempt at ensuring that more than proportionate share of additional water availability accrues to the small farmers. However, planning for employment generation will not always be so simple and obvious, and the planner will need wide comprehension and considerable ingenuity in devising technically and financially sound projects which will lead to growth and will at once also augment employment and income of the weaker sections.

It is erroneous to believe that additional investment is all that is needed for generating employment. Organization and institutional reform may be equally critical. For example, village crafts and industries are languishing because of the absence of proper organizations for supply of raw materials, marketing of finished products, innovative designing to suit the changing consumer demand, and need for upgrading the traditional technology and skills. The remedy for their inability to compete with the products of organized sector should first be sought through removal of these 'internal' weaknesses, and only subsequently, if need be, through the policy of reservations.

Sectors like forestry, animal husbandry, fisheries, etc. have immense potential for generating employment along with production and income which will have to be explored along the lines indicated above, by the sectoral planners.

Despite all efforts aimed at augmenting employment in the existing occupations through additional investments, development of infrastructure, institutional reforms etc., unemployment still persists, because of the failure to make significant impact on the hard core of the chronically unemployed labour force, who have no worthwhile productive assets or skills and no stable occupations. For these people a special public works programme for providing transitory unskilled employment will be necessary. The Employment Guarantee Scheme of the Government of Maharashtra provides an illustration and a valuable experience, but introduction of such a scheme would entail considerable preparatory work and organization to cope with the employment requirements and ability to design appropriate matching schemes. Finding worthwhile productive works on which mass of unskilled workers can be employed in successive years over a period of several years in future is no easy task. An employment guarantee programme should be conceived primarily as a programme of utilizing surplus manpower for conservation of the environment, and improvement and full utilization of the soil and water resources of each local area which should constitute an important element of the block-level planning. A detailed soil conservation survey of the block to identify the relevant works and to prepare plans and estimates of their cost and employment potential are essential ingredients of a block level plan, as also to open and execute such works on a systematic basis as and when the need arises. Assistance available under schemes such as 'Food for Work' should be fully utilized for taking up public works programme on a much bigger scale.

A careful record of the employment generated in the course of implementation of all development projects and programmes should be maintained, which will have to be comprehensive and its format will have to be carefully worked out. The number of (additional) mandays of employment generated, some economic and social characteristics of persons whose employment is augmented both through obtaining of new jobs or a longer duration of work in their existing occupations should all be noted, along with simultaneously collection of information for estimating unemployment. It is only then that over a period of a year or so, a large body of information on the employment or unemployment situation based on a factual records, will be built up, which will enable the planner to know the extent to which he is succeeding in augmenting employment, where and for whom, and the type of additional effort required in the realm of investment, organizations, institutions, technology, etc., to achieve better results. This will help improve the Planner's understanding of the responses of the unemployed or under-employed, his constraints and preferences.

The major difference between the approach suggested above and the 'traditional' approach to manpower budgeting is that instead of a prior data collection, data should be built up over a year—in fact continuously—from the actual experience gained through the action programme.

XI. A Critical Appreciation

Considering the time and the crucible of political dispensation in which the methodology evolved, it contained some of the most radical thinking of the time. The two crucial elements of the methodology, which were subsequently adopted in at least one operationalised methodology, related to: *one,* promoting a progressively more egalitarian structure of ownership of assets and *two,* building up of appropriate organization of the poor. In order to achieve the second, the methodology emphasized the re-orientation of existing institutions or organizations in order to protect the interests of the poor. The convergence of the rural growth centres and service centres constituted the heart of the methodology with regard to area planning.[14]

These were seminal ideas that were to later catch on and even continue to agitate the committed to this date. The methodology did not suggest any rigid pre-determined ways to build the organization of the poor, obviously because perhaps there can be none. Ways and means to build the organization of the poor depend upon, inter alia, local conditions, involvement and orientation of the people working with the poor, the network of inter-relationship and power-status structure obtaining in the area. The note appended to the *Report* on the alternative approaches followed and results achieved by some of the groups active in this field, though it leaves the solution to the question open ended, is worth reading.[15]

The methodology recognized that amongst the causes that have resulted in poverty and low productivity are absence of basic records of rights in land in many districts, lack of irrigation and deployment of credit. It, therefore, recommended, that block level plan should even encompass the preparation of such records of right. Twelve long years have gone by, yet the wisdom of the methodology in this regard remains undiminished even now, and this is a major problem with which we are grappling even today.

The methodology, however, bid not look deeply into the aspect of Panchayati Raj Institution and it did not take a "definitive stand" on the necessary institutional arrangements for planning at the sub-district level. This is probably because the Ashok Mehta Committee[16] was concurrently going into the functioning of the Panchayati Raj Institutions. There was, however, no bar to the methodology specifying only the *limited* input of these institutions in the planning process at the level under reference, and to the extent that it did not, it suffers from a defect.

A very important element of the methodology related to the building up of a resource inventory without compartmentalizing the operational task of full utilization of the resources. Facts and their analysis should not be a sequential process. Collation of facts, identification of constraints and determination of development potential are all parts of the same exercise in this methodology.[17] The *Status Paper*, talked about in the methodology, in respect of each major sector, would indeed be working operational plan for the sector including indication of projects to be undertaken during the plan period with all details including Cost-Benefit Analysis.

While the debate still continues whether environmental considerations ought to enter into planning at the sub-district (and district)level,[18] the methodology clearly placed emphasis on environmental protection. Despite the fact that this methodology may not be acceptable in its totality, it is still of immense importance that environmental considerations are given serious thought in all micro-level planning activities.

The methodology, however, did not catch on because of the lack of institutional arrangements to execute it, and then it was thought that the block was not the appropriate unit of planning: it was too small an areal unit. The Economic Advisory Council of the Prime Minister with Prof. Sukhomoy Chakravaty as the Chairman, even went on to argue that planning at the district level was of limited efficacy, and they therefore favoured a cluster of four districts on an average, as an appropriate areal unit for decentralized planning. In effect the Economic Advisory Council advocated a regional planning set up with an additional planning tier (without territorial tier of administration being coterminus with it) at the supra-district level.[19] Though these recommendations were not operationalised they did influence thinking on the subject, and abandoning the block as an unit of planning, another Committee was set up to go into the working of District Plans afresh.[20]

Significantly enough, the methodology laid considerable emphasis on growth and infrastructural development. While these are unexceptionable, several economists found that it would have been more appropriate for the methodology to emphasize "development" and not growth per se. Because there has been a shift in the thinking of the profession that development ought to be the goal of State Action (and not merely growth) resulting in the fructification of the right to live long and well, any methodology that intends to emphasize growth per se is likely to be at some discount, even if marginally so. Indeed the methodology seemingly uses the words "growth" and "development" interchangeably which does not make it quite clear which dimension it seeks to lay stress on.

Notes and References

1. Basic Source: Government of India: *Report of Working Group on Block Level Planning* (New Delhi: Planning Commission) 1978.
2. This was presaged in Venugopal Reddy Y.: "Regional Development Plan for Rayalaseema", in Misra, R.P., Urs, D.V. and Natraj, V.K.: *Regional Planning and National Development* (New Delhi: Vikas Publishing House) 1978.

3. This is at variance with the view of Prof. K.N. Raj, we have discussed in an earlier chapter.
4. Smaller the ambit of the area under planning greater the intensity of the planning effort. This view has been subsequently endorsed by the Food and Agriculture Organisation of the U.N. See F.A.O.: *Towards Improved Multi-Level Planning for Agricultural and Rural Development in Asia and the Pacific* (Rome: Food & Agriculture Organisation of the U.N.) 1985. See diagram on the cover page reproduced here as Figure 8.3.

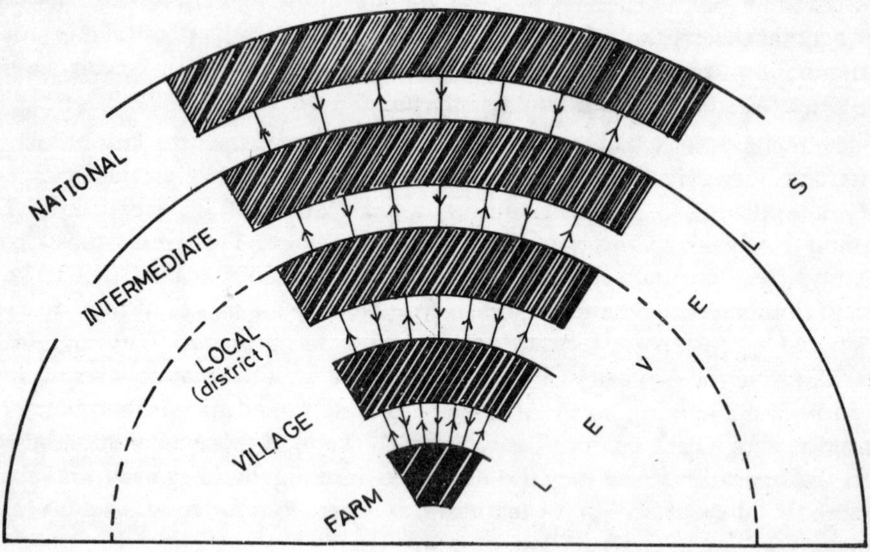

Figure 8.3. Hypothetical multi-level planning system.

5. Here district is not considered as a planning unit. Hence the briefing that is talked about is at the State Level Planning body.
6. See Chapter on "Methodology of Planning for Micro-Region" (V.S. Vyas's Approach) in this Volume and also Gupta, Ranjit (ed.): *Prelude to Block-Level Planning in Gujarat* (Ahmedabad: Centre for Management in Agriculture, Ahmedabad) 1980.
7. See Chapter on AVARD Methodology in this Volume.
8. Roy Prodipto and Patil B.R.: *A Manual on Block Level Planning* (New Delhi: MacMillan) 1977.
9 Recommendation on National "Minimum Needs" Programme, Government of India: *Fifth Five Year Plan* (New Delhi: Planning Commission).
10. *Ibid.*
11. These are elaborated in the Manual for Block Level Planning by Roy and Patil. See *Manual for Block Level Planning,* Edited by Prodipto Roy and B.R. Patil, (New Delhi: MacMillan 1977, Chapter 3, pp. 24-34.
12. (a) Gerard, Rushton et. al.: *Computer Programmes for Location-Allocation Problems* No. 6, Deptt. of Geography, University of Iowa, Iowa City, Iowa 52242, USA, July, 1973. (b) Banerjee, Shyamadas and Fisher H.B.,: "Hierarchical Locational Analysis for Area Planning in India" —Papers of the *Regional Science Association,* 1974, Vol. 33, pp. 177-

194. (c) Patel, Nitin S.: "Operations Research in Planning for Dharampur", IIM, Ahmedabad, (Mimeo) *Working Paper No. 166*, July, 1977.

13. *Report of the Working Group on Block Level Planning, Loc. cit.*.

14. This has been picked up much later in the West Bengal Methodology, we have discussed elsewhere in this book and is being aggressively re-emphasised once again in the current thinking on the subject. See Government of West Bengal: *Gram Bheethick Zela Parikalpna Podhoteegatoe Ruprekha* (Midnapure: District Planning Committee) 1985.

15. The note was prepared by Prof. Ranjit Gupta, a member of the Working Group, who subsequently developed the Dharampur Methodology, with B.M. Desai et al. See the Dharampur Methodology Chapter in this book.

16. See Government of India: *Report of the Committee on Panchayati Raj Institutions* (New Delhi: Department of Rural Development, Ministry of Agriculture and Irrigation) 1978.

17. The noted social scientist Dr. Pradipto Roy was a member of this Working Group. His ideas had clearly found acceptace in this methodology. See Roy, Prodipto et al.: *The Manual on Block-Level Planning*, (New Delhi: Mac Millan), which appeared one year before the publication of the Report of this Working Group, and which is still considered a classic.

18. See *Proceedings* of the International Expert Group Meeting on Decentralized Planning, 11th to 13th June, 1990 in Yugandhar, B.N. and Mukherjee, Amitava (ed.): *Readings in Decentralized Planning*, Vol. I. (New Delhi: Concept Publishing Co.) 1990, pp. 492 to 497, in the same volume "Decentralized Planning: Then and Now : 1973 to 1990", by Yugandhar, B.N. and Mukherjee, Amitava, pp. xv to xxxi.

19. Economic Advisory Council: *First Report of Decentralisation of Development and Implementation in the State*, 4th October 1983, text published in *Economic Times*, New Delhi, 14th January 1984.

20. Government of India: *Report of the Working Group on District Planning* (New Delhi: Planning Commission) 1984.

CHAPTER IX

STEPS IN PLANNING FOR TRIBAL BLOCK

(B. M. DESAI'S APPROACH[1])

I. INTRODUCTION

The methodology can be divided into two parts:

(a) the approach to action research and the objectives of the action plan for the development of a backward tribal area in Gujarat viz. Dharampur taluka in Valsad district, and

(b) the intervention strategy that have been followed to facilitate implementation of the action plan.

II. OBJECTIVES

As regards the first, this methodology adopted more or less the same objectives as suggested by the Dantwala Group[2] namely:

(a) To create a general and operational environment in Dharampur such that within a given period, say, five to seven years, all those who are below the poverty line are brought into the income earning stream and to the incomes that are above the threshold of poverty.

(b) To improve the quality of life of the people, especially the quality of education and health services, in a complementary way—complementary to the programme of income generation.

(c) To organize the programmes such that they do not contribute to a further accentuation of the social and economic inequalities, nor to the depletion of the natural, non-renewable resources of the area.

(d) To ensure the active participation of people at various levels in the organization of the regulatory, supportive, and developmental activities.

In reality these objectives may not all be achieved in full, and indeed measuring the extent of achievement itself may be difficult in many cases. It is also necessary to recognize that these objectives can come in conflict with each other, particularly the objective of providing a threshold income to the rural poor within a short period of time may prove inconsistent with the other set of objectives. It is necessary in such situations to prioritize the objectives. (The Desai et al. set the highest value on wide distribution of economic benefits among the needy).[3] If in so doing the rate of growth of the area is slowed down it will not be considered as unacceptable, because till the orbit of growth is widened to encompass the large masses of the working people, the type of development proposed looses much of its meaning.

III. STEPS

Though an action programme can be interpreted differently by different people, the fact remains that the action for any developmental programme in rural areas is more often than not instituted at the level of a household or an enterprise. An outside agency can rarely organize direct action; it can only influence those who will eventually implement programmes in fields and factories, in schools and health centres, in cultural, social, and political institutions. The role of action research is to *influence* the prime actors by appropriate interventions, which can be exercised in various ways: by influencing policy makers to take specific policy measures, by influencing agencies responsible for creating infrastructure or by influencing those responsible for providing supportive services, or by directly influencing the heads of households or enterprises in the allocation of resources, choice of technology, disbursement of surpluses, and so on. An intervention of this genre can be made through the system of markets and prices or through non-price measures of public investment in research and technology, extension, resources including skills formation and development, economic and social overheads and support institutions. In economically underdeveloped regions, generally non-price interventions become dominant, and as a matter of fact to make price mechanism effective, interventions measures that induce high, stable and self-sustained economic pay-off have to be undertaken to create a suitable responsive climate. Moreover, those non-price instruments that contribute maximum to the earlier discussed objectives should be given high priority.

An action programme of this kind is easier to organize if the objectives for which the actions are designed are clear and explicit. A clear aim structure does not necessarily imply laying down quantitative targets, although in certain cases, especially when the objective is in the realm of economic action, quantifiable targets are helpful in launching or evaluating programmes.[4]

Two more elements of the methodology that may be followed deserve mention. *First,* the main objective has been to create a facilitating or an uninhibiting environment for certain actions. No attempt need be made to prescribe for each individual household a pre-determined course of action, and indeed as a matter of strategy, it is preferable to have those interventions which are likely to influence a whole group.[5] Sheer economy of operations suggests the need for this approach. *Secondly,* emphasis has to be on activizing existing agencies and their functionaries rather than by-passing them or creating alternative, parallel agencies. However, this should not be construed to mean that RDRP is a systems' supportive programme. What is emphasized is that wherever existing arrangements are found wanting or are felt to create difficulties in achieving the given objectives other feasible alternatives should be identified and evaluated. The rationale for working with the existing agencies is thus to maximize to the extent possible the benefits from the investments, human and material, already made.

It also involves identification of area specific constraints, constraints to achieving the plan objectives, and making such interventions as would help relaxing them. Right from the national level the constraints can be classified for analytical convenience into two categories: institutional and economic. The institutional constraints could be in relation to land ownership structure, tenurial relations or conditions, and such other related dimensions, and the economic constraints could lie in the domains of lack of resources, the need for public investment to enable better exploitation of natural resources by individual households, problems of technology evolution and technology transfer, and so on. And then there may be social, political and economic factors inhibiting, say, occupational mobility, or, denial to the weaker sections of society ready access to the supportive institutions such as banks and cooperatives. Apparently, the focus of intervention will have to be on relaxing these constraints, ensuring at once that the interventions have to be such that the primary actors have some control over them, and (granted that resources are scarce) ensuring that the intervenor prioritizes the interventions in terms of their effectiveness or contributions to achieving the plan objectives.

IV. SUMMARY

To sum up, the main steps involved in this methodology are:

- Identification of tasks,
- Identification of agencies and instruments to achieve the tasks,
- Identification gaps in the present structures and prepare appropriate alternatives, and
- Identification methods of influencing the agencies chosen for achieving the given tasks.

V. SOME CLARIFICATIONS

There exists some 10 lakh people who are either unemployed or underemployed. Every year almost 2 lakh persons are added to these categories. Our planning efforts will therefore have to take care of 30 lakhs of people in the next 10 years. Assuming the investment-employment ratio at Rs. 5000 per additional job, the resources needed to provide employment opportunities in the next 10 years will be Rs. 1500 crores, a huge amount by any standard. The amount of resources that can be allocated for employment planning at block level is rather difficult to estimate at this stage, but we can have a rough estimate of the investment required on the assumption that it will be Rs. 5000 per job opportunity.

Notes and References

1. Extracted, with minor modifications, from *Rural Development for Rural Poor: Dharampur Project*, Vol. II, (Contours of Poverty and A Plan for Action), By B. M. Desai, Ranjit Gupta, T.K. Moulik, and V.S. Vyas, Centre for Management in Agriculture, Indian Institute of Management, Ahmedabad, July 1976.
2. Government of India *Report of the Working Group on Block Level Planning* (New Delhi: Planning Commission) 1978.
3. Gupta, Ranjit: *Prelude to Block Level Planning in Gujarat* (Ahmedabad: Centre for Management in Agriculture, Indian Institute of Management) 1980.
4. Bendavid-val, Avrom: *Local Economic Development Planning* (Chicago: American Planning Association) 1980, has categorically emphasized that the objectives should be clearly specified in quantifiable terms, which also helps in making proper assessment of target achievement.
5. Misra and Sundaram had argued very forcefully for adopting the group approach. See Misra R.P. and Sundaram, K.V.: *Multi-Level Planning for Integrated Rural Development in India* (New Delhi: Heritage Publishers) 1980.

CHAPTER X

METHODOLOGY OF PLANNING FOR THE MICRO-REGIONS

(DHARAMPUR METHODOLOGY)

I. INTRODUCTION

This is a simple methodology for planning at the micro level (of a block or a taluka), a methodology that has been devised as a part of an action-research programme of rural development for rural poor in a backward taluka, the Dharampur taluka of Gujarat.[1]

Three clarifications are in order here: *One,* though there is large degree of agreement on the objectives of decentralized planning, it seems that there is, still, some grey area about the basic approach to planning at the block or the taluka level. The planner's interest is neither in too general a plan nor in too specific a plan, because concern is not in global terms, like the rate of growth of income as in case of National Plans. What is of interest to the Planner is in generating incomes for those people who have been identified as the under-privileged sections, namely people below the poverty line. The view earlier held that the results of development at higher levels will percolate down to these people, has now been rejected comprehensively by experts for good reasons. The experience of planning for all these years is available to suggest that such percolation is very slow and tardy. There persists leakages and rigidities, which too are unsurmountable and, therefore, a direct intervention in favour of the poor becomes necessary, particularly so in favour of those groups, namely the weaker sections of society, who otherwise will not receive their share in the increased income. At the same time, the present methodology does not imply that there is need to approach each and every poor households to tell them what they need to do, because any attempt at planning along these lines will mean that the very purpose of decentralized planning will be defeated, which is to create a self reliant community. The scope of the plan, the methodology for which is being detailed below, is the organization of economic activities for the creation of relevant economic opportunities for those groups which are generally by-passed by the "autonomous" forces of economic growth.

Secondly, methodology aims at quick action. Its attempts is that an impact should be made on the economy of these groups within a reasonably short period of time. Therefore, the methodology eschews very elaborate time-consuming exercises, which is it not an impossible task, and there are several short cuts and less elaborate but good procedures. People who have worked in rural areas know that very often there *exists very good indicators which can be used for planning purposes and one need not therefore go into the type of rituals which may be necessary for writing a paper for* an academic journal. What the methodology aims at not an academic exercise, but an exercise for action and an action that has to be initiated within a given time frame. Therefore, one will have to think in terms of what is immediately feasible and then go on improvising as planning proceeds further.[2]

Finally, the methodology delineated in terms of simple steps is based in a large measure on experience gained in course of planning for Dharampur taluka in Gujarat. Although several other exercises of similar kind have been looked at, and lessons from them have been assimilated, and the elements which were found missing in the Dharampur exercise have been incorporated, but the basics applied in the Dharampur project have been retained.

II. THE METHODOLOGICAL STEPS: INTRODUCTORY

It needs to be emphasized at the beginning that even when one has a methodology and approach similar to the Dharampur Methodology, it does not mean that one's report will be the same as that on Dharampur, because of the simple reason that the priorities, allocations and the sequencing will change depending on the specific circumstances. But whatever might be the priorities, allocations or sequencing there has to be some system by which one will arrive at some judgement, for without a systematic approach one will not be able to cope with the problems of planning for an under-developed micro-region.

While starting any such exercise at the micro-level, say a block or taluka level, particularly when people who are entrusted with the planning exercise are not residing in or fully familiar with the area, its economy, polity or institutional framework, they have first to familiarize themselves with the regional background. The planners may be knowledgeable in their own way, many of them might be residing in the selected area for sometime, but let the fact be faced that most of people are not intimately acquainted with the area where they propose to work: their familiarity, at best, is only partial.

III. FIRST ELEMENT: AREA PROFILE

The first element then is an *area profile*, that is, a critical appraisal of the physical features, economy, society, institutional framework, political and administrative set up and the availability or lack of infrastructure. The purposes of drawing up the area profile are two fold: *one*, it provides the context for subsequent exercises, though it is not merely a status report, and *two*, to *identify constraints to development* of the area and the specific groups.

The constraints can be broadly identified in three major categories like physical, institutional and social constraints. The physical constraints, that is, the constraints introduced by the natural and physical features, includes constraints imposed by soil, aridity, climate, geology, hydrology and such other factors. That which is acting as a limiting factor and that which is acting as a constraint to major activity of the area, say, agriculture have to be determined.

All areas are not wholly or mainly dependent on agriculture, and certainly not all the sections of the local people are wholly dependent on agriculture, but a majority of the people are. Even if it is, some other activity, like forestry or animal husbandry, can be located where one can identify physical constraints imposed on the growth of that activity.

Another category is the institutional constraints, and the aspects that one ought to be looking at are the access that people have to the scarce resources, the profile of land ownership and tenancy, difficulty in obtaining credit, availability of facilities; the people who have access to these facilities and the marketing areas. If one concentrates on these three basic institutions, namely institutions pertaining to land, credit and marketing, one will be able to know a lot about the area and its people.

One should also list social constraints, where social factors should be defined in a broad way as for example the caste factors which come in the way of certain economic activities; the inter-caste or inter-religious harmony or lack of it, which inhibit development. One has to know something about the social handicaps to which various groups are subjected to. The main purpose of area profile is to sharpen our understanding of the key variables of socio-economic growth. This focus should not be lost. Most of the information has to be collected by discussions, through meetings with the knowledgeable people, but one must be able to locate the knowledgeable people, who have got a feel about the place, who have in depth knowledge about the physical, social and institutional features of the area. One has to meet and talk with a large number of people, representation a wide cross-section of population. When the Planning team wrote the area profile for Dharampur, four of them were constantly moving around in that area, talking with the people, having meetings among themselves, exchanging notes, deciding what questions remained unanswered and so on.

There are knowledgeable people in each area who have considerable knowledge about most of the aspects a planner should be interested in. In the intensive area profile exercise one should draw on the accumulated knowledge of the local people rather than rediscover the wheel, and the real skill lies in identifying the knowledgeable people and not the "wheel" and being sure about the questions the people may be requested to answer.

The purpose and the approach to Profile Note, is best described thus:

> "At the very outset we should be clear about what we consider the important 'building-blocks' of an economy or a society or a polity. Our main thrust should be to collect factual details—not only the quantitative details—on various ingredients of the system. For example, while working on the profile of the economy of an area, we should try to shift easily available material to give a coherent picture of its economic structure. The main items to be covered in that case would be, first, the availability of productive assets and their broad distribution within the

area and among different sections of the population. The second aspect would be the utilization of these assets with a view to grasp how the various sections of the population derive their livelihood? Thirdly, we should highlight the way in which the existing institutions affect the well-being of the poor. Since all these aspects will be discussed with the help of readily available data, the note should also specify the areas in which further probe should be made in order to collect relevant information by survey or by other techniques for developing the action plan.

"Thus the first major objective in preparing a profile note is to acquaint the researcher with the area. Another over-riding consideration is to identify various constraints which inhibit the development of a region or a people. In this respect also the profile notes will provide first approximation to the problems of the region. This exercise, however, would help the researcher to devise subsequent steps with greater facility."[3]

IV. SECOND ELEMENT: TARGET GROUP IDENTIFICATION

The second element, which is of critical importance, is the identification of the disadvantaged groups, and there exists various ways in which this can be attempted. If one has time and resources one may like to take a census of the household, but such a course need not be resorted to if there exists either paucity of money or of time, in which event it would be expedient to concentrate on a representative sample so that reliable estimates can be built. The sample, or for that matter census results where a census of households is resorted to, will provide the bare, stark, figures, which may leave important questions unanswered. It is possible to know more about the disadvantaged groups by supplementing the enquiry by discussions, by collecting indirect evidences, even by using proxies. It is possible, for example, that with the figures thrown up by sample surveys one may come to conclude that the number of people living below the poverty line in an area for which the plan was being prepared is 39 per cent of the total population. When one takes all the pain to identify each of the households of the landless labour, of marginal farmers and those pursuing rural arts and crafts, the number may work out to be 40 percent of the households in the area, which does not make a world of difference and this is the sort of difference which generally emerges between estimates arrived at through the two alternative methods. These differences are, nonetheless, very important and they should not be overlooked provided one has the time and one has the resources to do scientific, detailed surveys, but where time and resources are limited, which normally is the case one can straightaway start with certain broad indicators, and several such indicators from secondary data exists. The areas or blocks where there is Small Farmers Development Programme, information can be collected on land distribution, on number of landless households, number of households below one acre and so on.

Agricultural census which was conducted every ten years provides the same data, and it would not be surprising to note that several other censuses, surveys and enquiries are being conducted in the countryside. The information contained in the available reports may reveal a good deal about the approximate number and the major attributes of the target groups. Wherever one finds major gaps, a supplementary household survey can be conducted, but a proper collation of available information already existing or collected, should precede any fresh enquiry.

Experience has shown that it is possible to find out without detailed investigations, certain indicators which help in easily identifying the target groups. An expert who has rich experience of survey work in Latin America concluded that in Latin American countries, the poor can be identified as those who are "shirt-less": those who cannot afford the shirts are the poor, which in the Indian context may be redefined in terms of SHOE-LESSNESS AND UTENSIL-LESSNESS: the poor are the "shoe-less" or "utensil-less" people, though it is not necessary to rely totally on such gross indicators. This illustration may be an exaggeration but nevertheless it illustrates the point fairly well that there exists certain indicators by which one can make first approximation, which can later, if necessary, be made more exact by subsequent ground validation. One may start with such a list and then may screen the list to see whether some households are left out, or some households are included who should not have been in the list. For example, one may well take all scheduled castes and scheduled tribes households in an area as poor households, and then check whether there are some affluent households in these categories of people as well. Instead of embarking on a census or conducting a very elaborate survey it may be expedient to start with broad approximations and then start a process of elimination or inclusion. In Dharampur the planning team started with an elaborate survey, but at the end they found that the simplest criterion, to identify poor and not-so-poor was the fact of starvation, that is the indicator for poverty was "food-lessness". All that one required to enquire was whether any individual or family went without even one meal during the course of a particular month. In Dharampur during the month of August and September, hardly any employment is available, and by moving around in that area during these two months and just checking who are the people who do not get two meals a day, one could easily identify the poor households. Obviously in other areas as well there would be some very sensitive indicators that one should know and apply to identify the target groups, which, however, is not to plead against elaborate household surveys, and even if one were to do a statistical survey, findings will not be adequate and you will have to supplement these statistical surveys by informal enquiries.

V. THIRD ELEMENT: INTRODUCTORY OF RESOURCES

The third step (and these are not the sequential steps because the advantage of having a team working together is that one can simultaneously start several activities) or the *third element* in this methodology is to make an inventory of physical and human resources: very clear ideas about what is the resource base of the area for launching a developmental programme is important. The information on the availability of land, water, minerals and raw materials, the traditional skills available in area are to be systematically collected, for these are subsequently to be used for framing realistic programmes. While inventorising physical resources one should also know the extent to which, and the terms on which, the relevant target groups have an access to the physical resources. There may be abundance of very fertile lands in the planning area, for instance, but the target group may not be located on the fertile lands, or may not have access to fertile land, or may have access to fertile land on only very onerous terms.

VI. FOURTH ELEMENT: MAN-POWER BUDGETING

Then comes the fourth element of the plan, namely man-power budgeting. The man-power budgeting talked about in the methodology partakes the nature of partial budgeting. Econometrician may well disapprove the use of the term "budgeting" in this context, but the purpose of planning is served if the planners know the size of the labour force and what will be the accretion to labour force, say, over the span of the next five or ten years. At this stage the concern of the planner does not pertain to the balancing of demand for, and supply of, the manpower; but the concern relates to assessing the dimensions of the present tasks and those tasks which will have to be tackled in the near future. This can be achieved by answering simple questions, with regard to the size of labour force today, the rate of growth of population, and the participation rate, and thus arriving at the magnitude of the labour force at the end of the next five years or at the end of the next ten year period. This obviously indicates that this is the total universe and its segments, in which planners are interested and how this universe along with the segments is going to behave change with the flux of time.

VII. FIFTH ELEMENT : ON GOING PROJECTS

An important element in this methodology is to find out the details of the on-going activities: what are the major activities and what is the absorption of manpower resources in these activities. Admittedly, major activities in most of the rural areas in India are agriculture, animal husbandry (in some areas forestry and fisheries also), mining, cottage and small scale industries, public works construction and certain services. While recording labour absorption in on-going activities, the search is not merely for ascertaining the number of persons employed in these activities in a global sense, that is, in terms of so many 'man years', rather the employment in these activities have to be broken down by seasons, preferably by months, and investigate issues such as the different months of the year during which these activities are pursued in different sectors and the extent of employment generated in these activities. The latter will have to be estimated by using realistic, 'normal' coefficients, otherwise it will become a never ending exercise. First one has to ascertain for each month, what activities are pursued in the different sectors. Take for example agriculture, and let us take the major crops of the area (there may be 7 or 8 major crops in each area), which may cover about 90 per cent of the total cropped area. In every month what operations are done in regard to these crops and how much manpower is needed for the purpose, have to be worked out. A distinction has to be made in terms of irrigated and non-irrigated crops and mechanized and non-mechanized agricultural and agriculture-related operations. The knowledgeable people, say, experienced farmers or the agricultural officers, can provide reliable information. Using some realistic coefficients one can ascertain the disposition of labour for these activities, month by month. The same applies by and large to activities in other economic sectors. For the year-round activities, like the services, the task of estimating labour absorption is simple; where seasonal variations are the rule one has to be much more circumspect.

In addition, one will need to work out the public works component of the governmental activities. Details of the on-going plans have to be ascertained. Once again by application of labour coefficients for road building, soil conservation, afforestation, and so on it is possible to work out without much difficulty the labour absorption in these activities. This exercise also will have to be executed on a month to month basis, and this method of labour absorption estimates may result in a margin of error of, say 5 to 10 per cent, but that is within tolerable limits because a 5 to 10 percent margin of error is unavoidable even in much more elaborate exercises.

Following the two steps narrated above will lead to an identification of, *one*, the labour absorption in the economy and *two*, the labour availability in the economy. By focusing on the relative target groups, an estimate of the "gap" between the labour absorption potential and the labour availability in different groups of households, month by month, at the beginning of the plan period, would be possible.

VIII. SIXTH ELEMENT: GAP IN EMPLOYMENT

As the next step, this "gap" in employment is to be translated in terms of gap in the desirable level of incomes for different groups of households. The planners could concentrate on following four groups, namely, (i) landless labourers, (ii) marginal farmers, that is, those cultivating less than 1 hectare of land, (iii) rural artisans, and (iv) small farmers, namely, cultivating land between 1 to 2 hectare.

A list of the projects in an area which are identified as a part of the national, state or district plans needs to be then drawn up. The skill of the planner lies in estimating their impact on the employment and income levels of the target groups. For determining the threshold income level, one can take the national norm, viz., Rs. 40 per capita per month. And most of the people engaged in organized sector, those serving in formal organizations and the cultivators above 5 acres of holdings, may be assumed to be non-poor, and it is the remaining groups for whom the income gap has to be identified. Here the planner will be required not only to work out the direct employment and income generation effects, but also the secondary or link effects. For instance, while estimating employment and income generating impact of an irrigation project one has also to look into the secondary round of activities, like intensive agriculture or multiple cropping. It is difficult and probably meaningless to think in terms of an employment multiplier at the level of a block or a taluka. It is more realistic to estimate direct and the "linked" effects of the programmes.

IX. SEVENTH ELEMENT: INTRODUCTION OF ACTIVITIES

The next important element relates to identifying activities which will fill the "residual gap", after taking into account the planned activities. The process of identification of such activities can be simple, by the rule of thumb, or by more sophisticated technique. It is necessary to go into more precise methods at this stage. Firstly, because for the type of programme that the planners may have in view it may be expedient that the activities should satisfy several requirements, as for example, the activities should be labour intensive, quick maturing and non-exploitative all of which characteristics cannot be satisfied by simple intuitive judgements. Secondly, a proper exercise in project identification and formulation can result in a good deal of saving of the scarce resources. Just to cite one example, while estimating cost of services centres and road network in Dharampur, the figures suggested on the basis of conventional methods were exhorbitant, but by resort to a bit more scientific method of the standard OR Techniques, it was demonstrated that the same results can be obtained with one-third of the original cost. Wherever easily usable scientific methods are available their application should be unhindered. One need not, however, resort to use of scientific methods merely for the sake of novelty. It is in this context that some programming exercises become essential which can give relative weights to different activities, and can introduce various constraints. The simpler ways of identifying projects may turn out to be more wasteful.

X. EIGHTH ELEMENT: SUPPORTIVE SERVICES

Once having decided the nature of economic activities which are being planned for the respective target groups, the next element is to plan the supportive services for these activities, where comes the question of physical infrastructure, such as roads, power etc., and the supportive systems such as marketing, credit and so on. When one attempts at identifying an activity and it is not being done just to illustrate a point but in order to invest community's resources, it is essential to see that these resources are properly utilized. Resources, scarce as they are, cannot be properly utilized despite the project being well conceived, unless the supportive services are present. One has to ask oneself, "if I have agreed on the basis of whatever calculations, whatever exercises, that 'x' number of poultry units, carpentry shops or pumps repair workshops are to be set up, whether supportive services are available for sustaining them ? Or am I asking for something for which supportive services are not available and, therefore, they will be failures." Several of these schemes have failed because the supportive services were not planned properly, because one did not conceptualise the need for the services which are critically important for making the projects viable. A poultry unit without proper marketing arrangements has no future because after all there is a limit to the number of eggs that the owners of the poultry units can consume themselves. Thus, when one is proposing poultry units one has to ascertain the market for the eggs and ensure that the channel of communication and transport between producing areas and the marketing centres exists. The existence of an organization to transport these eggs to that market is equally important. It does not, however, mean that if supportive services are not available project should be rejected in *limine;* it only implies that the planner has to ascertain the extent to which it is possible to provide the supportive services as well.

XI. NINTH ELEMENT: BANKABLE PROJECTS

Once some notion is formed about the activities which can be suggested to bridge the gap between the existing and the threshold income, it is necessary to translate these in terms of bankable projects. The broad activities by themselves do not help because a stage comes when assistance of financing agencies will become necessary, or projects have to be defended before State government or other public agencies.[4] The type of plans being discussed here should contain a portfolio of bankable projects, for it would then become easier to convince the State authorities or the financial institutions to take up these projects for implementation. Methodology of project formulation is fairly well standardized, and is a type of exercise that can be done very easily and familiarity with this methodology is quite common.

XII. TENTH ELEMENT: QUALITY OF LIFE

It has to be realized that the type of activities being talked about so far though focused on raising the economic level of the needy sections are not enough. If we do not think in terms of raising the quality of life of the target group, who are the weaker sections of society, we will soon come back to the point where the economy, for which plans are being prepared, would relapse into the position from where the beginning was made. The target groups are also entitled for as much of support in terms of health care, nutrition, education, housing, as other groups which are less unfortunate and more privileged.[5] Indeed, the former groups need these facilities urgently and in greater quantum than the latter. In their case such services will not be available through the system of markets and prices: they will have to be provided as state supported activities, which brings in another aspect of planning, namely planning for social services.

There are two aspects of planning of social services, one the physical aspect of size and location and another the organizational aspects. While thinking about the first aspect the typical decision relates to a decision about the location of different types of services which can contribute to the improvement in the quality of life so that cost can be minimized. As a rough approximation, it is safe to assume that many of our village have a population of less than 500, which makes it inexpedient to have a primary health unit, a school, a post office, a cooperative society or a fair-price shop in each one of these villages. The decision with regard to locating those facilities, sometimes called "functions", has to be taken, and there are methods of deciding, which are again relatively simpler methods. The location of the activities which contribute to the improvement of the quality of life is an essential and a crucial activity in a plan for economic development and it is important to take these locational decisions carefully because these activities are mostly capital intensive, apart from the fact that it is difficult to evaluate their effectiveness. Whereas books of account reveal clearly whether an economic enterprise is succeeding or failing, in case of infrastructure investment the impact will not be known till one probes very deep. It is all the more necessary, therefore, to be careful in the initial stages while planning for these various services. Discussion about the organizational aspects may not be indulged in now, because that will take us to the quality of these services, not because a consideration of the quality aspect is less important, but because the planners have to decide on the question of what quality of service they are expecting from these institutions.[6]

XIII. ELEVENTH ELEMENT : MONITORING

Lastly comes the question of monitoring the programmes, so that after making all the desirable plans, the area for which planning is being done may not again slip back into the pattern which have been inherited from the past. Today even if it is ensured that only certain groups are benefited from an activity, soon the leakages would start and the benefits would start flowing, not to the target groups but, to the not-so-poor segment of the society, which suggests the need for a timely warning system. As in agriculture, where planners are now trying to develop the concept of timely warning system, in development plans as well, a system of timely warning has to be incorporated, which means keeping under close observations some critical sensitive indicators which can be easily identified. Unfortunately, not enough thought has been given to this aspect of planning, and answer to such questions, how can one determine whether the intended benefits have reached to the poor or not; or can it be done simply by going around, talking with people, or can there be other indicators, are still quite unsatisfactory and there is not much to offer barring some very tentative indicators. Nevertheless an exercise in monitoring the planned efforts and their impacts on the target groups will have to be done at all levels, at State level, at the district level and at the block or taluka level.

XIV. SUMMARY

These are the elements in a planning methodology which aims at reaching the rural poor in a micro-region, which even at the risk of sounding too simplistic is worth pondering over.

It is worth emphasizing that planning is a mechanism to achieve given objectives. Where the objectives are not clear, if the objectives are fuzzy, all these exercises will not carry us far. But if one's objectives are clear, one's direction is clear, then one can always improvise and chalk out a path. Before starting an exercise on local level planning, the questions that should be answered are: for whom are we planning and what type of structure will we like to have at the end of the plan period? Better still, make it explicit about the reason for which we not satisfied with the present system.

XV. ELABORATION OF CERTAIN POINTS

(a) For collection of information there are more than one sets of questionnaires.[7] These have been provided simply to illustrate the design of enquiry that may be adopted to prepare the action plan for a block or area. Besides enumerating the steps that may be followed, they contain the proformae and the tabulation design that may be used to analyse and present a wide range of data, and much of the information requirements of these questionnaires can be obtained from secondary or recorded sources. There is surely no question of compulsion. The planning teams are free to pick and chose whatever they feel might help them in preparing plans relevant to the needs and potential of the areas or blocks under plan.

(b) With regard to undertaking a survey and use of secondary data two points need clarification:

(i) Is a survey inescapable or can some alternative ways of collecting the required data be taken recource to?

(ii) How much flexibility would there be in instituting the survey ?

As regards sources of data, there is a need for collecting primary data, for it will help in planning our efforts better. It is agreed that the plan must be in consonance with the needs of the local people. What is it that we should or should not include in the data collection exercise can be best judged by the institutions involved in block planning. There might be several questions which are not included in these questionnaires but have relevance for a particular area, which explains why there ought to be complete freedom to add or delete whatever is felt meaningful.

As regards the specifics of the survey, it is the local institution, in cooperation with the district planning team, that should decide what needs to be done in the light of the local conditions obtaining. They are the best judges, and one cannot decide in advance which of the questions need be deleted and/or which new ones ought to be added. Nobody wants the survey to be of such a nature that it will not be sensitive to local wisdom. If that were the intention one could have requested Investigators to collect and process the information.

(c) The identification of homogeneous groups needs some comments. On homogeneity, people with different academic background may have different ideas. One trained in economics may have views which need not be always acceptable to others trained in other disciplines. The basic objective is to identify groups around an economic activity, a local activity which can be performed by a group of people, namely, the target group. Thus, basket-weavers could be one group; fishermen another; small farmers a third group; and so on, *but these groups again need not be multiplied into umpteen categories, because poverty does not have umpteen factors*, but, in terms of planning, certain groups can be identified on the basis of their activities. One would go in more for those groups (for the purpose of planning) which share a certain homogeneity, say, with respect to an activity which brings them together.

If you take the income criteria, it may be possible to identify those who have income less than a desirable level. The question then would relate to raising their incomes to that pre-determined level, and the planner starts with the hypothesis that their incomes can be augmented mostly through optimum utilization of labour, an asset which these households posses in abundance. Thus, starting with income, if it is possible to find out the employment pattern month by month for certain groups of people, and taking the growth potentials into account, perhaps it may be possible to estimate the additional income that can be or need to be generated.

(d) Regarding resource inventory there cannot be a rigid criterion, because the very concept of resource today is a dynamic concept. The local expertise, local knowledge. local acquaintance, local conditions can tell us better about the resources that are important with regard to planning for their relative area.

(e) Some mention can be made about the psychological factors such as incentive or motivation to work, which are applicable to all of us. There are some groups of people who have low motivation, while there are others who have high motivation. An illustration would clarify the point. Some experts were trying to find out what kind of access the poor have to the functionaries in Deogarh tehsil of Udaipur district, Rajasthan. Surprisingly, they found that the Patwari is the one functionary whom the largest number of the poor contacted. It was even more surprising that the landless labourers or marginal farmers went to the Patwari when they had nothing to do with Patwari or Talati, but it emerged, upon deeper probe that because there was a programme of land allocation for building houses, these poorer sections of society contacted the Patwari, which is indicative of the fact that if people are convinced that they can benefit from a programme, they will try to fully utilize it.[8]

Whether and how people are motivated thus depends a good deal on the quality and content of the programme: if employment or income generating opportunities are very limited, the poor in our society adopt quite justifiably a third party attitude and they do not get involved for they know that these opportunities are not for them. Here the organization of groups becomes important. One of the elements of group organization is that there should be *achievable opportunities*, which in itself will urge people to come together. In the example mentioned earlier, everyone without exception went to the Patwari of Deogarh Tehsil because there was an achievable opportunity, viz., allotment of house sites.

(f) The question of land reforms and institutional change is important. No plan at any stage can neglect the questions pertaining to land reforms, for land reforms constitute a necessary condition for the agricultural development of the country.[9] Wherever land reforms have been successfully implemented there has been better agricultural performance, and in all areas where there is a lukewarm attitude towards land reforms or where land reforms have been defeated, the performance of agriculture has been extremely poor. In some Asian countries like Indonesia, Malaysia and Thailand, the land holdings in these countries are smaller than ours, but the standard of living is higher though it may not be as high as Europe or America, but it is far better than ours, because these countries have evolved systems which have made it possible for a person having even one hectare of land to produce enough not only to make both ends meet but also to have surplus for investment in other sectors.

SOME OBSERVATIONS

Dharampur Methodology is one of the few methodologies that has been made by an academic and research institution. It is an example of how fruitful action research could be, in as much as the methodology evolved out of the Indian Institute of Management, Ahmedabad's attempt at evolving blue-print for rural development in four typical poor and under-developed areas in the country: a tribal, a drought prone, an area with severe institutional handicaps and a poverty ridden area. The Dharampur Methodology related to planning for a tribal area.

The methodology takes the preparation of the area Profile Notes (basically resource inventory highlighting resource potentials and problems) on physical social, economic and organizational dimensions of the area under plan, which would bring forth several problems requiring deeper research, which were then to be siezed upon for more detailed investigation through primary surveys.

Based on information available from both secondary sources and primary survey, an action plan for the area has to be chalked out.

The methodology advocates adoption of a strategy for economic development based on what is called income-employment approach, that is, additional income or employment needed per worker to ensure a threshold income, for which the households are to be stratified into three groups. Additionally, the methodology finds merit in providing necessary infrastructure (to strengthen the process of economic development) through spatial planning of services, which the essence of service-centre approach.

The methodology clearly envisges indicative plan because it disfavours detailed prescription for that would militate against this genre of planning where the dominant emphasis is on the beneficiaries themselves deciding the nitty-gritty of the schemes or programmes they want and the institutions they wish to statulise. The greater emphasis in the methodology to place reliance on local knowledge may be germane to this perspective. The researches in agricultural economics so far have revealed that the Indian farmers, given the state of art and given the constraints, acted rationally. This methodology, in very many words, extends this rationality to the rural poor and leaves a good deal of the decision making appertaining to their welfare on their judgement and wisdom.

The methodology thought well ahead of its time in that it attempted at measuring poverty using starvation as a measure ("foodlessness" vis-a-vis "shirtlessness" in Latin America) for locating the poverty line,[10] employed the criterion of a "threshold income" as the cut-off point and with this as the base, estimates are required to be made of both the proportion of labour force below the poverty line, and the additional employment necessary per capita, at normal wage rate so that threshold income is made available to the people below the poverty line in the area. The methodology, therefore, seeks to estimate the shortfall in employment opportunities through income analysis.

The forward looking elements in the Dharampur Methodology is brought out in sharpest focus where it talked about improving the quality of life. When economists and politicians were still struggling to come out of GNP as a measure of well-being, the methodology was hinting at improving the quality of life.[11] By so doing, the methodology advocated, and correctly so, the development of people, as opposed to development of the area, in any micro-level exercise.[12]

ANNEXURE I: DESIGN OF ENQUIRY

The annexure presents the details of the methodology to study the area's resources, growth constraints, development potentialities, social structure, functioning and structure of development administration and other agencies in the area, including the results of earlier development efforts etc. Most of this information, qualitative as well as quantitative, can be collected from secondary sources, a list of which is given at Annexure-II.

I. PHYSICAL FEATURE AND INFRASTRUCTURE

Resource inventory should include a descriptive but analytical study of the physical features and potentials of the area/region under planning namely its topography, rainfall, roads and rivers, land use, soils and land capability classes, irrigated areas by types of works, village settlements, location of markets (*hats*) and other institutions such as schools, health centres, and development offices which will help in mapping out a programme of action for tapping the physical potentialities of the area. Information should be supplemented by maps and charts, and though the bulk of data required is expected to be available with district development departments, including the census organisation, field investigation would be necessary to cover the gaps in the light of data collected from secondary sources.

A. Maps

1. Following maps could be obtained from district departments:

(a) Toposheet (scale : 1" = 1 mile);

(b) Road and river systems including power transmission lines.

(c) Sources, location and command of existing irrigation works.

(d) Location of public institutions like schools, block or taluka development offices, primary health centres, post offices, input supply centres, fair price or ration shops, power supply centres or power supply sub-centres, ranger's office and the like.

(e) Village settlements.

(f) Location and operational area of markets and weekly *hats*, which may have to be plotted in consultation with concerned departments.

(g) Soil survey maps, if available.

(h) Any other maps readily available.

B. Other Records

2. The following reports/publications which would be obtained from official sources will be found particularly useful:

(a) District Census Handbooks.

(b) District Gazetteer.

(c) Annual reports and plans of different district development departments, including PWD, Power and Electricity, TDO, BDO etc.

(d) Soil survey reports, if available; otherwise whatever data on soils are available with the Soil Conservation Officer.

(e) Geological survey reports revealing the mineral resources of the area/region.

(f) Any other reports describing the physical features and potentialities of the area under planning.

C.Data Collection

3. The following data from the above sources could be collected/compiled:

(a) Land use (for various years).

(b) Monthly rainfall and temperature data for 19__(Classify this data by crop seasons or quarterly intervals, January to March, April to June and so on— whichever fits in with the crop calendar or practices locally followed. Prepare three, four and five yearly moving averages of the data thus classified.)

(c) Number of irrigation works in use and their command by type of works; also number of works not in use but repairable by type of works. (Classify this data according to the natural regions in which area is divided, each region could be further divided into upland and lowland categories.)

(d) Hydrological data showing the irrigation potential of the rivers in the area/region.

(e) Capacity, supply and consumption of electric energy (19___) in the district and the block. (Consumption data to be recorded by source or use viz. agriculture, industry, domestic, street lighting etc.)

(f) Details of roads (Kutcha, Pucca, all-weather etc.) in the block/district, and the corresponding polymetric table of distances.

(g) Crop calendar locally followed showing the months when different crops (both major and minor) are sown, inter-cultured, and harvested.

(h) Soil survey data showing soil series, soil types, texture, pH value, reaction, capability classes etc. (If soil survey reports is not available, obtained whatever data are available with the District Soil Conservation Officer.)

(i) Any other relevant data e.g. seepage and evaporation rates, scale and incidence of soil errosion, recommended practices, including cropwise for cultivation etc.

Irrigation Survey

4. Prepare separate maps of each river showing its course or direction, water depth at different points during different seasons, location of

major pockets where loss of water is caused by run-off and uneven topography, suitable points for construction of check dams/barrage, cultivable land along the river banks etc.

5. Potentiality for drawing water from these rivers through lift irrigation devices and/or other means (specify), estimates of acreage which could be brought under irrigation. (What is the possibility of damage to such devices during monsoon? What measures may be taken to minimize this possibility?)
6. Number and location of major pockets where irrigation tanks could be built. (Also indicate the estimated command of such works.)
7. Number and location where check dams and bunds could be built. (Also indicate the estimated command of such works.)
8. Details of groundwater resources and their use potentials.

An indicative tabular design to record or present the various types of data listed in this section is given in the enclused set of 18 tables.

Physical Features and Infrastructure

1. *Area and Density of Population by Block/District*

Block	Total area (sq. Km.)	Total Population (000)	Density (per cultivable land)	Rural area/Population as Percentage of Block total	
				Area	Population

2. *Land Use Per Capita Cultivable Land*

Particulars	Area	Per cent
Land use (acres/hectares)		
Forest		
Cultivable waste		
Area not available for cultivation		
Cultivable land		
	Total :	
Total population		
Per capita cultivable land		

3. *Physiography of the Region*

4. *Soils (Description)*

5. *Soil Series and Their Characteristics by Physiographic Position*

Physiographic Position	Soil Series	Depth, Texture & Colour
1. Dissected Hilly Terrain		
1.1 Hill plateaus and escarpment slopes:		
(a) Pietmont plateaus (3-7% slope)		
2. Foothill slope (5-10% slope)		
3. Piedmont slope (3-5% slope)		
4. Flood Plain (1-3% slope)		

6. *Problems Limited Soil Use and Recommended Practices by Soil Association*

Soil Association	Problems	Recommended Practices

7. *Chemical Analysis of Soils*

Series of Association	Available Nutrient Nitrogen in form of Organic Carbon	Status in %P2 O5 K2OP^H EC

8. *Temperature in Fahrenheit*

	19...........	19...........	19...........
January			
Minimum			
Maximum			
April			
Minimum			
Maximum			
July			
Minimum			
Maximum			
October			
Minimum			
Maximu			

9. *Mean Temperature in Fahrenheit* (Decade Average: 19–19)

Month	Minimum	Maximum
January		
February		
March		
April		
May		
June		
July		
August		
September		
October		
November		
December		

10. *Rainfall and Water Resources (Description)*

11. *Annual Rainfall (Decade Average)*

Inch	Millimeter

12. *Monthwise Distribution of Annual Rainfall*

Month	Normal Rainfall	Average Annual Percentage of Rainfall (Post Rainfall Decade)
January		
February		
March		
April		
May		
June		
July		
August		
September		
October		
November		
December		
Annual		

13. *Annual Rainfall & Variation from Decade Average (%)*

Year	Annual Rainfall (Inch)	Variations from Decade Average(%)

14. *Estimated Potentials of Rivers and Alternative Sites for Irrigation Projects*

River Project Site	Type	Catchment area at size (Sq. Mile)	Gross Storage Capacity (Mc ft)	GCA (acres)	Power genera-tion	Estimated costs

15. *Groundwater Resources in the Block (Description)*

16. *Shops and trading Establishments (Weekly 'hats')*

Village	Shops/'Hat' days

17. *Communication (Roads)*

1) Condition
   ii) Length (Miles)
   iii) Places connected within the block their distances (in miles) from the starting point
   iv) Other roads connecting the Highway in the block

18. *Details of other roads in the Block*

Roads Running From	To	Total Length(mile)	on which Metalled Length (mile)	Unmetalled Length (mile)

19. *Power Supply*

i) No. of Villages electrified
ii) Total consumption of electric energy.

20. *Consumption of Electric Energy in the Block (19 -19)*

Village/ Town	Total Consumption (KWH)	Percentage distribution by uses			Existing Transformer with Capacity
		Agriculture	Industry	Domestic	

II. EDUCATION, HEALTH AND HOUSING

Education

1. Literacy rates according to census classification; number and proportion of school-going children (male and female), seasonal variations in school attendance, reasons for such variations, those who completed school education how and where are they generally placed?
2. Dropout rates by level or standard of education (primary, middle, secondary etc.) and type of educational institution, reasons for dropout at different levels, educational aspirations of those out of school (14-25 years), their problems and needs.
3. Who are the parents who send their children to school? Why do they send them to school? What do they expect of them? What are their problems with regard to educating their children? What is their background—social, economic and educational? Are they interested in getting themselves educated through some form or method?
4. The number of educational institutions presently functioning in the block by type and level (pre-primary, primary, middle, higher secondary, technical etc.), the system or method of education followed by them.
5. Who are the people manning these institutions—their background and academic attainments? What is their perception of the institutions and programmes they are manning? What do they expect of their students?
6. How about students and parents ? What is their perception of the educational programmes and institutions?

(In short, a qualitative but factual account of the education status of the people.)

Public Health

1. The rate and incidence of various kinds of diseases and ailments, wherever possible, by sex and broad age groups, seasons and peak periods of their occurance, yearly or any other periodic trends, birth rates, death rates and infant mortality rates, trends in such rates (say, during the past decade).
2. Availability of drinking water during different seasons/months. Sources of drinking water supplies and their adequacy. What is the situation in summer? Where do the people go or how do they get drinking water during summer? How many villages have no source of drinking water of their own? In which parts of the taluka these villages are concentrated? (Identify) The maximum, average and minimum distances from village to source of drinking water supply.
3. Sanitary conditions inside and outside huts; personal and public hygiene practices commonly followed.

Medical Care and Family Planning

1. Facilities available for medical care (traditional and modern, both public and private) in various parts of the block, number and regional distribution of private practitioners (quacks, qualified doctors etc.) and primary health centres and sub-centres.
2. Appropriate outturn of patients treated by such practitioners and health centres during different months or by peak and slack seasons—approximate distribution of such patients by type of disease during peak and slack seasons, approximation proportion of cases cured.
3. Number of beds available for indoor patients, facilities for handling delivery cases, number of such cases handled by different categories of doctors/medical centres, approximate distribution of delivry cases by peak and slack periods.
4. Nature and type of medical services normally rendered by primary health centre/sub-centres, background of key personnel manning these centres. What medical facilities are generally available during monsoon when communication system is disturbed, where do the patients go for treatment during this period and for what type of ailments?
5. Family planning facilities and services normally rendered, the extension agency set up for this purpose, and such other details revealing the present status of family planning.

Nutrition

1. List of food items, (including alcohol, fat, oil, milk, sugar/gur, vegetables, fruits, mahua etc.) generally consumed by different groups

during different seasons or months, approximate per capita or per household daily intake of these items during different seasons/months, nutritional value of such intakes.

2. The physical appearance of children, men and women belonging to different groups, their general stamina, nutritional deficiencies and maladies or diseases arising out of such deficiencies.

(Apart from knowledgeable persons, consult local doctors, both official and private.)

Housing

1. General housing conditions of different groups, physical description of these houses, (e.g. materials used, nature of construction, number of rooms, their areas or space, ventilation, attached courtyard and cattleshed or barn, hygienic conditions within and around the house etc.).
2. Approximate construction costs of different types of houses and such other details revealing the housing conditions and status.

Review of Programmes

A general review of the efforts made and the programmes undertaken in the foregoing fields will be useful. The programmes and activities to be reviewed are:

1. Education (from pre-primary to higher education through different institutional arrangements such as Ashramshala, primary-higher secondary schools, vocational training etc.).
2. Health and medical care, including drinking water, nutrition and family planning.
3. Provision for house sites.
4. Tribal welfare through development of forest and/or protection of rights of tribals to use forest products.
5. Other social welfare programmes if any.

A factual description of these programmes in the block in comparison to the district may be attempted. The review should reveal among other things the following:

1. The stated objectives of each of these programmes and the activities undertaken during the past decade (or, more wherever necessary) to realise them. (The special features of these programmes should also be indicated.)

2. Periodic (yearly, five-yearly etc.) progress and achievements in terms of monetary and physical targets, problems and difficulties encountered during various stages of programme implementation, comparative performance of each of these programmes in block/district.
3. People's perception of each of these programme. Also, their perception of the role of programme functionaries. How are these programmes linked with the needs of the people.
4. Functionaries' perception of programmes and people's need.
5. Overall, impressionistic assessment of the impact of each of these programmes in the block based on informal discussions with knowledgeable persons, both officials and non-officials.

General

Bibliography of all published and unpublished materials, including official reports, monographs etc. dealing with the problem/programmes under study, if prepared, will facilitate further probing.

III. ECONOMIC STATUS OF THE BLOCK/AREA

Introduction

The theme of this section may be woven around the following questions:

> What are the resources of the people in the block? How are these resources used by them in the past and at present? What constraints are faced by them in the use of resources? What is the pattern of past and existing development programmes that may have bearing on the use of resources?

To examine these questions date and observations could be obtained from secondary sources, published literature and also from interviews with knowledgeable persons and agencies. Reference period for quanitative variables could be 5 or 10 years preceding the survey year. Exceptions to this should be stated along with the variables concerned. The investigation should first seek information from secondary sources (such as District Census Handbook, Records at the District and Block Development Offices etc.) and then from primary sources (such as knowlegeable persons, mimeographed and other studies). At some stage of work particularly on questions for primary investigation, some selected individuals from different parts of the block may be interviewed. In the process of this work selected bibliography may also be prepared.

The outline should focus on the resources and their use pattern. In addition, it should cover some questions on migration and rural crafts and industries pursued by the people in the area. Wherever possible distinct characteristics by which various parts of the block differ in the resources and their use pattern may also be highlighted.

Aggregate Economy

Secondary Sources

1. Location and areas including the distinct geographical and locational characteristics of various parts of the block.
2. Rainfall and temperature in different months of years since 19___ to 19_____.
3. Land use pattern in various years since 19_____ to 19_______. This should also include information on net cultivable land and net irrigable land.
4. Population by sex, and its growth rate according to 1961 and 1971 censuses.
5. Occupational pattern according to 1961 and 1971 censuse.

Primary/Secondary Sources

Migration: Is migration a common source of earning livelihood in the block? Has its importance increased in recent times? Why? Who are the people (landless, small farmers, Harijans, tribals etc.) who migrate? Where do they migrate—outside the block and/or within the block? If within the block, from which areas do they migrate and where? What are the reasons for migration? In which months do they migrate? What are the activities migrants engage in?

Crop-Farming

Secondary Sources

1. Distribution of cultivators, their land holding, number of fragments, and ownership status in the year for which information is available. (Also include number of landless labourers.)
2. Bullock labour, 1966, 1971 and 1976, and 1976 censuses.
3. Farm implements by major types, 1966, 1977, and 1976 censuses.
4. Area under each crop in each season in various year since 19_____to 19____ also include not cultivable land and net irrigable land, 19____to 19_____.

5. Area under mixed cropping in various years. Names of crops grown in mix.
6. Area under double cropping in various years. Also find out method of calculating double cropping.
7. Production of each crop in each year since 19______ to 19_______.
8. Total use of different fertilizers, insecticides and pesticides in each year since 19_______ to 19________.
9. Total use of improved seeds by types of each crop in each year since 19___ to 19___.
10. Total availability of institutional credit (i.e. sum of maximum credit limit sanctioned for each credit/service cooperative) and its disbursement in various years since 19___ to 19____.
11. Prices of each crop at harvest times in each year since 19___ to 19____.
12. Procurement prices of each crop whose produce is procured, if at all, by government in the form of levy etc., in various years since 19___ to 19___.
13. Details of crop-farm development programmes for the latest year for which information is available. (See Table 1)
14. During the scarcity years which resources like tanks, roads etc. were created in the block? (Enquire separately about the reasons for each type of resource created.)
15. Obtain the details about Land Reforms with specific reference to (a) Abolition of Intermediaries, (b) Tenancy, and (c) Ceiling on holding.

Primary Sources

1. Is there increase in the number of landless people in recent years? If yes, why? and in which parts of the block/area?
2. Is there increase in the average size of holding in various parts of the block? If yes, why? and in which parts?
3. What crops are suitable to each soil type?
4. Do farmers keep (cultivable) land fallow in Kharif seasons? If yes, in which parts? and why?
5. What are the crop-rotations usually followed? What are the reasons behind them? Is there a marked change in this practice now compared to that in the past? If yes, indicate the nature of change and reasons for change.
6. What are the reasons for mixed cropping? Is there any change in this practice now compared to that in the past? If yes, indicate the nature of change and reasons for change.

Table 1

Type of programme	No. of villages covered	Area covered and employ ment gene-rated for items (a) to(e)	Financial costs and rate of subsidy given	Specific reasons for introduction	No. of villages which continued the programme its expiry	If some villages did not continue, why? (get as much detail as possible)	Future plan with reference to items in columns 2,3,4,6, &7
(1)	(2)	(3)	(4)	(5)	(6)	(7)	(8)
a) Bunding							
b) Soil conservation							
c) Contour ploughing							
d) Ridges & furrows							
e) Preparing Kyari Land:							
i) By manual labour							
ii) By bulldozer							
f) Distribution of improved and/or HYV seeds of various crops:							
i) Paddy							
ii) Jowar							
iii) Wheat							
iv)							
v)							
vi)							
g) Distribution of fertilisers by types							
i)							

(1)	(2)	(3)	(4)	(5)	(6)	(7)	(8)
ii)							
iii)							
iv)							
h) Distribution of pesticides and insecticides							
i)							
ii)							
iii)							
iv)							
i) Irrigation							
i) Wells							
ii) Oil engine							
iii) Elec. motor							
iv) Pipe lines							
v) Traditional lifts							
vi) Others (specify)							
j) Demonstration plots for							
i) Kyari Farming							
ii) HYV seeds							
iii) Fertilizers							
iv) Insecticides							
v) Pesticides							
vi) New crop							
vii) Others (specify)							

7. Was the crop-pattern different in the past? Which were the other crops grown? Why are they not grown now? What factors led to the introduction of new crops?
8. What crops compete with each other in a given season? Why?
9. Describe the operations carried out in various types of soils for various crops in each month from July to June.
10. Indicate the use of labour on an acre of land of each major crop in various months and for various operations.
11. What are the marketing facilities for paddy, wheat, jowar, negli, sugarcane and any other major crop in the block? (This may include existence of regulated markets and their location, privatre traders in 'hats' and in the local villages etc.)
12. What are the credit facilities available to the farmers?

Orchard-Farming

Secondary and Primary Sources

1. Acreage under and number of trees of different types (mango, chiku, etc.) in each year since 19___ to 19____. If this information is already covered above, please do not repeat.
2. Production of main fruits in each year since 19_____ to 19_____.
3. Describe the calendar of work for a typical orchard in its initial and later stages of growth.
4. Describe the marketing facilities for major fruits.
5. What are the areas (i.e. number and location of villages) where potentialities for developing orchards exists?
5. What are the areas (i.e. number and location of villages) where potentiality for developing orchards exists?
6. Which villages are assisted in this regard by the block and / or Development Office?

Dairy Farming

Secondary Sources

1. Number of milch animals by types and breeds, 1966, 1971 and 1976 censuses.
2. Birth rate and death rate of milch animals, 1966, 1971, and 1976 censuses.

3. Area under grass and other fodder crops (specify) in each year since 19____ to 19_____. (If this information is already covered above, please do not repeat.)
4. Details of Development Programmes for the latest year for which information is available. (see Table 2).

Primary Sources

1. Is dairy-farming pursued by most farmers? Why is it pursued as subsistence-oriented or market-oriented activity? What constraints are faced by farmers in this activity?
2. What are the water facilities in the block? Please describe them with reference to their quality, adequacy, in different months of a year and their source.
3. Is the grass produced in the block sold? If yes, why and where? Does this practice cause shortage of fodder for the animals in the block? If yes, why? Is this practice followed? How the problem of shortage tackled if at all? What are the possible solutios? What are the possible solutions? What are the marketing facilities for dairy-products?

Poultry-Farming

Secondary Sources

1. Number of poultry birds by types, 1956, 1971 and 1976 censuses.
2. Birth rate, death rate of each type of bird, 1966, 1971 and 1976 censuses.
3. Are there commercial units of poultry farming in the block? If yes, obtain details such as their number, location, and their source of financial and technical support for latest year for which information is available.
4. Details of development programmes for the latest years. (See Table 3.)

Primary Sources

1. Are poultry-birds kept by most people including landless labourers in the block? Why? Is this activity pursued mainly as subsistemce-oriented or market oriented activity? What constraints are faced in this activity?
2. What are the marketing facilities for eggs, chicks, and manure?

Forests

Secondary and/or Primary Sources

1. Classification of forests in different parts of the block/region under Indian Forest Act.

Table 2

Type of programme	No. of villages covered	No. of farmers covered	Fin. cost & rate of subsidy	Specific reasons for introducing	No. & name of villages which contd. the activity after the expiry of the programmes	Specific reasons why other villages did not continue	Future plans details w.r.t. 2,4,6 and 7.
a) Better breed milch animal							
b) Better breed bull							
c) Distribution of traditional breed milch animal							
d) Distribution of fodder and feed							
i) Green							
ii) Dry							
iii) Feeds (specify)							
e) Others (specify)							

Table 3

Type of Programme	No. of villages covered	No. of farmers covered	Fin. cost & rate of subsidy	Specific reasons for introducing	No. & name of villages which contd the activity after the expiry of the programmes	Specific reasons why other villages did not continue	Future plans with reference to colmns 2,4,6 and 7.
(1)	(2)	(3)	(4)	(5)	(6)	(7)	(8)

2. If not classified, why? and in what specific terms it has been advantageous and disadvantageous to the area concerned? (This latter question requires probing into the objectives behind classification.)
3. Details of forest resources by type of forest trees and their products since 19___ to 19___. (See Tables 4a & 4b.)
4. Are the rights to cultivate forest land given? If yes, why? If no, why? How the royalty for rights is fixed? How are people selected for this purpose?
5. Number of forest labourers' cooperatives, their functions, area and villages under jurisdiction. How does a typical forest coop function in terms of its decisions to cut the forest, employing resources including labour needed to cut the forest, arrangements for extracting and marketing forest products (main and subsidiary products), the payment of costs and receipt of revenue.

Rural Crafts and Industries

Secondary and/or Primary Sources

1. What are the different rural crafts and industries pursued at present in the block? Are these pursued as full-time occupations? If not, what is the extent of dependence on this activity?
2. Were there other crafts and rural industries in the past? Why are they not pursued at present? Is there any scope to revive them? What measures need to be taken to revive them?
3. What are the raw materials used what products are made by the existing units? Where from raw materials are obtained? Where the products are marketed?
4. Details of development programmes for the latest year for which information is available. (See Table 5.)

IV. SOCIAL STRUCTURE

1. Structure

Give a brief historical background of the social groups (caste, religious, ethnic groups etc.). This may include the following:

a) A kaleidoscopic account of caste/ethnic origins.
b) Extent of fusion and fission of social groups in the area.
c) Points of culture contacts—institutions and practices which resulted from culture contacts.

Table 4 (a) (For the latest Year)

Type of trees	Name of Products	Acreage*	Production		Revenue earned by department	Months in which employment is generated		Details of use of each product (as raw material, intermediate product, final consumption	Private or Government	
			Qty (specify units for each)	Value.		Months	No. of days		Owned	Managed
1. Production of trees										
	Timber									
	Firewood and									
	Charcoal									
	Khair									
	Bamboos									
	Grass									
	Timru Leaves									
	Mahuda Flowers									
	Others (specify)									

* Acreage must add upto about 174, 901.

Table 4(b)

Type of Product	Area covered	Villages covered	Financial cost and rate of subsidy	Specific reason for introduction	Year in which benefits would begin to acrue-	By products that may accrue	Amount of employment that generated
1. *Plantation of trees*							
a) Teak							
b) Khair							
c) Cashewnuts							
d) Bamboo							
e) Eucalyptus							
f)							
2. Others (specify)							

Table 5

Type of Programme (including the name of craft, rural industry)	No. of Villages covered	Financial costs and rate of subsidy	Specific reason for introduction	No. of villages which contd the programme after its expiry	If some villages did not continue, why?	Future plans w. r.t. columns 2,3 & 6.

d) Map out the distribution of specific cultures (institutions and practices) among the social groups.

e) Assimilation of social groups into major religious groups.

2. If there are tribals in the area, include significant anthropometric information on the tribes such as:

a) Tribals groupings and ethnic homogeneity (both structurally and functionally).

b) Hierarchy of tribal groups based on ethnic considerations.

c) Tribal demography over the years: trends in population growth.

d) Age, sex and religion structure of the tribal groups

3. The profile note should include some information on the pattern of life such as:

a) Kinship and clan groupings with corresponding terrirotial limits. This will include totemic ties, territorial contigüity or mythical origin of the clans determining inter and intra-group affiliation as a function of common residence within a territorial limit. Also, the nature of ties should be assessed: whether totemic ties or political ties or feudal ties.

b) Inter-group relations, both formal and informal.

c) Dwelling and settlement patterns (spatial distribution) of the social groups (both within a village and without) corresponding to clan hierarchies (if any).

d) Family structure: whether nuclear, joint or extended; whether patrilineal or matrilineal; authority and decision making power in the family; whether discrimination according to sex and age; laws of inheritance.

e) Marriage types: whether intra or inter-clan; intra or inter-villages; endogamous or exogamous; selection of spouses; marriage season; marriage expenses, monogamy or polygamy; child marriages; ceremonies; remarriage.

f) Births and deaths: ceremonies and expenses.

g) Religious institutions and organisations; faiths; worship patterns; feasts and festivals; sacrifice; family deity; religious head (priests, shadhus, gurus, and their remunerations).

V. DEVELOPMENT ADMINISTRATION, AGENCIES AND INSTITUTIONS

Developmental Organizations

1. Assessment of the role played by block / district development administration:

a) Historical review of the development administration in the block/taluka/tehsil.

b) Major programmes/activities of development administration over the year (description and wherever possible analysis in terms of monetary and physical targets and achievements).

c) Reasons for any shift in the activities.

d) Background of the key personnel manning the development departments/organizations (age, education, experience, local/non-local, general orientation)

2. Description and analysis of the structure of developmental organizations and the processes and procedures followed by them:

a) Structure of development administration—personnel, hierarchy, functional divisions and responsibility, control system.

b) Organizations at higher levels from which the district/block level administration draws ideas and resources, the relationship between the two, the nature of authority and the manner in which it is exercised, feedback and correctional devices.

c) Procedures and processes followed in executing major activities. (This can be illustrated by two or three different types of activities e.g. resource supply activity—fertilizer supply; extension activity—propagation of new seeds; control activity—supervision over cooperative loans.)

d) Formal and informal relationship of development administration with non-governmental agencies and institutions.

3. Apart from the developmental activities funelled through block development organization, a number of other governmental agencies function more or less independently of the former at the block level. Among these are:

* Public Works Department
* Irrigation Department (other than minor irrigation)
* Electricity Board
* Forest Department
* Education Department (higher education)
* Health Department (major health projects)
* Social Welfare Department
* Revenue Department (taccavi loan operation

The following aspects need to be studied about each of these departments:

(a) The main activities it pursued in the past decade or so. (Description and wherever possible analysis in terms of monetary and physical targets and achievements.)
b) Reasons for any shift in the activities.
c) Field level organizations of each department.
d) Background of the key personnel.
e) Formal and informal relationship of the department with the block administration.

4. Besides official developmental organisations, there may be some social and political (e.g. voluntary agencies and trade unions) organizations in the area participating in the development process. It would be desirable to prepare profile/case studies of important organizations of this type.

Protective Measures

1. Various measures have been taken to safeguard the legitimate rights of scheduled castes, economically poor or backward classes etc. Measures have also been taken to protect them from exploitation by vested interests. These measures are mainly in the fields of protection against alienation of land and usurious moneylenders. The questions which need to be asked are:

a) Which are the agencies charged with these functions?
b) How effectively they are functioning?
c) If there functioning is not effective, does the fault lie with their organizations or somewhere else?

2. The weaker sections, especially landless labourers and tenant farmers, are sought to be protected and helped by the state in a variety of ways wuch as:

a) Minimum Wages Act.
b) Protection of tenants and land to tiller legislation.
c) Provision of house sites.
d) Imposition of ceiling and redistribution of land.

It is pertinent to enquire as to:

a) Which are the agencies set up to implement these measures?
b) What has been their record?
c) If their records is not satisfactory, is it because of organizational or some other defects?

Land Records

1. Give a brief description of the nature of land tenure in the area.
2. Whether cadastral survey and settlement have been completed. If yes, when? If not, why?
3. What is the position of land records in the area? Do the records show the names of all persons having interest in land? Are they uptodate? What steps are necessary to update the records?
4. Has any surplus land been acquired under the ceilings legislation? If yes, how much? Is there some more surplus land to be acquired? If yes, why has it not been acquired? How much of the acquired land has been distributed and to whom?

Land Restoration

1. Is there a law prohibiting land alienation? If so, obtain a copy of it (including rules, executive instructions and uptodate amendments).
2. Is adequate legal protection available for the rural poor in regard to restoration of land from moneylenders, petty traders or other non-tribals?
3. Obtain the following information (for the last five years):

(*Year*)

a) Number of cases brought forward at the beginning of the year.
b) Amount involved under item (a).
c) Number of cases disposed of during the year.
d) Amount involved under item (c).
e) Number of cases pending at the end of the year.
f) Amount involved under item (e).

4. Will long-term loans at cheap rates for purchase of ownership rights help in solving the problem of land restoration to the poor?
5. Which agency is best suited to provide such long-term loans and why?

Debt Relief Legislation

1. Is the area covered by any debt relief legislation? Obtain copies of the relevant legislation.
2. What are the provisions for regulating debts?
3. What is the maximum rate of interest chargeable under legislation? Can moneylender collect interest in excess of the principal? If so, how much?
4. What are the penal provisions?

5. Who is the competent authority to enforce the legislation?
6. Obtain the following information (for last five years):

(*Years*)

   a) Number of cases brought forward at the beginning for the year.
   b) Amount involved under item (a).
   c) Number of cases disposed of during the year.
   d) Amount involved under item (c).
   e) Number of pending cases at the end of the year.
   f) Amount involved under item (e).

7. It would be useful to consult knowledgeable persons—officials, practitioners, and villagers—and obtain their views and suggestions on the following:

   a) Whether it is possible to scale down debts.
   b) Approximate estimate of the amount required for scaling down debts.
   c) The steps needed to be taken to strengthen the credit structure: Cooperatives, commercial banks, and other institutions. (Make a brief but qualitative study of these instititions, their working and operational achievements/problems/limitations/ and effectiveness in terms of providing production and consumption credit to villagers, particularly the poor).

8. What are the methods adopted by moneylender, commission agents etc. to keep the poor under control?

ANNEXURE II: SOURCES OF INFORMATION

PHYSICAL FEATURES AND INFRASTRUCTURE

Particulars	Sources
1. Area and density of population	District Census Handbook (DCH)
2. Land use and per capita cultivable land	-do-
3. Physiography of the region	l Survey Officer, Deptt. of Agri.
4. Soil (description)	-do-
5. Soil series and their characteristics by Physiographic position	-do-
6. Problems limiting soil use and recommended practices by soil association	-do-

7. Chemical analysis of soils	-do-
8. Rainfall, climate and temperature	(i) DCH, (ii) Gazetteer, (iii) Agriculture Department
9. Annual rainfall	-do-
10. Monthwise distribution of rainfall	-do-
11. Annual rainfall and variation from decade average (%)	-do-
12. Estimated potentials of rivers and alternative sites for irrigation projects	Superintending Engineer/Water Resources Investigation Division/ Irrigation Department
13. Groundwater resources in the block	Director, Groundwater Resources Investigation
14. Shops and trading establishments	DCH
15. Communication (roads)	PWD/Zila Panchayat/Panchayat Samiti
16. Details of other roads in the block	-do-
17. Power supply	Chief Engineer, District Ele. Board
18. Consumption of ele. energy by uses	-do-

SOCIAL STRUCTURE

1. Percentage distribution of population by caste group	DCH/Research studies or surveys if available
2. Settlement patterns	Books
3. Household, family and Neighbourhood	Books
4. Activity pattern	-do-
5. Child bearing and socialization	-do-
6. Social Hierarchy	-do-
7. Leadership	-do
8. Constraints and directions for development	-do-

ECONOMIC STRUCTURE

1. Average annual rainfall	(See 8-11 under Infrastructure)
2. Soil type	Soil Survey Officer
3. Geographical area	District Census
4. Distribution of workers by occupational categories, comparision between towns	DCH
5. Climatic condition in the block and comparison with district	-do-
6. Structural holding in the area	DCH
7. Cropping pattern	Season and Crop Reports
8. Per acre yields of selected crops	-do-
9. Agricultural implements and equipment in the area	Livestock Census Reports
10. Crop calendar of selected crops	Season and Crop Reports

11. Use of modern inputs in the area	Extension Officers for Agriculture
12. Forest of the region	Working Plan Division of Forests
13. Distribution of sound and unsound sample species by girgh classes	-do-

HEALTH AND EDUCATION

1. Daily per capita consumption(gms)	Diet Atlas of India, National Institute of Nutrition, Hyderabad, 1971.
2. Distribution of Malaria cases by age	Malaria Unit Office
3. Distribution of patients treated at Primary Health Centres by type of disease	Primary Health Centres
4. Birth and death rate per thousand population	Primary Health Centres
5. Literate and educated as percentage of population	District Census Handbook
6. Preparation of literate rural population by age and sex.	-do-
7. Primary education: Number of schools, students and teachers	Education Department
8. Dropouts at successive stages of primary education	Inspector of Schools/ Education Department/School Records
9. Dropouts at successive stages of secondary education	

DEVELOPMENT ADMINISTRATION

1. Classification of village level functionaries by age, place of origin and educational qualifications	Block records

Notes and References

1. Gupta, Ranjit (ed.): *Prelude to Block Level Planning in Gujarat* (Ahmedabad: Centre for Management in Agriculture, Indian Institute of Management) 1980.
2. These are called impact projects. See Misra R.P.: *District Planning: A Hand Book* (New Delhi: Concept Publishing Co.) 1990.
3. *Ibid.*, pp. 106-107.
4. In Dharampur the planners stopped at the level of identifying the activities though they did suggest some projects by way of illustration, which they admitted was a mistake.

5. This is what A.K. Sen much later rechristened as the right to live long and well and Partha Das Gupta and others have started talking about well-being and quality of life. World Bank: "What Do We Know About the Poor", being Chapter 2 of *World Development Report* 1990 (Washington, D.C.: World Bank) June 1990, particularly p. 38. See Das Gupta, Partha *Coromandal Lecture* delivered in January 1990 at New Delhi, and Sen, Amartya: *Food for Thought and Survival* (Bombay : Forum for Free Enterprise) January 1989.
6. In Dharampur project the planners explicitly spelled out the qualitative aspect of education and health services, which may find universal agreement but one should be clear about the quality of service one is aiming at.
7. Questionnaires have been provided in Gupta, Ranjit, *loc. cit.*, in Roy, Prodipto and Patil, B. R.: *A Manual for Block Planning* (New Delhi: Mac Millan) 1977 and in AVARD: *Block-Level Planning* (New Delhi: Vikas) 1978.
8. By the same logic, if people do not perceive a service or good provided as being usefull, there would be no demand for it. The classic case is of houses built under Indira Awas Yojana, for weaker sections where people do not move into these relatively better houses and prefer to hold on to their hearth and home.
9. See Raj, K.N.: "Land Reforms and Agricultural Development in Kerala", *Gandhi Marg*, Vol.5, No. 11, February 1984, pp. 759-766; Saxena, N. C.:"Land Reforms and Rural Development", *Administrator*, The Quarterly Journal of the Lal Bahadur Shastri National Academy of Administration, Mussoorie, Vol. 27, No. 1, Jan-March 1982, pp. 1-17; and the classic work of Appu, P.S.: "Land Reform and Agricultural Growth", *Community Development and Panchayati Raj*, Vol. 5, No. 3, January 1974, pp. 105-108.
10. Sen has brought this to sharp focus subsequently. Sen, Amartya: *Poverty and Famines: An Essay on Entitlement and Deprivation* (Oxford: Clarendon Press) 1981 and Dreze, Jean and Sen, Amartya: *Hunger and Public Action* (Oxford: Clarendon Press) 1990.
11. The elements that go into measuring the quality of life have now been enlarged and crystallised subsequently. See World Bank Report and Das Gupta's work mentioned earlier.
12. Karnataka Model still adheres primarily to area development. See Nanjundappa, D.M.: "Planning From Below", *Yojana*, Vol. 33, pp. 75-78 and *Report of the Expert Group on Perspective Plan 2001*, 1989, (Chairman: L.C. Jain) for a view of Karnataka's Decentralised model.

INDEX